Harrods
COOKERY BOOK

MARILYN ASLANI

EBURY PRESS
LONDON

Published by Ebury Press
Division of The National Magazine Company Ltd
Colquhoun House
27–37 Broadwick Street,
London W1V 1FR

First impression 1985
Second impression 1985
Third impression 1986
Fourth impression 1987
Paperback edition 1988

ISBN 0 85223 486 4 (hardback)
0 85223 700 6 (paperback)

Filmset by Advanced Filmsetters (Glasgow) Ltd

Printed and bound in Italy by New Interlitho, S.p.a., Milan

Marilyn Aslani and Ebury Press would like to thank
the following:
Pat Alburey
Mary Cadogan
Sue Peart
Jane Suthering
Hilary Walden

Edited by Laurine Croasdale, Coralie Dorman
Art Director Frank Phillips
Designer Mike Leaman
Stylist Mary Jane Kemp
Photography by Paul Kemp
Cookery by Susanna Tee, Maxine Clark, Janet Smith

CONTENTS

INTRODUCTION

The Harrods tradition of selling the finest food began just 136 years ago, when Henry Charles Harrod bought a small grocery business from his friend Philip Burden in the then less than fashionable Knightsbridge area. Now a tourist landmark, Harrods stands on 4½ acres of the choicest property in London.

Its slogan—Enter a Different World—could hardly be more appropriate, for Harrods is more of a small town than a department store. Twelve entrances offer access to 230 selling departments where more than 4,000 members of staff attend to the various needs of their customers. On any one day, up to 30,000 customers will enter this different world, a further 19,000 will dial the Harrods number and hundreds of thousands of pounds' worth of transactions will be made.

Although it may not strictly be true, the saying still goes that you can buy anything at Harrods from a pin to an elephant. Because of its origins as a grocers, Harrods has

remained true to that tradition and the Food Halls continue to attract tourists from all over the world.

Situated in the very heart of the store, the Food Halls occupy a large central section of the shop floor. The grandeur of the Edwardian mosaic tiles and original plaster ceilings blend with the marble floors to off-set the variety of produce so skilfully displayed. A stroll through the several, linked rooms could reveal politicians, celebrities and even the odd VIP browsing through the merchandise; local, regular customers dashing in to stock up on everyday groceries; keen cooks and gourmets searching out a rare and elusive ingredient; and visitors who have come simply to marvel at the displays.

The Harrods tradition of personal service lives on alongside the ringing of the checkout tills. You can still place an order for almost anything, and your order will be taken with the same efficiency whether you are sending a couple of

Above: *In 1911 building work was completed and Harrods now occupied its present-day site.*

Left: *This photograph, taken in 1889, shows extensions from 87–105 Brompton Road.*

Previous page: *1936 Christmas display of poultry and fish.*

cases of champagne to the Far East—or asking for one soft bread roll to be delivered to Kensington.

What is now a unique and flourishing business started in a very small way. Henry Charles Harrod first went into business as a wholesale grocer and tea dealer in 1835 in Stepney, East London. His business grew rapidly, and when one of his customers, Philip Burden, apparently ran into financial difficulties, Harrod took over his grocery shop in Brompton Road, and moved into living quarters above.

Knightsbridge at that time was becoming fashionable, and business prospered. In 1861, Harrod's son, Charles Digby, joined the business and expanded it further by improving the service and advertising in newspapers.

Seven years later, in 1868, the family was forced to leave their home above the shop in order to provide more space for the burgeoning business. A new shop front was fitted, and a two-storey extension was built in the garden.

By all accounts, Charles Digby Harrod was an extremely hard-working and ambitious man, and he expected similar dedication from his staff, stressing that they should always arrive at work with a clean face. However, he was not without his compassionate side, and if he saw a regular customer in financial embarrassment, Charles Digby was known to waive the bill entirely, murmuring to his salesman, "See that he has what he needs and send the bill to me."

And so the business grew, and with it, its reputation for excellence and customer service. In 1877 the leases of 101 and 103 Brompton Road were acquired, and a sign saying "Harrod's Stores" was erected above the shop front. Additions to the range of merchandise were made, and with the help of a cousin, William Kibble; fresh vegetables, fruit and provisions were brought in daily from Covent Garden market.

One freezing night in early December 1883, when building work on the expansions was almost complete, tragedy struck. A fire broke out, and in a few short hours, a lifetime's work was reduced to ashes. The *Chelsea Herald* of Saturday, 8th December 1883, reported the incident in ghoulish detail:

9

Harrod's stores are now a heap of ruins. The alarm was raised shortly before midnight, and at half past one in the morning, the fire was at its height. From the raised pavement on the west side of Brompton Road a considerable crowd watched the scene of splendidly terrible character. Only the skeleton of the three large shops and the stores at the back remained, but the fire raged in a seething mass, shooting high up in the air from the inner portion, whilst the flames clung tenaciously to the window frames, mouldings and other woodwork, thus outlining the structure as if by an intentional illumination.

Even in what must have been his blackest hour, for Charles Digby Harrod, the customer still came first. Shortly after the inferno, his customers received a letter thus:

Harrod's Stores,
101/103/105 Brompton Road,
7th December 1883

Madam,

I greatly regret to inform you that, in consequence of the above premises being burnt down, your order will be delayed in the execution a day or two. I hope, in the course of Tuesday or Wednesday next, to be able to forward it.

In the meantime may I ask you for your kind indulgence.

Your obedient servant,

C. D. Harrod.

PS All communications to be addressed to 78 Brompton Road.

While rebuilding on a grander scale began on the original site immediately, Charles Digby rented premises across the street, and, with the help of an acquaintance, Edgar Cohen, succeeded in fulfilling all the Christmas orders.

Nine months later, in 1884, the newly built store was opened. Once again, the *Chelsea Herald* was quick to chronicle the event:

Stretching for a long way into the distance is the tea and grocery counter, where pyramids of tea and sugar, mountains of coffee are mixed up with tins of biscuits, breeches' paste, blancmange, glycerine, lobsters, plate powder, sugar candy, boot top powder, wax vestas, salt, prawns, phosphor paste, oysters, milk, knife polish, house flannel, dog biscuits, mustard, and a thousand and one other articles.

Next on the right comes the fruit and flower department and here is to be a collection that will hold its own against any Covent Garden shops.

Beyond this is a stall where poultry and game are to be on view, and we are informed that arrangements have been made for a constant and daily supply direct from the country, and to complete this side of the place, there is a long counter where cheeses and general provisions are to be found.

Customers remained loyal to Harrod, and shortly after reopening, the first credit accounts were opened by a few selected patrons, including Oscar Wilde, Lily Langtry and Ellen Terry. A staff of 200 were employed at this time, and the shop day began at 7 a.m., and ended at 9 p.m., excepting Fridays and Saturdays, when the store remained open until 10 and 11 p.m. respectively.

Notwithstanding the earlier setbacks, expansion continued apace. In 1891 counters for fish and cooked meat were added to the food department, and in 1897 a French confectionery counter was opened. This counter proved so popular that Harrod's catalogue in 1902 included the following statement: "The directors beg to call special attention to their 'own make' cooking and eating chocolates. These are all made on the premises, on French principles, by French workmen, from the finest materials obtainable, and absolute purity and perfect cleanliness are guaranteed. Part of the machinery used in manufacture may be seen in the Department." An impressive list of chocolates followed, including 17 different brands of plain and milk chocolates from 5½d to 4/- per pound.

Henry Charles Harrod lived to see the success his son achieved before he died in 1885. His father's death, combined with the strain of rebuilding the store, may have influenced Charles Digby's decision to sell, and in November 1889 Harrod's Stores was floated as a public company. Charles Digby remained in charge for a further 18 months, until Richard Burbidge was appointed General Manager.

By now, the store stretched from 87 to 105 Brompton Road and, as a result of Richard Burbidge's foresight and enthusiasm, the building was finally completed in 1911 and Harrods now occupied the full island site it stands on today. A new store front had been built to encompass the expansion and a terracotta facade was supplied by Royal Doulton.

Within the store, re-decorating was also taking place. Two new Halls—for the flowers, fruit and vegetables, provisions, grocery and bakery departments—were opened, decorated with green and brown tiles by Malkin, and large dome topped mirrors. For the Meat Hall, tiles were commissioned for the walls from Royal Doulton. Appropriately for a room that should house meat, fish, poultry and game, W. J. Neatby—Royal Doulton's head of architecture from 1890 to 1907—used Parian ware tiles in a design entitled "Scenes from the Hunt", consisting of 20 medallions depicting farming and hunting, set in an overall pattern of birds, fishes and trees.

The Food Halls continued to prosper, despite two World Wars, rationing and staff shortages. Few changes were made until the early 1970's when two refits resulted in 50 per cent more space, giving the Food Halls a total of 45,000 square feet. On 4th October, 1983, Her Royal Highness The Princess Anne officially opened the newly-extended Food Halls.

And so, to this day, the Food Halls have retained their unique atmosphere. To wander through them is a feast for all the senses. In the Fruit and Vegetable Hall you can breathe in the delicate fragrance of mangoes and pineapples, admire the ripe melons displayed alongside wild strawberries, kumquats and shiny hot-house grapes. In this room the seasons merge, bringing ugli fruit, apricots and passion fruit to cheer us in the dead of winter.

Then there is the charcuterie counter, decked with hundreds of sausages and salamis; the salad bar and pasta shop which sells over 500 lbs of pasta every week—and the Dairy, where over 500 different types of cheese rest on cool marble slabs. In the Bakery, you can now choose from over 170 different varieties of bread, with even the more

unusual organic loaf selling at a rate of 200 loaves per day.

The new Pantry, on the lower ground floor, stocks a huge range of teas, including no less than 24 flavours of fruit tea, including mango and kiwi. The rich aroma of coffee permeates the room, as a choice of 17 blends are ground to customers' requirements. The most expensive and the rarest of the beans is the high grown, Jamaican Blue Mountain coffee, which comes from a small growing area and sells at £12 per lb.

In the Confectionery, glass counters containing regiments of hand-made chocolates are handled by white-gloved assistants, who wrap the confectionery in presentation boxes decorated with flowers and ribbons. With over 100 different types to choose from, it is hardly surprising that 130 tons of chocolate are sold each year.

In the Meat Hall, 30 butchers stand behind marble counters, ready to advise and cut prime joints of meat. Renowned for its fresh fish and shellfish, the fish department is the most photographed in the building. As in the meat and poultry departments, a fresh display is dressed daily at around 7.30 a.m., upon the buyer's return from Billingsgate Fish Market. The display takes $1\frac{1}{2}$ hours to dress, and is made up of 60 fish, reflecting the produce available that day.

Even for those who are not connoisseurs, the wine department is a must to visit. It stocks at any one time, between a quarter and half a million pounds' worth of wine,

Above: *Clever, eye-catching displays such as the All England Egg Week, photographed in the post-war era, have remained one of the Food Hall's most popular attractions.*

spirits and liqueurs. This is the department which, in 1977, had on display what is believed to be the largest bottle of port in the world; a bottle of 1963 vintage port which will not be ready for drinking until 2020. Called Nebuchadnessar, it contained the equivalent of 48 bottles of ports, and would have retailed at that time at £6,000.

Like a huge bustling market under one roof, Harrods Food Halls account for a high per cent of the store's transactions, with a turnover which runs into tens of millions.

And yet, after a century of continued success, Henry Charles and Charles Digby Harrod's original aspirations of excellence in both quality and service are undiminished. The store's exacting high standards are maintained with the same precision now as they were one hundred years ago. This is one reason why Harrods is proud to have been appointed purveyor of provisions and household goods to Her Majesty the Queen. It is testimony to the hard work and vision of Henry Charles Harrod, his son Charles Digby and the Burbidge family, that Harrods is what it is today: the store with a difference.

THE MEAT HALL

MEAT

MEAT

◆

*In this most famous and splendid of the Food Halls, 30 butchers
stand ready to prepare the superb cuts of meat brought in daily
from Smithfield market. Tender and succulent, the quality never wavers,
and is perfect for traditional dishes like Steak and Kidney Pie or
something with a slightly more exotic flavour, such as Lamb Kebabs
Marinated in Yogurt and Onion.*

STEAK AND KIDNEY PUDDING

*There are many variations of this classic British pudding. In this recipe,
which has a straightforward method, the suetcrust pastry absorbs the meat juices
and is quite delicious.*

Serves 4–6

INGREDIENTS

*suetcrust pastry, made with
350 g (12 oz) flour (see
page 249)*

*500 g (1 lb) shin of beef, trimmed
weight, cut into 2.5 cm (1 inch)
cubes*

*175 g (6 oz) ox kidney,
trimmed weight, coarsely
chopped*

1 onion, finely chopped

5 ml (1 tsp) flour

salt and pepper

15 ml (1 tbsp) mushroom ketchup

*450 ml (¾ pint) beef stock, cold
(see page 246)*

Divide the pastry into 3 and reserve one-third. Roll out the pastry on a lightly floured board into a 36 cm (14 inch) circle. Lightly grease a 1.8 litre (3 pint) pudding basin and line it with the dough: fold the circle in half, then in half again, place it in the basin, open out and press the pastry into the shape of the basin. The dough should overlap the edge a little. Roll out the remaining dough into a 20 cm (8 inch) circle and reserve.

Mix the beef, kidney and onion with the flour, and season. Place this mixture in the lined pudding basin. Mix the mushroom ketchup with the cold stock and pour it over the meat.

Moisten the edge of the pastry with a little cold water and place the circle of dough on top of the pudding. Gently press the lining and the top layer of pastry together and leave it overlapping the basin by about 1 cm (½ inch). Cover the top of the basin with a pleated circle of greased greaseproof paper or aluminium foil and secure with string.

Immerse the pudding in a pan with enough boiling water to come two-thirds up the side of the basin. Steam for 20 minutes, reduce the heat and steam gently for another 3½–4 hours. Serve from the basin, wrapped in a white starched napkin.

STEAK AND OYSTER PIE

STEAK AND OYSTER PIE

*During the last century oysters were cheap and plentiful and were often used in
pies to pad out the more expensive ingredients. Canned oysters may be
used instead of fresh ones if these are unavailable.*

Serves 4

Carefully prise open the oysters and remove from the shells, reserving the liquid.
Coat the steak in flour mixed with salt, pepper and cayenne pepper.

Melt the butter and fry the onion until soft. Remove from the heat and set
aside.

Roll out two-thirds of the pastry on a lightly floured surface to 3 mm ($\frac{1}{8}$ inch)
thick and use to line a 1.5 litre ($2\frac{1}{2}$ pint) pie dish. Place a pie funnel in the middle.

Place half of the steak in the lined pie dish with half the onion. Arrange the
oysters on top and sprinkle over the liquid. Cover with the remaining onion and
steak, then add the stock. Brush the edges of the pie with the beaten egg. Roll out
the remaining pastry and cover the pie. Press gently to seal, then trim and crimp
the edges. Re-roll the trimmings and cut into decorative shapes. Brush the pie
with beaten egg, position the shapes and brush these with beaten egg. Make a
small hole around the pie funnel.

Bake at 190°C (375°F) mark 5 for $1\frac{1}{2}$ hours. Serve hot.

INGREDIENTS

6 fresh oysters

*750 g (1$\frac{1}{2}$ lb) rump steak,
    trimmed and cut into 5 mm
    ($\frac{1}{4}$ inch) thick strips*

40 ml (2$\frac{1}{2}$ tbsp) flour

salt and pepper

pinch of cayenne pepper

25 g (1 oz) butter

1 medium onion, finely chopped

*puff pastry, made with 225 g
    (8 oz) flour (see page 248)*

*200 ml (7 fl oz) beef stock
    (see page 246)*

1 egg, lightly beaten

CROWN ROAST OF LAMB
WITH TARRAGON

CROWN ROAST OF LAMB WITH TARRAGON

The distinctive flavour of fresh tarragon enhances the taste of the lamb.
It is a decorative main course if filled with watercress and garnished with cutlet frills.

Serves 8

INGREDIENTS

2 best ends of lamb, about 1.8 kg
  (4 lb) containing 8 cutlets each
50 g (2 oz) butter
1 shallot, sliced
90 ml (6 tbsp) dry white wine
2 sprigs of fresh tarragon
15 ml (1 tbsp) flour
300 ml (½ pint) beef stock
  (see page 246)
salt and pepper
1 bunch watercress, to garnish

Trim off as much fat as possible from the skin side of the cutlets. Cut all the meat and fat between the rib ends to expose 5 cm (2 inches) of the bone. Reserve the trimmings. Bring the ends of the racks together and sew at the base and near the bones. Bring the other ends together, fat side inwards and sew. Tie with string and place in a roasting tin. Wrap the exposed bones with aluminium foil.

Place the butter, shallot, wine and tarragon in the roasting tin. Roast at 200°C (400°F) mark 6 for 50 minutes. Remove the trimmings from the centre and baste the meat. Return to the oven for 10 minutes then transfer it to a warmed serving dish to rest in a warm place.

Pour off all but 15 ml (1 tbsp) of the fat from the pan. Stir in the flour, then the stock, and bring to the boil. Simmer for 3 minutes and adjust the seasoning.

Remove the aluminium foil from the bones and place a cutlet frill on each. Fill the crown with watercress and serve hot with the gravy.

ROAST BEEF WITH SMOKED OYSTER STUFFING

This smoked oyster stuffing is extremely quick and easy to prepare. Its
splendid rich flavour really complements a good joint of beef.

Serves 4–6

In a saucepan, melt the butter and fry the shallots until soft. Remove the shallots with a slotted spoon and add them to the oysters. Reserve the butter. Season with black pepper only, as the oysters are already quite salty. Lay the meat out flat and spread the stuffing over evenly. Re-roll the meat, and tie with string in several places to retain the shape. Place the meat on a rack in a roasting tin. Brush with the olive oil and reserved melted butter.

Roast the beef at 220°C (425°F) mark 7 for 20 minutes. Reduce the temperature to 170°C (325°F) mark 3 and cook for an additional 15 minutes per 500 g (1 lb) for rare meat or 20 minutes per 500 g (1 lb) for medium rare. Cover with aluminium foil and leave to rest in a warm place for 10 minutes before carving.

To make the sauce, put all the ingredients into a bowl and mix thoroughly. Serve the beef with the pan juices, and horseradish and green peppercorn sauce.
Note
This sauce is also delicious with cold beef or smoked trout.

INGREDIENTS
25 g (1 oz) butter
2 shallots, finely chopped
50 g (2 oz) canned smoked oysters,
 drained and roughly chopped
freshly ground black pepper
1.5 kg (3 lb) rib of beef, boned
15 ml (1 tbsp) olive oil
HORSERADISH AND GREEN
PEPPERCORN SAUCE
225 ml (8 fl oz) crème fraîche or
 soured cream
15 ml (1 tbsp) grated fresh
 horseradish
10 ml (2 tsp) green peppercorns,
 crushed
15 ml (1 tbsp) lemon juice
salt

RUMP STEAK AND HERB STUFFING

Finely chopped mushrooms, celery and fresh herbs are combined for this stuffing.
Quick and easy to prepare, this dish is ideal to make when there
is a shortage of time.

Serves 4

Melt the butter in a frying pan and fry the shallots until soft. Add the mushrooms and celery stalk and fry for 5 minutes. Transfer the vegetables to a bowl and add the breadcrumbs, pepper, herbs, the celery leaves, brandy and cream. Mix together well.

Place the steak on a board with the fat farthest from you. Insert a sharp knife about 2.5 cm (1 inch) in from one end of the steak and slice horizontally to within 2.5 cm (1 inch) of the other end of the steak, to make a pocket for the stuffing.

Place the stuffing into the pocket then sew up with thick cotton thread or string. Place the meat on a hot, ungreased cast-iron frying pan and seal for 2 minutes on each side. Reduce the heat and cook for 4 minutes on each side. The meat will be sealed outside but pink and juicy inside. Place the steak on a serving plate, remove the thread, and carve into thick slices across the grain. Serve hot.

INGREDIENTS
25 g (1 oz) butter
2 shallots, finely chopped
50 g (2 oz) mushrooms, finely
 chopped
1 small celery stalk, plus leaves,
 finely chopped separately
50 g (2 oz) fresh breadcrumbs
pepper
2.5 ml (½ tsp) finely chopped
 fresh thyme
15 ml (1 tbsp) chopped fresh
 parsley
15 ml (1 tbsp) brandy
30 ml (2 tbsp) single cream
1 kg (2 lb) rump steak, in one
 piece, about 4.5 cm (1¾ inches)
 thick

ROAST BEEF AND YORKSHIRE PUDDING

*Yorkshire pudding was originally cooked under the joint to catch the juices
as the meat cooked and then served as a first course with thick gravy.
Mustard and horseradish sauce are the traditional accompaniments for roast beef.*

Serves 4–6

INGREDIENTS

2 kg (4½ lb) beef joint on the bone
lard or dripping
pepper
YORKSHIRE PUDDING
100 g (4 oz) plain flour
pinch of salt
100 ml (4 fl oz) milk, at room
temperature
100 ml (4 fl oz) water, at room
temperature
1 large egg, at room temperature
15 ml (1 tbsp) melted fat, taken
from the beef pan
GRAVY
10 ml (2 tsp) flour
300 ml (½ pint) beef stock
(see page 246)
salt and pepper

To make the Yorkshire pudding, sift the flour and salt into a bowl. Mix the milk, water and egg together and gradually whisk them into the flour. Continue mixing until the batter is smooth and free of lumps. Leave to stand for 30–40 minutes.

Place the joint on a rack in a roasting tin, smear with lard and season with pepper. Cook the beef at 220°C (425°F) mark 7 for 20 minutes. Reduce the temperature to 190°C (375°F) mark 5, and continue to roast for 15 minutes per 500 g (1 lb) for rare meat, 20 minutes per 500 g (1 lb) for medium and 25 minutes per 500 g (1 lb) for well done. When the meat is cooked, transfer it to a warmed serving plate and leave it to rest for 20 minutes before carving.

While the meat is resting, put the fat from the beef into a 23 cm (9 inch) square and 4–5 cm (1½–2 inch) deep baking tin. Place the tin in the oven to melt the fat (it must be very hot before the batter is poured into it), then whisk the batter and immediately pour it into the hot tin. Bake in the centre of the oven, or on the top shelf, at 220°C (425°F) mark 7, for 35 minutes. Do not open the oven door during the first 20 minutes of the cooking time. Serve cut into portions with the roast beef.

For individual puddings, pour the batter into 10–12 patty tins and bake as above for 15–20 minutes.

To make the gravy, the meat juices alone may be used. For a thicker gravy, skim some of the fat from the surface and place the tin over moderate heat. Sprinkle 10 ml (2 tsp) of flour into the tin and stir it into the pan juices, scraping up the brown sediment. Cook over high heat, stirring constantly, until the flour has browned slightly. (When the meat is carved, any juices from the meat can be added to the gravy). Add up to 300 ml (½ pint) of beef stock to the tin and stir well. Bring it to the boil, simmer for 2–3 minutes and season to taste. Pour into a sauce boat and keep hot.

Note

A meat thermometer is an invaluable piece of equipment, as it eliminates the guesswork. Inserted into the thickest part of the meat the pointer on the dial will reach 60°C (140°F) for rare, 71°C (160°F) for medium and 77°C (170°F) for well done.

FILLET OF BEEF WITH FOIE GRAS

Use only the finest beef fillet for this impressive dish. Because of the richness of the pâté de foie gras, only a small amount is needed. Serve with steamed broccoli and new potatoes.

Serves 4

INGREDIENTS

40 g (1½ oz) butter, chilled
15 ml (1 tbsp) olive oil
600 g (1¾ lb) beef fillet,
    cut into 4 tournedos
salt and pepper
1 shallot, finely chopped
100 ml (4 fl oz) port
100 ml (4 fl oz) Madeira
15 g (½ oz) canned or bottled
    truffles, drained and finely
    sliced, with the juices reserved
150 ml (¼ pint) beef stock
    (see page 246)
25 g (1 oz) pâté de foie gras, diced

Melt 15 g (½ oz) of the butter with the oil in a large frying pan and fry the tournedos for 2–5 minutes on each side, depending on whether you like them rare or well-done. Season, remove from the pan and keep hot.

Fry the shallot in the fat in the pan until soft, then add the port, Madeira and truffle juices. Boil rapidly until reduced by half. Stir in the beef stock and boil rapidly until reduced slightly. Add the truffles and pâté de foie gras and simmer very gently for 2 minutes. Adjust the seasoning to taste. Remove from the heat and stir in the remaining butter, a little at a time. Serve at once with the steaks.

BEEF WELLINGTON

This classic dish is said to have been a favourite of the Duke of Wellington.

Serves 4–6

INGREDIENTS

900 g (2 lb) beef fillet, in one piece
10 ml (2 tsp) brandy
salt and pepper
75 g (3 oz) butter
1 onion, finely chopped
175 g (6 oz) mushrooms,
    finely chopped
puff pastry, made with 225 g
    (8 oz) flour (see page 248)
75 g (3 oz) smooth pâté —
    chicken, duck or goose liver
1 egg, lightly beaten
SAUCE
25 g (1 oz) butter
30 ml (2 tbsp) onion, finely
    chopped
50 g (2 oz) mushrooms, finely
    chopped
15 ml (1 tbsp) flour
300 ml (½ pint) beef stock (see
    page 246)
150 ml (¼ pint) red wine

Trim the fat from the beef and brush with brandy. Season with pepper. Melt the butter in a frying pan, add the beef and fry for 2 minutes turning to seal all over. Remove the beef from the pan and roast in the oven at 200°C (400°F) mark 6 for 15 minutes.

Meanwhile, fry the onion in the fat in the pan for 10 minutes. Add the mushrooms and fry for 4–5 minutes or until most of the moisture has evaporated. Season and cool. Remove the meat from the oven and allow to cool completely.

Roll out the pastry to a large rectangle. Mix the pâté with 30 ml (2 tbsp) of the onion and mushroom mixture and spread it over the top of the beef. Place the meat, pâté side down, in the centre of the pastry. Cover the meat with the remaining mushroom mixture. Brush the edges of the pastry with the beaten egg and wrap the fillet in the pastry. Press the edges to seal and place, join side down, on a baking sheet.

Re-roll the pastry trimmings and cut into leaves and a flower. Brush the pastry with egg. Place the leaves and flower on the pastry and brush with beaten egg. Bake at 200°C (400°F) mark 6 for 20 minutes or until the pastry is golden brown. Transfer to a warmed serving dish.

Meanwhile, make the sauce. Melt the butter and fry the onion for 5 minutes, then add the mushrooms and cook for a further 3 minutes. Stir in the flour and cook for 1 minute. Gradually stir in the stock and red wine, bring to the boil, then simmer for 10 minutes. Season to taste. Strain the sauce if preferred, and serve with the beef.

BRAISED BEEF OLIVES

*These thin slices of topside are rolled around a herb and green olive stuffing
to make a delicious casserole.*

Serves 4—6

Flatten the beef slices with a meat bat or rolling pin. Set aside and make the
stuffing.

Mix the pork with the breadcrumbs. Melt the butter in a frying pan and fry the
onion until soft. Allow to cool slightly. Add to the pork mixture with the parsley,
olives, marjoram and lemon rind. Season to taste and bind with the egg.

Spread the stuffing over the beef slices and roll up, starting from one short
edge. Tie with string in two or three places.

Heat the oil and half of the butter in a flameproof casserole. Fry the beef olives
for 2 minutes or until browned all over. Remove from the casserole. Add the
onion, celery and carrots, and fry for 5 minutes. Return the beef olives to the pan,
add the stock and bring to the boil. Reduce the heat, cover and simmer for $1\frac{1}{2}$
hours. Remove the beef olives from the casserole, and remove the string. Keep
hot.

Pour the wine into the casserole. Knead the remaining butter with the flour,
and stir into the liquid, a little at a time. Simmer, stirring, for 5 minutes. Return the
beef olives to the casserole to re-heat. Transfer with the vegetables and pan juices
to a warmed serving dish. Serve hot, sprinkled with chopped parsley.

INGREDIENTS

4 slices beef topside, about 150 g
   (5 oz) each
15 ml (1 tbsp) oil
25 g (1 oz) butter
1 onion, finely chopped
1 celery stalk, finely chopped
2 carrots, finely chopped
300 ml ($\frac{1}{2}$ pint) beef stock
   (see page 246)
30 ml (2 tbsp) dry white wine
15 ml (1 tbsp) flour
15 ml (1 tbsp) chopped fresh
   parsley, to garnish

STUFFING

100 g (4 oz) minced pork
50 g (2 oz) breadcrumbs
25 g (1 oz) butter
1 small onion, finely chopped
30 ml (2 tbsp) finely chopped fresh
   parsley
6 green olives, stoned and finely
   chopped
2.5 ml ($\frac{1}{2}$ tsp) dried marjoram
finely grated rind of 1 lemon
salt and pepper
1 egg, lightly beaten

VEAL CHOPS WITH PORT AND MUSHROOM SAUCE

*The veal chops in this dish are beautifully complemented by a creamy
mushroom sauce, the taste of which is heightened by a touch of port.*

Serves 4

Melt the butter in a pan and fry the chops for 5 minutes on both sides. Season
with black pepper. Place the chops in a serving dish and keep hot.

Add the mushrooms to the pan juices and cook for 2 minutes. Stir in the port,
stock and cream, and bring to the boil. Boil until the sauce has reduced and
thickened. Adjust the seasoning and spoon the mushrooms and sauce over the
chops. Sprinkle with the chopped parsley and serve.

INGREDIENTS

50 g (2 oz) butter
4 veal chops, about 225 g (8 oz)
   each
salt and pepper
175 g (6 oz) mushrooms, sliced
30 ml (2 tbsp) port
100 ml (4 fl oz) chicken stock
   (see page 247)
100 ml (4 fl oz) double cream
15 ml (1 tbsp) chopped fresh
   parsley

FILLET OF BEEF WITH ANCHOVY SAUCE

A fillet of beef is always popular. The anchovy essence in this sauce provides a sharp taste to offset the richness of the beef.

Serves 6

INGREDIENTS

1.3 kg (2½ lb) beef fillet, in one
    piece
pepper
30 ml (2 tbsp) olive oil
3 slices unsmoked streaky bacon,
    rinded and halved
150 g (5 oz) butter, melted
45 ml (3 tbsp) dry white wine
2 shallots, finely chopped
1 bay leaf
SAUCE
4 egg yolks
40 ml (2½ tbsp) dry white wine
25 g (1 oz) cold butter
15 ml (1 tbsp) anchovy essence

Trim the beef of excess fat and tie with string in about four places, to keep the shape. Season with pepper.

Heat the olive oil in a large frying pan and fry the meat, turning, until sealed all over. Transfer to a small roasting tin. Cover with the bacon and pour over the melted butter and white wine. Add the shallots and bay leaf. Cook at 220°C (425°F) mark 7 for 10 minutes. Baste, then reduce the temperature to 190°C (375°F) mark 5, and cook for a further 15–20 minutes, if you like the meat rare, or up to 30–35 minutes for well-done.

Meanwhile, prepare the sauce. Place the egg yolks in a bowl and whisk until smooth. Whisk in 25 ml (1½ tbsp) of the wine and half of the butter. Set the bowl over a pan of hot water and cook, stirring constantly, for 10–15 minutes or until thickened. Whisk in the remaining butter, a little at a time. Cover and keep warm.

Transfer the meat to a warmed serving plate. Remove the string and the bacon, and leave to rest in a warm place for 10 minutes before carving.

Scrape any sediment from the base of the roasting tin and strain the juices. Stir in the remaining wine and the anchovy essence, then gradually beat into the sauce. Carve the meat into slices and serve with the sauce.

LAMB CASSEROLE WITH CARAWAY SEED DUMPLINGS

Cheaper cuts of lamb may be used for this casserole, but chump chops are best as they have a lower percentage of bone and fat. When available, chump ends are a good buy as they are extremely economical.

Serves 4–6

INGREDIENTS

800 g (1¾ lb) chump chops,
    trimmed of fat
30 ml (2 tbsp) seasoned flour
2 onions, finely chopped
3 carrots, diced
salt and pepper
1.2 litres (2 pints) stock or
    water, hot
15 ml (1 tbsp) chopped fresh
    parsley
DUMPLINGS
100 g (4 oz) plain flour
50 g (2 oz) grated beef suet
large pinch of salt
2.5 ml (½ tsp) caraway seeds
about 75 ml (5 tbsp) cold water

Coat the chops in the seasoned flour.

Place half the onions and carrots in the base of a casserole. Place the meat on top, then put the remaining vegetables on top. Season, then pour over the stock. Cover the pan and cook the casserole in the oven at 180°C (350°F) mark 4 for 2½ hours.

To make the dumplings, mix the flour, suet, salt and caraway seeds together in a bowl. Add sufficient water to make a firm, stiff dough. Divide the mixture into 8 equal portions and shape into balls.

Add the dumplings to the casserole and cook for 30 minutes. Sprinkle with chopped parsley and serve.

ROAST LAMB WITH
CHERRY PILAF

ROAST LAMB WITH CHERRY PILAF

*A half leg or whole shoulder of lamb may be used for this recipe.
The lamb is accompanied by deep pink rice which has been tinted by the cherry juices.*

Serves 4

Place the lamb on a rack in a roasting tin, smear all over with half the butter and season. Roast at 180°C (350°F) mark 4 for 20 minutes per 500 g (1 lb), plus 20 minutes.

Meanwhile, make the cherry pilaf. Place the cherries and sugar in a pan. Cook over gentle heat, stirring, until the sugar has dissolved. Cover and simmer for 10 minutes, then drain and reserve the juice. Cook the rice in a large pan of boiling salted water for 5 minutes. Drain and rinse under cold running water. Drain well.

Spread the remaining butter over the base of a heavy-based saucepan and sprinkle over the oil. Spread one-third of the rice over the base of the pan and top with one-third of the cherries. Do not allow either the rice or cherries to touch the sides of the pan from now on. Continue to make layers, building them up into a pyramid, ending with a layer of rice. Spoon the cherry juice evenly over the rice. Wrap the saucepan lid in a clean tea-towel, cover the pan and cook over gentle heat for 25 minutes.

About 20 minutes before the lamb is cooked, brush it with the redcurrant jelly and stir the port into the pan juices. When cooked, transfer it to a warmed serving plate and rest in a warm place for 10 minutes.

Plunge the base of the pan in which the rice was cooked in cold water for 30 seconds. Spoon the rice on to a serving plate, leaving the bottom layer behind. If this crust is not too dark, it may be served with the rice, but the sugar in the syrup tends to burn this layer slightly. Keep hot.

Skim the fat from the pan juices, strain and serve with the meat, carved into slices and garnished with the rosemary. Serve with the rice.

INGREDIENTS

*1.5 kg (3 lb) half leg or shoulder
  of lamb*
50 g (2 oz) butter, softened
salt and pepper
*350 g (12 oz) fresh black cherries,
  stoned weight*
100 g (4 oz) sugar
*350 g (12 oz) basmati rice, rinsed
  and drained*
15 ml (1 tbsp) groundnut oil
45 ml (3 tbsp) redcurrant jelly
75 ml (3 fl oz) port
sprigs of rosemary, to garnish

LAMB KEBABS MARINATED IN YOGURT AND ONION

*Marinating the lamb in yogurt breaks down the tough fibres in the meat,
making it as tender as butter. Serve in warm pitta bread with shredded lettuce and salad,
instead of rice, if preferred.*

Serves 4

INGREDIENTS

500 g (1 lb) lamb fillet, in one piece
1 onion, grated
300 ml (½ pint) natural yogurt
salt and pepper
RICE
225 g (8 oz) rice
50 g (2 oz) butter
4 egg yolks

Trim the fat off the meat then cut it in half horizontally. Cut the 2 pieces into 7.5 cm (3 inch) strips across the grain. Place in a shallow container with the onion, yogurt and pepper. Cover with clingfilm and marinate in the fridge for a minimum of 12 hours and up to 2 days.

Thread the meat on to skewers. Cook under a hot grill for about 15 minutes, turning frequently. Season with salt. Meanwhile, cook the rice in boiling salted water for 15 minutes or until tender. Spoon the rice on to individual serving plates. Each guest should mix the rice with butter and a raw egg yolk, then top with a kebab. Serve hot.

LAMB KEBABS MARINATED IN YOGURT AND ONION

PORK LOIN WITH TRUFFLES AND THYME

This dish combines the flavours of fresh herbs and truffles, one of the world's most sought after delicacies. By using bottled truffle trimmings, you can enjoy the taste without the vast expense.

Serves 4

Remove the rind from the pork, leaving a layer of fat, and make an incision down the eye of the meat to form a shallow pocket. Drain the juices from the truffles and reserve. Mix the truffles, garlic, thyme, butter and seasoning together and place in the incision in the pork. Secure at 2.5 cm (1 inch) intervals with string, cover and chill for 24 hours.

Place in a roasting tin and season. Roast at 190°C (375°F) mark 5 for 1–1¼ hours. It is cooked if the juices run clear when a skewer is inserted into the centre.

Remove the pork from the roasting tin, pour off the excess fat and stir in the flour. Cook, stirring, for 1 minute. Stir in the wine and cook over moderately high heat for 1 minute. Stir in the truffle juices and stock, and simmer for 5 minutes. Season to taste. Slice the pork, pour over a little of the sauce and serve the remaining sauce separately. Garnish with sprigs of watercress.

INGREDIENTS

1.5 kg (3 lb) loin of pork, boned
50 g (2 oz) truffle trimmings
1 garlic clove, crushed
2.5 ml (½ tsp) chopped fresh thyme
25 g (1 oz) butter
salt and pepper
15 ml (1 tbsp) flour
60 ml (4 tbsp) dry white wine
300 ml (½ pint) chicken stock
  (see page 247)
watercress sprigs, to garnish

PORK LOIN WITH TRUFFLES AND THYME

BAKED HAM GLAZED WITH HONEY, ORANGE AND GINGER

*This is an excellent way of cooking ham, as it absorbs the flavour of the glaze
and remains succulent and tender.*

Serves 8

Soak the ham in sufficient cold water to cover for 3 hours then discard the water. Place the ham, onion stuck with cloves, bay leaf, peppercorns and 225 ml (8 fl oz) of the white wine in a saucepan. Add sufficient cold water to cover. Bring to the boil, cover the pan and boil gently for 1 hour.

Meanwhile, make the glaze. Place the brown sugar, 30 ml (2 tbsp) of the orange juice, honey, ginger and mustard in a bowl and mix well.

Drain the ham and discard the vegetables. Reserve the stock for soup if it is not too salty. Remove the skin from the ham, score the fat into a diamond pattern, and stud with cloves. Place the ham in a baking dish and pour the remaining wine and orange juice into the pan.

Cover the ham with one-third of the glaze. Bake at 200°C (400°F) mark 6 for 45 minutes. Baste the ham with the pan juices, and glaze 3–4 times during cooking. Discard the pan juices and serve the ham hot or cold. Garnish with orange slices and curly endive.

INGREDIENTS

*2 kg (4 lb) smoked middle cut
     gammon*
1 onion stuck with 3 cloves
1 bay leaf
6 peppercorns
300 ml (½ pint) dry white wine
40 g (1½ oz) dark brown sugar
100 ml (4 fl oz) orange juice
15 ml (1 tbsp) clear honey
2.5 ml (½ tsp) ground ginger
15 ml (1 tbsp) Dijon mustard
whole cloves
*orange slices and curly endive,
     to garnish*

LAMB WITH GARLIC POTATOES

*This dish has the most wonderful aroma and is easy to cook. The meat
is placed directly on to the oven rack to roast, enabling the garlic-flavoured
juices to seep down into the dish of potatoes below.*

Serves 4–6

Grease a large, shallow baking dish. Crush 2 garlic cloves and layer with the potatoes and seasoning. Dot with the butter, reserving 15 g (½ oz). Cut the remaining garlic into slivers. Pierce the meat with a sharp knife in several places and insert the garlic slivers. Push the sprig of rosemary into the centre of the lamb. Rub the remaining butter over the meat and season well.

Place the meat directly on to the oven rack with the dish of potatoes beneath it on the shelf below. The juices will drip down on to the potatoes as the meat cooks. Roast at 190°C (375°F) mark 5 for 1½ hours. Serve with the potatoes and a green vegetable or salad.

INGREDIENTS

3 large garlic cloves
1.3 kg (2½ lb) potatoes, thinly sliced
salt and pepper
65 g (2½ oz) butter
1.5 kg (3 lb) half leg of lamb
large sprig of fresh rosemary

LAMB STUFFED WITH ROQUEFORT CHEESE AND MINT

*A boned shoulder of lamb is much easier to carve and produces neat slices
of meat and stuffing.*

Serves 6–8

INGREDIENTS

*1.5 kg (3 lb) shoulder of lamb,
  boned*

*175 g (6 oz) Roquefort cheese,
  crumbled*

2 sprigs fresh mint, finely chopped

*65 × 7.5 cm (26 × 3 inch) strip of
  pork fat*

25 g (1 oz) butter

45 ml (3 tbsp) mint jelly

150 ml (¼ pint) port

*150 ml (¼ pint) beef stock
  (see page 246)*

salt and pepper

Lay the lamb, skin side down on a flat surface. Score a cross, about 7.5 cm (3 inches) wide, in the centre of the meat. Mix the cheese with the mint and place it in the centre of the meat. Pull the edges of the meat up and around the filling to make a neat round. Wrap the strip of pork fat around the meat, overlapping the ends, to cover completely. Tie tightly with string in 8 even wedge-shaped sections.

Weigh and smear the joint all over with butter. Place in a roasting tin. Roast at 180°C (350°F) mark 4, allowing 25 minutes per 500 g (1 lb) plus 25 minutes. The lamb is cooked when a skewer is inserted into the base and the juices run clear.

About 15–20 minutes before the end of the cooking time, remove the string and the fat. Brush the lamb with the mint jelly. Stir the port into the pan and return the joint to the oven, basting several times during the remaining cooking time. Transfer the joint to a warmed serving plate and leave in a warm place to rest for 15 minutes.

Pour the fat off the pan juices and stir in the stock. Simmer, stirring frequently, over moderately high heat, for 10 minutes, until slightly reduced. Adjust the seasoning and serve with the meat.

PORK ROASTED IN HONEY, SOY SAUCE AND SHERRY

*Marinating pork in this way makes it beautifully sweet and tender. Cook it
directly on the oven rack with a tray of water placed underneath to catch the drips.
This not only prevents burning, but keeps the pork moist during cooking.*

Serves 6

INGREDIENTS

1.5 kg (3 lb) boned half leg of pork

pepper

MARINADE

200 ml (7 fl oz) clear honey

45 ml (3 tbsp) medium dry sherry

90 ml (6 tbsp) light soy sauce

45 ml (3 tbsp) hoisin sauce

*45 ml (3 tbsp) ground yellow bean
  sauce*

Remove the rind from the meat but leave as much fat on as possible. Lay the meat out flat and cut it into 4 equal-size strips. Slash diagonally 3 or 4 times. Season with pepper.

To make the marinade, mix 175 g (6 oz) of the honey with the remaining ingredients in a shallow container. Place the meat in the marinade, cover with clingfilm and marinate in the fridge overnight.

Place a tray filled with about 2.5 cm (1 inch) water in the oven. Remove the meat from the marinade and place it directly on to the oven rack with the tray underneath. Roast at 190°C (375°F) mark 5 for 30 minutes.

Remove each piece of meat, one by one, dip it into the marinade, and return it to the oven. Roast for a further 15 minutes, dip in the marinade and return to the oven. Repeat once more. Cook for a further 10 minutes. Remove the meat from the oven and immediately brush it with the remaining honey. Serve hot or cold.

LOIN OF VEAL WITH TURMERIC AND LEMONS

The addition of turmeric gives the meat a delicate golden tinge.
Lamb is also very successful cooked in this way. If liked, during the last 30 minutes
of the cooking time, arrange new potatoes, carrots and baby onions around
the meat and cook in the pan juices.

Serves 6

Heat the oil in a large flameproof casserole and brown the meat all over to seal. Stir in the turmeric and seasoning and fry for 1 minute. Pour over the lemon juice and 75 ml (3 fl oz) water and bring to the boil. Reduce the heat, cover the pan and simmer very gently for 2–2½ hours, or until tender. Add more water if the mixture gets too dry.

To serve, slice the meat and serve with the pan juices.

INGREDIENTS
30 ml (2 tbsp) groundnut oil
1.5 kg (3 lb) loin of veal,
  boned and rolled
5 ml (1 tsp) turmeric
salt and pepper
juice of 1 lemon
water

NOISETTES D'AGNEAU CHASSEUR

This is a delicious combination of tender lamb with lightly sautéed mushrooms,
shallots and white wine. Accompany with a red or white Burgundy.

Serves 4

Melt the butter with the oil in a large frying pan and fry the noisettes for 2–5 minutes on each side, depending on whether you like them rare or well-done. Remove from the pan and keep hot.

Pour off all but about 30 ml (2 tbsp) of fat from the pan. Fry the shallot and garlic in the fat until soft. Add the mushrooms and fry for 3 minutes. Stir in the brandy and wine and cook over high heat for 1 minute.

Mix the stock, arrowroot and tomato purée together and stir it into the pan with the tomatoes and tarragon. Simmer gently for 10 minutes.

Adjust the seasoning and stir in the parsley. Serve at once with the noisettes.

INGREDIENTS
15 g (½ oz) butter
15 ml (1 tbsp) olive oil
12 lamb noisettes, about
  2.5 cm (1 inch) thick
2 shallots, finely chopped
1 garlic clove, crushed
100 g (4 oz) button mushrooms,
  thinly sliced
15 ml (1 tbsp) brandy
150 ml (¼ pint) dry white wine
150 ml (¼ pint) chicken stock
  (see page 247)
5 ml (1 tsp) arrowroot
5 ml (1 tsp) tomato purée
4 tomatoes, skinned, seeded and
  chopped
7.5 ml (1½ tsp) chopped fresh
  tarragon or basil
salt and pepper
15 ml (1 tbsp) chopped fresh
  parsley

PORK CHOPS WITH ARTICHOKE HEARTS

These thick pork chops from the loin are simmered in a wine and tomato sauce, delicately flavoured with marjoram, and garnished with whole artichoke hearts.

Serves 4

INGREDIENTS

25 g (1 oz) butter

30 ml (2 tbsp) olive oil

1 slice unsmoked streaky bacon, rinded and finely chopped

2 shallots, finely chopped

1 large garlic clove, crushed

4 pork loin chops, about 225 g (8 oz) each

1.25 ml (¼ tsp) dried marjoram

300 ml (½ pint) dry white wine

salt and pepper

25 ml (1½ tbsp) tomato purée

75 ml (3 fl oz) water

400 g (14 oz) canned artichoke hearts, drained

In a flameproof casserole, melt the butter with the oil and fry the bacon, shallots and garlic, for 3 minutes. Add the pork chops, sprinkle with marjoram, and fry for 3 minutes on each side to seal. Pour in the wine and season. Cook, uncovered, for 10 minutes.

Blend the tomato purée with the water and stir into the liquid in the pan. Bring to the boil, reduce the heat, cover and simmer for 30 minutes. Add the artichoke hearts, cover and simmer for a further 10 minutes. Serve hot.

STEAK TARTARE

Steak Tartare is raw fillet or rump steak which is minced finely and served with a variety of chopped vegetables. The meat is shaped into individual rounds and garnished with raw egg yolks in their shells.

Serves 4

INGREDIENTS

500 g (1 lb) lean fillet or rump steak, finely chopped or minced

salt and pepper

Worcestershire sauce

30 ml (2 tbsp) sunflower seed oil

1 small onion, finely chopped

1 green pepper, seeded and finely chopped

15 ml (1 tbsp) capers, chopped

30 ml (2 tbsp) fresh parsley, finely chopped

4 egg yolks, in their half shells

lettuce leaves, to garnish

mayonnaise, to serve

Mix the minced beef with seasoning, Worcestershire sauce to taste and the oil. Mix thoroughly, then form into 4 rounds. Arrange on individual plates and surround with small mounds of onion, green pepper, capers and parsley.

Make a shallow indentation in the centre of each mound and place an egg yolk in its shell inside. Garnish with lettuce leaves and serve with mayonnaise.

RAISED PORK AND APPLE PIE

Raised pork pies are a traditional English dish with sage and apple used as a tasty addition. During the 18th century apples were commonly used in savoury pies.

Serves 8–10

Place the veal knuckle, salt, peppercorns and bouquet garni in a large pan with enough cold water to cover. Bring to the boil, skim off any scum, cover then simmer for 2 hours. Strain the stock through a muslin, then skim off the fat when cool and reserve.

Sift the flour and a pinch of salt into a mixing bowl. Bring the lard and water to the boil, remove from heat and quickly stir it into the flour to form a dough. Cool slightly, then knead the dough until smooth. Cut off one-third of the dough and place it under an upturned bowl until required.

Flour the inside of a pie mould or an 18 cm (7 inch) round spring-form cake tin. Roll out the dough and line the base and sides of the tin.

Mix the bacon, pork, seasoning and sage together and add 30 ml (2 tbsp) of the veal stock to moisten. Press half the mixture into the pastry case. Cover with apple slices and press the remaining mixture over the top.

Roll out the remaining pastry to cover the pie. Brush the edges of the pie with water, place the lid in position and press the edges together to seal. Mark around the edge of the pie with a fork and make a hole in the centre. Brush with beaten eggs. Re-roll the trimmings and cut them into leaves. Arrange on top of the pie and brush with the egg. Place on a baking sheet.

Bake at 190°C (375°F) mark 5 for 1 hour. Reduce the temperature to 180°C (350°F) mark 4 and bake for a further 1–1¼ hours. Remove the outside of the mould or tin and brush the sides of the pie with beaten egg, then return to the oven for about 10 minutes until golden. Pour the veal stock carefully through the hole in the centre of the pie and leave for 2–3 hours until the stock has set to a jelly. Remove from the mould to serve.

INGREDIENTS
1 veal knuckle, chopped
salt and pepper
6 black peppercorns
bouquet garni
500 g (1 lb) plain flour
100 g (4 oz) lard or butter
175 ml (6 fl oz) cold water
100 g (4 oz) streaky bacon, rinded and diced
750 g (1½ lb) lean pork, cut into 1 cm (½ inch) cubes
10 ml (2 tsp) chopped fresh sage or 5 ml (1 tsp) dried
175 g (6 oz) cooking apple, peeled, cored and thinly sliced
beaten egg, to glaze

FILLET OF VEAL IN PASTRY

*This cut of meat is extremely tender. The fillet is spread with chicken pâté,
pistachio nuts and ham, then rolled and encased in puff pastry.*

Serves 4

INGREDIENTS

25 g (1 oz) butter

*500 g (1 lb) boned and rolled fillet
of veal (grenadin)*

salt and pepper

*100 g (4 oz) smooth chicken liver
pâté*

*25 g (1 oz) shelled pistachio nuts,
skinned and roughly chopped*

*4 large slices Parma or
Westphalian ham*

*puff pastry, made with 100 g
(4 oz) flour (see page 248)*

1 egg, beaten

SAUCE

150 ml (¼ pint) dry white wine

*150 ml (¼ pint) chicken stock
(see page 247)*

*50 g (2 oz) button mushrooms,
sliced*

15 ml (1 tbsp) redcurrant jelly

Melt the butter in a roasting tin, add the veal and turn until it is well coated with the butter. Roast in the oven at 190°C (375°F) mark 5 for 20 minutes. Remove from the tin and leave until cold. Reserve the meat juices in the roasting tin.

Season the veal with salt and pepper. Combine the pâté and pistachio nuts and spread the mixture over the veal. Completely wrap the veal in the ham.

Roll out the pastry on a lightly floured board to a rectangle large enough to completely encase the meat. Place the meat in the centre, wrap the pastry around and seal the edges well by brushing with water and pressing together. Re-roll the trimmings and use to garnish. Brush beaten egg over the pastry and place, seam side down, on a dampened baking sheet. Bake at 220°C (425°F) mark 7 for 25 minutes or until crisp and golden. Transfer to a warmed serving dish.

To make the sauce, add the wine, stock and mushroom slices to the juices in the roasting tin and boil rapidly until reduced by half. Stir in the redcurrant jelly and season to taste. Serve with the veal.

PORK LASAGNE

This delicious pasta dish, flavoured with marjoram and Italian cheese,
is best served piping hot with a green side salad.

Serves 6–8

Heat the oil in a frying pan and fry the bacon, onion and garlic for 5 minutes. Add the pork and cook, stirring, until browned. Stir in the tomato purée, then the wine, water, seasoning, bay leaf and marjoram. Bring to the boil, cover, reduce the heat and simmer for 1 hour.

Place a layer of lasagne in a greased shallow oblong dish. Top with a layer of meat, then some ricotta cheese. Continue in this way, ending with a layer of pasta.

For the sauce, melt the butter and stir in the flour. Cook, stirring, for 1 minute. Remove from the heat and gradually stir in the milk. Add the bay leaf, salt, pepper and nutmeg. Cook over a gentle heat, stirring constantly, for 5 minutes. Pour over the lasagne. Sprinkle with Parmesan cheese and dot with the butter. Bake at 200°C (400°F) mark 6 for 30–40 minutes or until the topping is golden brown. Serve hot.

INGREDIENTS
30 ml (2 tbsp) olive oil
50 g (2 oz) unsmoked streaky
  bacon, rinded and finely
  chopped
1 onion, finely chopped
1 garlic clove, crushed
500 g (1 lb) minced pork
30 ml (2 tbsp) tomato purée
100 ml (4 fl oz) red wine
300 ml (½ pint) water or stock
salt and pepper
1 bay leaf
2.5 ml (½ tsp) dried marjoram
225 g (8 oz) lasagne (see page 251)
350 g (12 oz) ricotta cheese
30 ml (2 tbsp) finely grated
  Parmesan cheese
25 g (1 oz) butter
BECHAMEL SAUCE
25 g (1 oz) butter
25 g (1 oz) flour
450 ml (¾ pint) milk
1 bay leaf
pinch of grated nutmeg

PAUPIETTES DE VEAU

Paupiettes are thin slices of meat or fish which are stuffed and rolled.
These paupiettes are filled with Parma ham and fresh tarragon and cooked
in a subtle wine sauce.

Serves 4

Place the veal escalopes between two sheets of greaseproof paper and flatten with a meat bat or rolling pin. Lay the escalopes flat and cover with the ham, trimming to fit if necessary. Season and place 2 tarragon sprigs on each. Roll up and secure with wooden cocktail sticks. Coat lightly in seasoned flour.

Melt 25 g (1 oz) of the butter in a sauté pan and fry the shallots and any ham trimmings until the shallots are soft. Add the veal rolls and fry until evenly browned all over. Stir in the wine, tomato purée and stock. Season to taste. Cover the pan tightly and cook over gentle heat for 20 minutes or until tender. Transfer the veal rolls to a warmed serving dish and remove the cocktail sticks. Keep hot. Boil the pan juices until reduced and thickened. Taste and adjust the seasoning. Stir in the remaining butter, heat until melted, then pour it over the veal rolls and serve.

INGREDIENTS
4 veal escalopes
4 slices Parma ham
salt and pepper
8 sprigs fresh tarragon
seasoned flour
40 g (1½ oz) butter
5 shallots, finely chopped
150 ml (¼ pint) dry white wine
10 ml (2 tsp) tomato purée
60 ml (4 tbsp) veal stock

VEAL MEATBALLS WITH CAPER AND CREAM SAUCE

Serve with buttered noodles and a green vegetable such as mangetout or French beans.

Serves 4

INGREDIENTS

500 g (1 lb) minced lean veal
1 small onion, finely chopped
15 ml (1 tbsp) chopped fresh
*   parsley*
salt and pepper
pinch of grated nutmeg
50 g (2 oz) fresh white
*   breadcrumbs*
1 egg, lightly beaten
seasoned flour
50 g (2 oz) unsalted butter
60 ml (4 tbsp) white wine
15 ml (1 tbsp) drained capers
150 ml (¼ pint) sour cream
chopped fresh parsley, to garnish

Mix the veal, onion, parsley, seasoning, nutmeg and breadcrumbs together. Mix in the lightly beaten egg.

Shape the mixture into 16 oval balls and toss in the seasoned flour. Melt the butter in a large frying pan and fry the meatballs for 15 minutes, or until evenly browned and cooked through.

Remove from the pan with a slotted spoon and keep hot while preparing the sauce. Pour off half the fat from the pan, then add the wine, scraping the base of the pan to loosen any sediment. Bring to the boil.

Reduce the heat and stir in the capers and sour cream. Heat gently but do not allow the sauce to boil. Taste and adjust the seasoning. Arrange the meatballs on a warmed serving plate, pour the sauce over the top and sprinkle with parsley.

VEAL CHOPS WITH GRUYERE CHEESE AND SAGE

The veal chops are fried in breadcrumbs, seasoned with sage leaves
to give a distinctive flavour, and then topped with melted cheese.

Serves 4

INGREDIENTS

75 g (3 oz) fresh breadcrumbs
salt and pepper
5 fresh sage leaves, finely chopped
4 veal chops, about 225 g (8 oz)
*   each*
1 egg, lightly beaten
100 g (4 oz) butter
75 g (3 oz) Gruyère cheese, finely
*   grated*
4 fresh sage leaves, to garnish

Mix the breadcrumbs with seasoning and the chopped sage leaves.

Coat the chops first in the beaten egg, then in the breadcrumbs, pressing them on lightly.

Melt the butter in a frying pan and fry the chops over moderate heat for 4 minutes on each side, or until the coating is crisp and golden brown. Remove the chops from the pan, and place them in a flameproof serving dish. Sprinkle the cheese over the chops. Cook under a hot grill for 2 minutes or until the cheese melts and bubbles.

Place a sage leaf on top of each chop and serve at once.

MEAT PILAF

Saffron threads are the dried stigmas of the crocus flower and there are varying grades of quality. The very best saffron is a burnished orange colour, and in some countries, it is more expensive to buy per 1 oz (25 g) than gold, as 70,000–80,000 crocus flowers are needed to make 500 g (1 lb) of saffron.

Serves 6–8

INGREDIENTS

75 g (3 oz) butter

1 large onion, finely chopped

750 g (1½ lb) braising steak, trimmed and cut into 4 cm (1½ inch) cubes

75 ml (5 tbsp) tomato purée

cold water

2.5 ml (½ tsp) saffron threads

5 ml (1 tsp) hot water

salt and pepper

750 g (1½ lb) French beans, trimmed and cut into 5 cm (2 inch) pieces

1 kg (2 lb) basmati rice

extra butter and natural yogurt, to serve (optional)

Melt 50 g (2 oz) of the butter in a frying pan and fry the onion until golden. Add the meat and cook, stirring, for 5 minutes or until browned. Stir in the tomato purée and cook for 2 minutes. Stir in 900 ml (1½ pints) cold water, bring it to the boil, cover and reduce the heat. Simmer for 2 hours or until the meat is tender and the sauce has reduced and thickened sufficiently to just cover the meat.

Place the saffron threads in a mortar and pound with a pestle until they are ground to a fine powder. Place in a small bowl, add the hot water and leave to infuse for 10 minutes.

Add the saffron and water mixture, seasoning and French beans to the meat and simmer for 10 minutes. Cook the rice in boiling salted water for 5 minutes. Drain the rice immediately, rinse in cold water then drain thoroughly.

Melt the remaining butter with 75 ml (3 fl oz) cold water in a large deep saucepan with a tight-fitting lid. Spoon a 5 cm (2 inch) layer of rice over the base of the pan. Using a slotted spoon, place some of the meat and bean mixture on top of the rice layer. Do not spread the meat to the edges of the pan. Continue making alternate layers of meat and beans and rice, in a pyramid shape, ending with a layer of rice. Pour the sauce very gently over the top of the rice pyramid. Push the handle of a wooden spoon down through the centre of the rice. Wrap the saucepan lid in a tea towel and cover the pan.

Cook over a moderately low heat for 30–35 minutes, stirring occasionally. Plunge the base of the pan into cold water to prevent further cooking. Spoon on to a warmed serving dish and serve hot. The crunchy rice at the base of the pan should be served on a separate plate.

ROAST PORK WITH BLUE CHEESE SAUCE

In this dish the roast pork flavour is complemented by this surprisingly easy-to-make cheese sauce. Stilton cheese is used in this recipe, although Roquefort or Danish blue can be substituted.

Serves 4–6

INGREDIENTS

1 kg (2 lb) loin of pork

12 sage leaves

oil

salt and pepper

60 ml (4 tbsp) hot water or vegetable water

150 ml (¼ pint) sour cream

75 g (3 oz) Stilton cheese, crumbled

Wipe the meat with damp kitchen paper. Slightly loosen the skin and fat from the meat at both ends of the joint and tuck the sage leaves underneath. Brush the skin with oil and sprinkle with salt.

Roast at 180°C (350°F) mark 4 for 35 minutes per 500 g (1 lb) plus 35 minutes. Transfer to a warmed serving dish and keep hot while preparing the sauce.

Pour off all but 30 ml (2 tbsp) of the fat from the roasting tin. Pour the remaining 30 ml (2 tbsp) and the sediment into a small pan with the water. Bring to the boil, stirring. Reduce the heat and stir in the sour cream and Stilton cheese. Stir over gentle heat until the cheese has melted. Do not allow to boil. Adjust the seasoning.

Carve the meat into thin slices and serve the sauce separately.

CHARCOAL GRILLED VEAL WITH DIJON BUTTER

The Dijon butter may also be served with steak, pork or lamb chops.

Serves 4

Brush the veal cutlets with the oil and season with pepper.

For the Dijon butter, place all the ingredients in a blender or food processor and blend for a few seconds until just mixed. Alternatively, beat the butter by hand until smooth, then beat in the remaining ingredients. Season and chill until firm.

Heat a charcoal grill until hot. Lay the cutlets on the grill and cook for 2–3 minutes on each side, depending on the heat from the grill.

Remove from the heat and season with salt. Arrange the cutlets on a serving plate and garnish with lemon slices and parsley. Place a pat of the Dijon butter on each cutlet and serve immediately.

INGREDIENTS
*8 thin veal cutlets, about
   100 g (4 oz) each
75 ml (3 fl oz) olive oil
salt and pepper
½ lemon, thinly sliced
4 parsley sprigs*
DIJON BUTTER
*100 g (4 oz) unsalted butter,
   softened
½ shallot, finely chopped
25 ml (1½ tbsp) Dijon mustard
15 ml (1 tbsp) chopped fresh
   parsley*

PORK AND BEAN CASSEROLE

If a thicker sauce is preferred, strain the casserole and boil the sauce to reduce to the required consistency. Return the meat and beans to the sauce and re-heat gently.

Serves 4–6

Rinse the beans and drain. Heat 30 ml (2 tbsp) of the oil in a large frying pan, add the pork and fry until brown all over. Transfer to a flameproof dish. Add the remaining oil to the pan and fry the onion until soft. Add to the dish with the beans, bay leaf, cloves, thyme, stock, lemon juice and tomato purée. Bring to the boil, cover and simmer for about 2 hours or until the meat and beans are tender, stirring occasionally. Remove the bay leaf and cloves—and thyme, if possible.

Add the tomatoes, season and simmer for 1–2 minutes to heat through. Sprinkle with chopped parsley before serving.

INGREDIENTS
*225 g (8 oz) dried haricot, pinto
   or black eyed beans, soaked
   overnight and drained
45 ml (3 tbsp) oil
750 g (1½ lb) pork shoulder, cubed
1 onion, chopped
1 bay leaf
6 cloves
few sprigs of fresh thyme
450 ml (¾ pint) chicken stock
   (see page 247)
45 ml (3 tbsp) lemon juice
15 ml (1 tbsp) tomato purée
4 tomatoes, skinned and chopped
salt and pepper
chopped fresh parsley, to garnish*

THE MEAT HALL

FISH

FISH

— ❖ —

With at least 40 different types of fish on show from Scotch salmon and Cornish sturgeon to king prawns from the Indian Ocean, it is hardly surprising that visitors flock to look at the renowned display which changes daily. Delicious to eat, tempting to look at, fish makes the ideal starter to a meal or an impressive main course dinner dish.

SPAGHETTI WITH ANCHOVY AND OREGANO SAUCE

This is a tasty spaghetti dish tossed in an anchovy and oregano sauce. Serve with a generous amount of freshly grated Parmesan cheese.

Serves 4

INGREDIENTS

90 ml (3½ fl oz) olive oil
2 garlic cloves, crushed
50 g (2 oz) canned anchovy fillets, drained
500 g (1 lb) spaghetti
10 ml (2 tsp) finely chopped fresh oregano
salt and pepper
45 ml (3 tbsp) chopped parsley
grated Parmesan cheese, to serve

Heat the oil in a small saucepan and fry the garlic until golden. Reduce the heat to very low, stir in the anchovies and cook gently until the anchovies have completely disintegrated.

Meanwhile, cook the spaghetti in plenty of boiling salted water until al dente.

Stir the oregano and pepper into the sauce. Drain the spaghetti well and turn into a warmed serving dish. Pour over the sauce, sprinkle with the parsley and gently toss together. Serve with plenty of Parmesan cheese.

SHELLFISH SALAD

This salad is very colourful and quick to prepare. If fresh mussels are unobtainable, prawns or clams can be used instead.

Serves 6

INGREDIENTS

12 fresh mussels
500 g (1 lb) scallops
150 ml (¼ pint) white wine
1 yellow pepper, seeded
12 black olives
50 ml (2 fl oz) white wine vinegar
15 ml (1 tbsp) Dijon mustard
1 garlic clove, crushed
salt and pepper
175 ml (6 fl oz) sunflower seed oil

Wash the mussels under cold running water and cut off the 'beard'. Discard any that do not close when the shell is tapped sharply. Steam the mussels for about 3 minutes, or until the shells open.

Poach the scallops in the white wine for 1 minute, then drain. Arrange the mussels and scallops in a large serving bowl. Cut the yellow pepper into fine shreds and add to the bowl with the olives. Pour the vinegar into a screw top jar and add the mustard, garlic, salt and pepper. Stir well and add the oil. Place the lid on the jar tightly and shake the dressing until thoroughly mixed. Pour the dressing over the salad and toss well.

DEEP-FRIED SCAMPI WITH
RADICCHIO SALAD

DEEP-FRIED SCAMPI WITH RADICCHIO SALAD

*The addition of ale makes a light batter to coat the scampi. Radicchio
adds colour and a sharp bite to the salad.*

Serves 4

Sift the flour, mustard and salt into a bowl and make a well in the centre. Pour in the oil and light ale then gradually draw the flour into the liquid. Beat well to form a smooth batter. Cover with clingfilm and leave to rest for 30 minutes.

Whisk the egg white until stiff then fold it into the batter. Add the scampi to the batter in batches and carefully turn them over to coat thoroughly. Remove with a slotted spoon, allowing the excess batter to drain off. Heat the oil in a deep-fat fryer to 180°C (350°F). Place the scampi in the basket, lower it into the oil and cook for 3 minutes.

Drain the scampi on kitchen paper and keep hot. Continue in the same way until all the scampi has been cooked.

Arrange the radicchio and fennel on the side of each serving plate. Cut the strips of green pepper in half and add these to the plates with the walnuts. Mix the olive oil, vinegar, sugar and seasoning together and pour it over the salads. Divide the scampi between the plates and serve with wedges of lemon.

INGREDIENTS
100 g (4 oz) flour
pinch of mustard powder
salt and pepper
30 ml (2 tbsp) vegetable oil
*150 ml (¼ pint) light ale or bitter
  beer*
1 egg white
350 g (12 oz) peeled scampi
oil, for deep frying
1 radicchio lettuce
*½ fennel bulb, cut into julienne
  strips*
*½ green pepper, peeled, seeded and
  cut into julienne strips*
25 g (1 oz) walnuts, chopped
45 ml (3 tbsp) olive oil
15 ml (1 tbsp) tarragon vinegar
pinch of sugar
lemon wedges, to serve

41

CREAMY CLAM CHOWDER

CREAMY CLAM CHOWDER

*An all-American favourite, this creamy and substantial soup, with potatoes
and dried pork, will satisfy any mealtime appetite.*

Serves 4

INGREDIENTS
16 clams
75 g (3 oz) salt pork, diced
1 onion, finely chopped
15 ml (1 tbsp) flour
*225 g (8 oz) potatoes, peeled
    and diced*
450 ml (¾ pint) milk

To open the clams, hold each one in your hand, well protected by a thick cloth, with the hinge facing outwards. Insert the point of a sturdy short bladed knife in the hinge and give a short quick upward twist. Strain and reserve the clam liquid. Remove all the clams from their shells and reserve.

Cook the pork in a heavy-based saucepan until the fat runs. Reserve the pork and strain 30 ml (2 tbsp) of the fat into a saucepan. Add the onion and fry until soft and lightly browned. Add the flour and cook, stirring, for 2 minutes. Add the potatoes and clam liquid, cover and simmer for about 10 minutes or until the potatoes are almost tender.

Chop the clams, add them to the pan, cover and cook for 8–10 minutes. Stir in the milk, season and cook for a further 5 minutes. Sprinkle with the reserved pork and serve at once.

MONKFISH TERRINE WITH TOMATO CREAM

Monkfish has a firm white flesh and a distinct rich flavour. It is often referred to as 'poor man's lobster'. Other suitable fish for this recipe are; sole, whiting or cod.

Serves 4

Remove the stalks from the watercress and discard them. Place the leaves in a small saucepan and just cover with boiling water. Bring back to the boil, then drain and rinse in cold water. Squeeze dry to remove as much water as possible. Purée or finely chop the leaves.

Roughly chop the fish and place in a blender or food processor. Purée until smooth, then slowly add the egg white and cream whilst the machine is still running, until the mousse mixture is firm.

Add the lime rind and juice and seasoning. Divide the mixture in half and stir the watercress purée into one half.

Grease a 500 g (1 lb) loaf tin and line the base with greased greaseproof paper. Spread the watercress mousse evenly over the base of the tin, arrange the prawns down the centre and top with the fish mousse. Level the surface, cover with aluminium foil and place in a roasting tin. Pour in enough boiling water to come half-way up the sides of the loaf tin. Bake at 150°C (300°F) mark 2 for about 45 minutes or until just firm to the touch.

For the tomato cream, mix the tomato purée and lime juice together. Whisk the cream until it just holds its shape and fold in the tomato mixture. Season to taste. Chill until required.

Remove the terrine from the oven and take out of the roasting tin. Leave to cool, then pour off any liquid on the surface.

Unmould on to a plate and remove the lining paper. Cut into 8 slices and arrange 2 slices on 4 individual plates. Serve with a little tomato cream and garnish with watercress.

INGREDIENTS
1 bunch watercress
250 g (9 oz) monkfish fillet,
  well chilled
1 egg white, well chilled
150 ml (¼ pint) double cream,
  well chilled
grated rind and juice of 1 lime
salt and pepper
75 g (3 oz) peeled prawns
watercress, to garnish
TOMATO CREAM
2 tomatoes, skinned, seeded and
  puréed
5 ml (1 tsp) lime juice
100 ml (4 fl oz) double cream
salt and pepper

PRAWN NEWBURG

Serve on a large bread croustade as a starter, or on a bed of rice as a main course, with fresh watercress.

Serves 4

Place the slices of bread on a baking tray.

Melt half the butter and brush over the bread. Bake at 150°C (300°F) mark 2 for 25 minutes.

Meanwhile, melt the remaining butter in a pan and add the Madeira and brandy. Simmer for 5 minutes, then add the prawns. Season and simmer for 2 minutes. Remove from the heat.

Mix the egg yolks with the cream and stir into the pan. Cook over a gentle heat for 5 minutes, stirring, until the sauce thickens. Do not allow the mixture to boil or it will curdle.

Spoon the prawns and the sauce on to the baked bread and sprinkle with paprika. Serve hot with watercress.

INGREDIENTS
four 2 cm (¾ inch) thick slices
  white bread, crusts removed
50 g (2 oz) butter
45 ml (3 tbsp) Madeira
10 ml (2 tsp) brandy
350 g (12 oz) peeled prawns
salt and pepper
2 egg yolks
150 ml (¼ pint) double cream
2.5 ml (½ tsp) paprika
watercress, to serve

SOUSED HERRINGS

These herrings, strongly flavoured by the white wine vinegar, make a tasty hors d'oeuvre.

Serves 4

INGREDIENTS

4 herrings, cleaned, boned and
    filleted
salt and pepper
15 ml (1 tbsp) chopped fresh
    parsley
15 ml (1 tbsp) chopped fresh chives
1 small onion, sliced into rings
6 black peppercorns
2 bay leaves, crumbled
4 parsley stalks
300 ml (½ pint) white wine vinegar

Lay the herring fillets out flat, season and sprinkle with parsley and chives. Roll up the herrings from the head to the tail with the herbs on the inside. Secure with wooden cocktail sticks. Pack into a fairly shallow ovenproof dish. Scatter over the onion rings, peppercorns, bay leaves and parsley stalks. Pour over the vinegar and sufficient water to cover the rolls.

Cover with greaseproof paper and cook at 170°C (325°F) mark 3 for 45 minutes–1 hour or until the flesh flakes easily. Leave the herrings to cool in the liquid, then chill until required.

GREY MULLET WITH CUMIN AND COURGETTES

*Grey mullet has delicate white flesh and is found in warm coastal waters.
English grey mullet comes from the south west. This agile fish is capable
of leaping sideways to great heights, and is often referred to in France as
'poisson sauteur', the leaping fish.*

Serves 4

INGREDIENTS

1.5 kg (3 lb) grey mullet (about 4
    fish), cleaned
600 ml (1 pint) water
45 ml (3 tbsp) olive oil
1 large onion, finely chopped
2 garlic cloves, crushed
5 ml (1 tsp) ground cumin
large pinch of cayenne
15 ml (1 tbsp) tomato purée
400 g (14 oz) canned tomatoes,
    coarsely chopped
30 ml (2 tbsp) finely chopped fresh
    parsley
500 g (1 lb) potatoes, peeled and
    cut into bite-sized chunks
salt and pepper
500 g (1 lb) courgettes,
    thickly sliced

Cut the heads and tails off the fish and cut the bodies in half lengthways. Place them, with the heads and tails, into a large saucepan. Add 600 ml (1 pint) water, bring to the boil, cover and simmer gently for 20 minutes.

Meanwhile, heat the oil in a frying pan and fry the onion and garlic until soft. Stir in the cumin and cayenne, then the tomato purée. Stir for 1 minute before stirring in the tomatoes. Add the parsley then set aside.

Remove the fish from the pan, and discard the heads and tails. Skin the fish and remove any bones. Reserve the flesh. Strain the liquid and add it to the tomatoes. Bring to the boil, then add the potatoes and salt. Simmer, covered for 15 minutes. Stir in the courgettes and cook for a further 15 minutes, adding more water if necessary. Add the fish to the pan and simmer for 5 minutes. Adjust the seasoning and serve hot with crusty bread.

DEVILLED WHITEBAIT WITH DEEP-FRIED PARSLEY

Devilled Whitebait with Deep-Fried Parsley

Coated in flour seasoned with spices, these young fish are deep fried and then eaten whole.

Serves 4

Sift the flour, curry powder, ginger, cayenne pepper and salt together into a large plastic bag. Put a quarter of the whitebait into the bag and shake well to coat them in the flour mixture. Lift the fish out and shake in a sieve to remove excess flour. Repeat with the remaining whitebait.

Heat the oil in a deep-fat fryer to 190°C (375°F). Put a single layer of whitebait into the frying basket and lower it into the pan. Fry for 2–3 minutes, shaking the basket occasionally, until the whitebait make a rustling sound as they are shaken. Tip out on to a warmed plate lined with kitchen paper. Fry the remaining whitebait in the same way. Allow the fat to reduce in temperature to about 186°C (365°F). Deep-fry the parsley for a few seconds until it stops sizzling. Drain on kitchen paper then sprinkle with sea salt.

Divide the whitebait between four individual warmed plates. Scatter over the parsley sprigs and garnish with the lemon wedges.

INGREDIENTS

60 ml (4 tbsp) flour
1.25 ml ($\frac{1}{4}$ tsp) curry powder
1.25 ml ($\frac{1}{4}$ tsp) ground ginger
1.25 ml ($\frac{1}{4}$ tsp) cayenne pepper
salt
600 g (1$\frac{1}{4}$ lb) whitebait, fresh or frozen
oil, for deep-frying
15 g ($\frac{1}{2}$ oz) parsley sprigs
sea salt
2 lemons, cut into wedges

SMOKED SALMON PATE WITH MELBA TOAST

This delicious pâté is quick to make, using a food processor, or blender.
Smoked salmon trimmings may be used, which are far more economical
than slices.

Serves 6–8

Put the butter in a small saucepan and heat gently until melted. Leave for 5 minutes to cool slightly. Place the salmon in a blender or food processor. With the machine running, pour in the melted butter and mix until the salmon is a smooth paste. Remove the mixture from the bowl, season to taste, then stir in the lemon juice and cream.

Spoon the pâté into a serving dish and garnish with the smoked salmon and cucumber slices. Chill for 30 minutes before serving.

To make the melba toast, toast the bread slices on both sides under a hot grill. Using a serrated knife, cut off the crusts and slide the knife between the toasted edges to split the bread. Cut each piece into two triangles, then toast the untoasted side until golden and the edges curl.

Serve the pâté with the melba toast.

INGREDIENTS
100 g (4 oz) butter
225 g (8 oz) smoked salmon
salt and pepper
15 ml (1 tbsp) lemon juice
150 ml ($\frac{1}{4}$ pint) double cream,
lightly whipped
8 thin slices white bread
extra smoked salmon and
cucumber, to garnish

POTTED SALMON

Serve this recipe with thin slices of brown bread and butter and lemon.

Serves 4–6

Put the salmon into a shallow ovenproof dish and pour over the wine. Season and add the bay leaf and mace. Cover tightly and cook at 170°C (325°F) mark 3 for 45 minutes–1 hour or until the flesh flakes easily.

Leave the salmon to cool in the liquid. Remove with a slotted spoon and drain well. Flake the salmon then purée in a blender or food processor with half of the butter. Pack firmly into 2 pots, cover and chill for at least 1 hour.

Meanwhile, melt the remaining butter in a small heavy-based saucepan over gentle heat until it stops foaming. Remove from the heat and stand until all the sediment has sunk to the bottom. Carefully pour off the clear liquid and pour it over the surface of the salmon mixture. Leave in a cool place to set, then cover and chill until required.

INGREDIENTS
600 g (1$\frac{1}{4}$ lb) tail piece of salmon
75 ml (3 fl oz) dry white wine
salt and pepper
1 bay leaf
2 blades of mace
225 g (8 oz) butter, softened

SMOKED EEL PATE

Smoked eel has a distinct earthy flavour which is greatly enhanced by the
addition of horseradish. Serve the pâté with melba toast (see above) or crackers.

Serves 8

Place the eel fillets in a blender or food processor. With the machine running, pour in the melted butter and mix until the eel is a fine paste. Remove the fish from the bowl, stir in the lemon juice, and season to taste. Stir in the horseradish and the sour cream. Mix all the ingredients well, then transfer it to a serving dish.

INGREDIENTS
225 g (8 oz) smoked eel fillets
100 g (4 oz) butter, melted and
cooled
15 ml (1 tbsp) lemon juice
salt and pepper
5 ml (1 tsp) grated fresh
horseradish
150 ml ($\frac{1}{4}$ pint) sour cream

SMOKED SALMON PATE WITH MELBA TOAST

LANGOUSTINE SOUFFLES

These individual soufflés can be served as a light, appetizing starter or as a luncheon dish served with a crisp green salad.

Serves 6

INGREDIENTS

225 g (8 oz) raw langoustine tails,
  shelled
300 ml (½ pint) fish stock (see
  page 246)
40 g (1½ oz) butter
2 shallots, finely chopped
30 ml (2 tbsp) flour
2 egg yolks
pinch of cayenne pepper
pinch of grated nutmeg
45 ml (3 tbsp) toasted breadcrumbs
3 egg whites
pinch of salt
whole langoustines, to garnish
  (optional)

Poach the langoustine tails in the fish stock for about 2 minutes. Drain and roughly chop. Reserve the fish stock.

Melt the butter and fry the shallots until soft. Stir in the flour and cook for 1 minute. Remove from the heat and gradually stir in the fish stock. Cook, stirring, until the sauce has thickened. Simmer for 1 minute, then remove from the heat and beat in the egg yolks. Stir in the langoustine tails and season well.

Grease 6 individual 175–200 ml (6–7 fl oz) ramekins and coat the insides with toasted breadcrumbs. Chill.

Whisk the egg whites with the salt until stiff, then fold them into the sauce. Spoon into the prepared ramekins.

Arrange on a preheated baking sheet and bake at 180°C (350°F) mark 4 for about 20 minutes or until risen and golden. Serve immediately garnished with langoustines if liked.

TAGLIATELLE WITH CRAB AND ASPARAGUS CREAM SAUCE

This quick-and-easy recipe turns tagliatelle into a special meal.
This sauce is also delicious served with other pasta shapes.

Serves 4

Steam the asparagus until just tender, then drain and rinse under cold running water. Roughly flake the crabmeat. Melt the butter and fry the shallots until soft then stir in the ham. Add the asparagus, crabmeat, half the cream and seasoning. Bring gently to a simmer over moderate heat, stirring carefully until the sauce has thickened slightly. Reduce the heat and simmer gently while cooking the pasta.

Cook the pasta in plenty of boiling salted water until al dente. Drain well, then return to the pan with the remaining cream and half the Parmesan cheese. Toss over a low heat until well mixed. Transfer to a warmed serving dish and make a hollow in the centre of the pasta. Pour the crab and asparagus sauce in the centre and sprinkle with the remaining Parmesan cheese. Serve at once.

INGREDIENTS
175 g (6 oz) fresh asparagus,
  trimmed and cut into 2.5 cm
  (1 inch) lengths
175 g (6 oz) crabmeat, white and
  dark mixed
75 g (3 oz) butter
3 shallots, finely chopped
1 thin slice ham, finely chopped
225 ml (8 fl oz) double cream
salt and pepper
25 g (1 oz) finely grated
  Parmesan cheese
350 g (12 oz) tagliatelle
  (see page 251)

RISOTTO DE COQUILLES ST JACQUES

Golden saffron powder subtly flavours this flavoursome risotto of fresh scallops
and julienne vegetables.

Serves 4

Melt 50 g (2 oz) of the butter in a large saucepan and fry the shallots until soft. Add the rice and cook, stirring until transparent. Add the saffron and 150 ml ($\frac{1}{4}$ pint) of the white wine then bring it to the boil. Stir in 300 ml ($\frac{1}{2}$ pint) of the stock and simmer gently for about 15 minutes or until all the liquid has been absorbed and the rice is tender, adding a little more stock if necessary.

Separate the coral roe from the scallops. Cut each scallop in half horizontally. About 5 minutes before the rice is cooked, melt the remaining butter in a frying pan and stir-fry the leek and fennel for 3 minutes or until just tender. Remove from the pan and keep hot. Add the scallops and coral and fry quickly on both sides until just opaque. Season generously. Pour over the remaining white wine and simmer gently for 2 minutes.

Stir the Parmesan cheese into the risotto and adjust the seasoning. Pile the risotto into a serving dish. Top with the leek, fennel and scallop mixture and garnish with the fennel leaves. Serve at once.

INGREDIENTS
90 g (3$\frac{1}{2}$ oz) butter
3 shallots, finely chopped
225 g (8 oz) short-grain risotto rice
1.25 ml ($\frac{1}{4}$ tsp) saffron powder
200 ml (7 fl oz) dry white wine
about 400 ml (14 fl oz) fish stock
  (see page 246)
salt and pepper
16 fresh scallops
100 g (4 oz) leek, cut in julienne
  strips
100 g (4 oz) fennel, cut in julienne
  strips
25 g (1 oz) freshly grated
  Parmesan cheese
fennel leaves, to garnish

LANGOUSTINE SOUFFLES

STUFFED SEA BASS BRAISED IN WHITE WINE

Attractively garnished with fresh fennel leaves and served with a thick creamy sauce,
this sea bass is a hearty and satisfying meal.

Serves 4

INGREDIENTS

2 fennel bulbs, trimmed and
  thinly sliced
150 ml (¼ pint) water
1 sea bass, about 1 kg (2 lb),
  cleaned
50 g (2 oz) fresh white
  breadcrumbs
30 ml (2 tbsp) milk
75 g (3 oz) butter
2 shallots, finely chopped
10 ml (2 tsp) finely chopped fresh
  parsley
5 ml (1 tsp) finely grated lemon
  rind
2 egg yolks
salt and pepper
150 ml (¼ pint) full-bodied dry
  white wine
30 ml (2 tbsp) dry white
  vermouth
50 ml (2 fl oz) double cream
fennel leaves, to garnish

Cook the fennel in the water in a covered pan for 10 minutes.

Meanwhile, cut the fins and gills from the fish. To remove the bones, place it underside downwards with the sides of the fish spread slightly outwards on the work surface. Press firmly along the backbone with the thumbs. Turn the fish over, cut through the backbone at the head and tail, then carefully lift the the backbone out. Remove any extra bones.

For the stuffing, soak the breadcrumbs in the milk then squeeze dry. Melt 25 g (1 oz) of the butter and fry the shallots until soft. Stir into the breadcrumbs with the parsley, lemon rind, egg yolks and seasoning. Spoon the stuffing into the cavity in the fish and sew up with fine string or cotton or secure with wooden cocktail sticks.

Place the fish in a shallow, greased ovenproof dish and pour over the wine and vermouth. Drain the fennel and add it to the dish. Dice the remaining butter, sprinkle over the fish and season. Cover with buttered greaseproof paper and cook at 170°C (325°F) mark 3 for 30–40 minutes or until the flesh flakes easily.

Carefully transfer the fish to a warmed serving plate. Remove the fennel from the cooking liquid with a slotted spoon and place on the dish with the fish. Cover and keep hot.

Strain the cooking liquid into a saucepan and boil until reduced to a light, syrupy consistency. Stir in the cream and continue to boil until slightly thickened. Adjust the seasoning. Remove the thread, or cocktail sticks, from the fish and spoon the sauce over. Garnish with fennel leaves and serve at once.

PLAKI

This dish can be found in Greece and throughout the Middle East.
Whole sea bass is an ideal choice, but halibut, grey mullet, sea bream, cod,
John Dory or haddock are all good alternatives.

Serves 4

INGREDIENTS

1 kg (2 lb) fish, left whole or
  cut into thick steaks
juice of 1 lemon
60 ml (4 tbsp) olive oil
2 large onions, thinly sliced
3 garlic cloves
400 g (14 oz) canned tomatoes,
  drained and finely chopped
175 ml (6 fl oz) dry white wine
15 ml (1 tbsp) rigani or oregano
1 bay leaf
salt and pepper
75 ml (5 tbsp) chopped parsley

Place the fish in a baking dish and pour over the lemon juice. If using a whole fish, pour some of the juice inside it. Heat the oil in a frying pan and fry the onions and garlic until golden. Add the tomatoes, breaking them up with a fork and cook for a further 5 minutes. Add the wine, rigani or oregano, bay leaf and seasoning. Bring to the boil, remove from the heat, add the parsley and cool for 5 minutes. Pour the sauce over the fish and bake uncovered, at 180°C (350°F) mark 4, for 40 minutes. Serve accompanied by hot crusty bread.

STIR-FRIED PRAWNS

*Make this dish with raw prawns if possible. If unavailable, add cooked prawns
at the end of the cooking time—although they will not have the same
'crunch' that raw prawns have.*

Serves 4

INGREDIENTS

225 g (8 oz) raw prawns, shelled
  and veins removed
2.5 ml (½ tsp) salt
60 ml (4 tbsp) groundnut oil
2 large spring onions, white part
  finely sliced and green part cut
  into 1 cm (½ inch) slices
2 large garlic cloves, finely
  chopped
5 ml (1 tsp) finely chopped
  fresh root ginger
225 g (8 oz) tomatoes, skinned and
  finely chopped
30 ml (2 tbsp) light soy sauce
2.5 ml (½ tsp) sugar
2.5 ml (½ tsp) potato flour
15 ml (1 tbsp) medium dry sherry
  or shaohsing wine
175 g (6 oz) mangetout
few drops sesame oil

Place the prawns in a dish and sprinkle over half of the salt.

Heat a wok until it is very hot, then add the oil. Add the prawns and stir-fry for 1 minute. Remove from the wok with a slotted spoon and reserve. Add the white spring onion, garlic and ginger to the wok, and stir-fry for a few seconds. Add the tomatoes, the remaining salt, soy sauce and sugar. Stir, cover the wok with a lid and reduce the heat. Cook for 3 minutes.

Uncover and stir in the potato flour mixed to a paste with the sherry, green spring onions and mangetout. Stir-fry for 2 minutes, add the prawns and stir-fry for 1 minute more. Sprinkle with sesame oil and serve immediately.

BAKED TROUT WITH HAZELNUTS AND DILL

*This is a delicious way to cook trout. The fish are baked in wine
and seasoned with dill, then served with hazelnuts and butter.*

Serves 4

INGREDIENTS

4 trout, about 275 g (10 oz) each,
  cleaned
40 ml (8 tsp) lemon juice
salt and pepper
4 sprigs of fresh dill
100 ml (4 fl oz) dry white wine
1 shallot, finely chopped
75 g (3 oz) hazelnuts
50 g (2 oz) butter
lemon wedges and parsley sprigs,
  to garnish

Cut the fins from the fish then sprinkle 30 ml (6 tsp) of the lemon juice over the skin and the cavities. Season inside and out and put a sprig of dill in each cavity. Place the trout in an ovenproof dish large enough to hold them tightly in one layer. Pour over the wine and add the shallot. Cover the dish with greased greaseproof paper, then bake at 180°C (350°F) mark 4 for 20–25 minutes or until the flesh flakes easily.

Meanwhile, place the hazelnuts under a moderately hot grill for about 5 minutes or until the skins dry out and flake. Rub off the skins and chop. Melt the butter, add the hazelnuts and cook over moderately high heat, stirring frequently, until golden brown. Add the remaining lemon juice and seasoning.

Carefully transfer the trout to 4 warmed serving plates. Boil the cooking juices rapidly until reduced to about 45 ml (3 tbsp). Spoon the juices over the fish, then over the hazelnuts and butter. Serve at once.

INDIVIDUAL MUSSEL SOUFFLES

These soufflés make a very elegant beginning to a dinner party meant to impress.
To save time, cook the mussels and mix with the sauce in advance.

Serves 4

Scrub the mussels well and remove the beards. Tap any which have opened—if they do not close, discard them. Place the mussels in a saucepan with the wine. Cover and cook over high heat for 5–7 minutes, until all the shells have opened. Discard any closed shells.

Drain the mussels and return the liquid to the pan. Add the garlic, shallot and herbs, and boil rapidly until reduced to 150 ml ($\frac{1}{4}$ pint). Strain through a muslin cloth and reserve.

Remove the mussels from their shells. Combine the cornflour, water and egg yolks, and add it to the reduced liquid in a small saucepan. Cook gently, stirring, until thickened. Stir in half the butter, then add the lemon juice and pepper to taste.

Grease 4 individual 175–200 ml (6–7 fl oz) ramekin dishes and coat the sides with Parmesan cheese. Chill.

Whisk the egg whites until stiff, then fold them into the sauce mixture until evenly combined. Spoon half the mixture into the prepared ramekin dishes. Sprinkle the mussels on top and finish with the remaining soufflé mixture.

Place the ramekins on a preheated baking tray and bake at 180°C (350°F) mark 4 for about 20 minutes until risen and golden. Serve immediately.

INGREDIENTS
750 g (1½ lb) fresh mussels
150 ml (¼ pint) white wine
1 garlic clove, chopped
1 shallot, chopped
sprig of fresh thyme
sprig of fresh parsley
1 bay leaf
10 ml (2 tsp) cornflour
15 ml (1 tbsp) water
2 egg yolks
25 g (1 oz) butter
15 ml (1 tbsp) lemon juice
pepper
30 ml (2 tbsp) grated Parmesan
   cheese
3 egg whites

THON A LA PROVENCALE

Tuna fish are found in the warmer parts of the Atlantic and Mediterranean seas.
The flesh is firm and is eaten fresh, salted, smoked or canned in oil or brine.

Serves 4–6

Place the tuna steak in a shallow dish and lay the anchovies on top. Mix 50 ml (2 fl oz) olive oil, lemon juice and pepper together and pour it over the fish. Leave to marinate for 1 hour. Melt 25 g (1 oz) of the butter in a flameproof casserole and fry the onion until golden. Add the garlic and fry for a further 2 minutes, then add the tomatoes and the bouquet garni, and cook for 5 minutes.

Drain the fish. Heat the remaining olive oil and fry the fish for 1 minute on each side. Add the fish to the casserole and pour over the white wine. Bring to the boil, cover, then cook in the oven at 180°C (350°F) mark 4 for 40 minutes, basting frequently.

Remove the fish from the casserole and discard any skin and bones. Remove the bouquet garni.

Knead the remaining butter with the flour. Gradually stir in the flour a little at a time over gentle heat, and cook until the sauce has thickened.

Pour the sauce over the fish and serve.

INGREDIENTS
750 g (1½ lb) whole tuna steak
6 anchovy fillets, soaked in cold
   water for 10 minutes and
   drained
55 ml (2¼ fl oz) olive oil
50 ml (2 fl oz) lemon juice
pepper
40 g (1½ oz) butter
1 onion, finely chopped
1 garlic clove, crushed
500 g (1 lb) tomatoes, peeled and
   finely chopped
bouquet garni
175 ml (6 fl oz) dry white wine
15 ml (1 tbsp) flour
few capers (optional)

SALMON TROUT STEAKS WITH WATERCRESS SAUCE

*This recipe may also be made with fresh salmon. Reserve some of the
larger watercress leaves, dip them in a little oil, and arrange them around the
border of each plate as a garnish.*

Serves 4

INGREDIENTS

300 ml (½ pint) dry white wine

600 ml (1 pint) water

bouquet garni

salt and 6 peppercorns

1 small onion, sliced

1 small carrot, sliced

30 ml (2 tbsp) double cream

175 g (6 oz) butter, diced

*2 bunches watercress, 4 small
   sprigs and some large leaves
   reserved for garnish*

4 salmon trout or salmon steaks

10 ml (2 tsp) lemon juice

½ lemon, thinly sliced, to garnish

Bring the wine, water, bouquet garni, seasoning, onion and carrot to the boil in a
large shallow pan. Simmer for 20 minutes, or until the vegetables are tender.

Strain 75 ml (3 fl oz) of the court bouillon into a small saucepan and boil until
reduced by two-thirds. Stir in the double cream and boil gently for 2 minutes.
Gradually whisk in the butter.

Plunge the watercress, including the stalks, into boiling water. Drain
immediately, then refresh in cold water. Drain and squeeze as much water as
possible from the watercress. Chop the watercress finely and add it to the
sauce. Keep hot. Strain the remaining court bouillon and return it to the pan. Add
the fish steaks and cook gently in the court bouillon for 12–15 minutes or until
the flesh flakes easily. Drain.

Stir the lemon juice into the sauce.

Arrange the reserved watercress leaves around the edge of each plate, pour
over the sauce and place the fish on the top. Garnish with watercress sprigs and
lemon slices.

BAKED SCAMPI AND SPINACH IN PERNOD SAUCE

*Spinach, chard or lettuce leaves wrapped around fish or shellfish help retain
the natural juices and flavour of the seafood.*

Serves 4

INGREDIENTS

*about 24 large fresh spinach
   leaves, central core removed*

350 g (12 oz) peeled scampi tails

25 g (1 oz) butter

60 ml (4 tbsp) dry white wine

pinch of cayenne pepper

salt and pepper

1 shallot, finely chopped

60 ml (4 tbsp) Pernod

*150 ml (¼ pint) fish stock
   (see page 246)*

100 ml (4 fl oz) double cream

*30 ml (2 tbsp) freshly grated
   Parmesan cheese*

Pour boiling water over the spinach leaves. Drain, then immediately drop them
into iced water. Dry well. Wrap the scampi in the leaves and arrange them in a
single layer in a shallow ovenproof dish, greased with half the butter. Pour over
the white wine and add the cayenne and seasoning. Cover and bake at 190°C
(375°F) mark 5 for 20 minutes. Drain the juices and reserve. Transfer the scampi
to a flameproof serving dish and keep hot.

Melt the remaining butter and fry the shallot until soft. Stir in the Pernod and
bring to the boil. Add the fish stock and pan juices, and boil rapidly until reduced
by half. Add the cream and continue boiling until reduced and thickened slightly.

Adjust the seasoning to taste. Pour the sauce over the scampi and sprinkle with
Parmesan cheese. Cook under a hot grill until golden brown.

PRAWN AND SPINACH ROULADE

This dish can be served warm or cold as a starter or light lunch dish.

Serves 4—6

Wash the spinach and cook with just the water clinging to the leaves for 5 minutes in a covered pan or until soft. Drain in a sieve and press out all excess water using the back of a wooden spoon. Finely chop, then place in a bowl with the nutmeg, cheese and seasoning. Mix well.

Whisk the egg whites until stiff. Beat the egg yolks into the spinach mixture, then gradually fold in the whites. Pour into a greased and lined 28 × 18 cm (11 × 7 inch) Swiss roll tin. Shake the tin to level the mixture. Bake at 190°C (375°F) mark 5 for about 15 minutes or until firm to the touch.

Meanwhile, make the filling. Melt the butter in a pan and fry the mushrooms until soft. Stir in the flour and cook for 1 minute. Remove from the heat and gradually stir in the milk. Return to the heat and cook gently, stirring, until thickened and smooth. Stir in the tomatoes, prawns, dill and lemon juice, and cook until heated through. Season well.

Invert the roulade on to a sheet of greaseproof paper and carefully remove the lining paper. Spread the sauce over the roulade. Starting from one short edge, roll up firmly using the paper to lift the roulade. Serve warm or cold garnished with whole prawns (if liked) as a starter or light lunch dish.

INGREDIENTS

500 g (1 lb) fresh spinach
pinch of grated nutmeg
25 g (1 oz) grated Parmesan cheese
salt and pepper
4 large eggs, separated
25 g (1 oz) butter
50 g (2 oz) button mushrooms,
    chopped
25 g (1 oz) flour
200 ml (7 fl oz) milk
2 tomatoes, skinned, seeded and
    finely chopped
175 g (6 oz) peeled prawns, thawed
    if frozen
5 ml (1 tsp) chopped fresh dill
    (optional)
30 ml (2 tbsp) lemon juice
whole prawns, to garnish
    (optional)

55

QUENELLES OF HALIBUT WITH SAFFRON SAUCE

*Quenelles are like poached mousseline dumplings and can be made from fish,
shellfish, meat, poultry or game. The saffron sauce adds a delicate golden hue to the dish.*

Serves 4

INGREDIENTS

250 g (9 oz) halibut fillet, skinned
and boned weight, well chilled

1 egg white, well chilled

150 ml (¼ pint) double cream,
well chilled

15 ml (1 tbsp) lemon juice

salt and pepper

450 ml (¾ pint) fish stock
(see page 246)

chervil or parsley sprigs,
to garnish

SAUCE

15 g (½ oz) butter

2 shallots, finely chopped

150 ml (¼ pint) fish stock (see
page 246)

2 generous pinches saffron threads

75 ml (3 fl oz) dry white wine

100 ml (4 fl oz) double cream

Roughly chop the fish and place in a blender or food processor. Purée until
smooth, then slowly add the egg white and cream whilst the machine is running.
When the mixture is firm, stop the machine, add the lemon juice, season and mix
once again. Chill until required for cooking.

With two wetted spoons, shape the mixture into 12 ovals (quenelles). Poach
the quenelles in the fish stock for 5–7 minutes until just firm to the touch. Drain
and keep warm. Reserve the fish stock for another recipe.

Meanwhile, make the sauce. Melt the butter and fry the shallots until soft. Add
the fish stock, saffron and white wine, then simmer gently for 5 minutes. Add the
cream and simmer gently for 5 minutes more. Strain the sauce.

Pour the sauce on to 4 individual plates, arrange 3 quenelles on each and
garnish with chervil or parsley sprigs.

CREAMY SEAFOOD PIE

*Any firm white fish may be used for this recipe such as haddock, cod, plaice
or halibut. The vegetables may be varied or omitted altogether. Prawns can
also be added to the fish and a little cheese stirred into the sauce.*

Serves 6

Cook the potatoes in boiling salted water for 20 minutes. Drain well. Add half the butter and mash. Season to taste and beat in the egg. Set aside.

Place the fish fillets, milk, onion, carrot, peas and bay leaf in a saucepan. Season lightly, bring to the boil, cover and simmer for 15 minutes. Remove the pan from the heat and discard the onion and bay leaf. Strain and place the fish and vegetables in an ovenproof dish. Reserve.

Melt half the remaining butter in a saucepan and stir in the flour. Cook for 1 minute. Remove the pan from the heat and gradually stir in the strained milk. Cook, stirring constantly, until the sauce has thickened and is smooth. Stir in the nutmeg and the cream. Adjust the seasoning, then pour the sauce over the fish and vegetables. Mix them together in the dish and sprinkle over the parsley.

Spread over the potatoes to completely cover the filling and dot the surface with the remaining butter.

Bake at 200°C (400°F) mark 6 for 10–15 minutes or until the potato topping has browned.

INGREDIENTS
1 kg (2 lb) potatoes
100 g (4 oz) butter
salt and pepper
1 egg, beaten
1 kg (2 lb) white fish fillets,
  skinned
450 ml (¾ pint) milk
1 small onion, halved
1 carrot, diced
100 g (4 oz) peas
1 bay leaf
25 g (1 oz) flour
pinch of grated nutmeg
30 ml (2 tbsp) single cream
30 ml (2 tbsp) chopped fresh
  parsley

GRILLED MACKEREL WITH SAGE SAUCE

This is a delicious way to serve mackerel; it is also very quick and easy to prepare.

Serves 4

Cut the fins from the mackerel and cut 3 diagonal slits in the skin across both sides of the fish. Season the fish inside and out, then place in a dish large enough to hold them in a single layer.

Mix the oil, lemon juice and wine together and pour over the fish. Cover and leave to marinate in a cool place for 1½ hours, turning the fish occasionally.

Remove the mackerel from the marinade. Cook under a hot grill for 5–8 minutes each side, depending on the thickness of the fish, until the flesh flakes easily. Transfer to a warm dish, cover and keep hot. Carefully remove the oil from the top of the marinade. Pour the cooking juices into a saucepan, add the vermouth and sage leaves and simmer for 2–3 minutes. Season to taste and pour over the mackerel.

INGREDIENTS
4 mackerel, cleaned
salt and pepper
150 ml (¼ pint) olive oil
30 ml (2 tbsp) lemon juice
75 ml (3 fl oz) dry white wine
75 ml (3 fl oz) dry vermouth
5 ml (1 tsp) very finely chopped
  fresh sage

QUENELLES OF HALIBUT WITH SAFFRON SAUCE

TAGLIATELLE WITH SEAFOOD AND CHAMPAGNE SAUCE

A scrumptious sauce made with salmon, monkfish and dry champagne
transforms fresh pasta into a special occasion dish.

Serves 4

INGREDIENTS

16 fresh mussels, scrubbed and
   beards removed
150 ml (¼ pint) fish stock (see
   page 246)
1 red mullet, about 300 g (11 oz)
   filleted
175 g (6 oz) monkfish fillet
175 g (6 oz) fresh salmon fillet,
   skinned
4 large uncooked Pacific prawns,
   shelled
4 fresh scallops
225 g (8 oz) tagliatelle (see page
   251)
75 g (3 oz) butter
salt and pepper
50 g (2 oz) leek, cut in fine
   julienne strips
150 ml (¼ pint) champagne or dry
   sparkling white wine
300 ml (½ pint) double cream
pinch of cayenne pepper
12 fresh basil leaves, shredded
   (optional)

Discard any open mussels which do not close when tapped. Place the mussels and fish stock in a pan, cover and cook over high heat for several minutes or until the mussels open. Discard any closed mussels. Leave to cool in the stock then remove the mussels from their shells. Strain the stock through fine muslin and reserve. Cut the fish fillets into 1.5 cm (½ inch) strips. Remove the vein from each prawn and cut in half. Separate the coral from each scallop and cut the scallops in half crossways.

Cook the tagliatelle in boiling salted water with a dash of oil for 2–3 minutes or until al dente. Drain and toss in half the butter. Season to taste and keep hot. Melt the remaining butter and fry the leeks, prawns and scallop coral for 30 seconds. Add the fish fillets, champagne and reserved stock, and simmer for 1 minute. Carefully remove all the fish from the pan and keep warm. Boil the liquid rapidly until reduced by half. Add the cream and boil rapidly until reduced and thickened. Adjust the seasoning and add the cayenne pepper. Return the fish to the sauce with the mussels, scallops and basil. Warm through gently for about 3 minutes.

Serve at once with the tagliatelle.

KEDGEREE

A classic English breakfast dish of smoked fish in creamy rice,
seasoned with cayenne pepper and nutmeg.

Serves 4

INGREDIENTS

500 g (1 lb) smoked haddock
100 g (4 oz) long-grain rice
salt and pepper
2 large eggs, hard-boiled, peeled
   and chopped
30 ml (2 tbsp) lemon juice
pinch of cayenne pepper
pinch of grated nutmeg
150 ml (¼ pint) single cream
50 g (2 oz) butter, diced
30 ml (2 tbsp) finely chopped fresh
   parsley
parsley sprigs, to garnish

Place the haddock in a large shallow pan and poach in water to cover for about 15 minutes or until tender. Drain, skin, bone and roughly flake the fish.

Meanwhile, cook the rice in boiling salted water for about 15 minutes or until tender.

Carefully mix the haddock, rice and eggs together. Stir the lemon juice, cayenne pepper and nutmeg into the cream. Stir it into the haddock and rice, and adjust the seasoning. Spoon the mixture into a greased ovenproof dish, dot with the butter and cook at 180°C (350°F) mark 4 for 25 minutes. Stir in the chopped parsley and garnish with parsley sprigs.

SQUID RISOTTO

If wished the risotto may be pressed into a buttered mould, left to stand for a few minutes, then unmoulded on to a serving plate.

Serves 4

INGREDIENTS

500 g (1 lb) small squid
60 ml (4 tbsp) olive oil
225 g (8 oz) red onions, chopped
2 garlic cloves, crushed
350 g (12 oz) short-grain risotto rice
1 medium red pepper, seeded and chopped
150 ml (¼ pint) dry white wine
600 ml (1 pint) fish stock (see page 246)
10 ml (2 tsp) tomato purée
salt and pepper
5 ml (1 tsp) lemon juice
25 g (1 oz) fresh parsley, finely chopped

To prepare the squid, carefully remove the tiny silvery ink sacs inside the body and place in a small bowl. Pour a small amount of boiling water over and press the sacs to squeeze out the ink. Leave to soak.

Wash the squid well and cut the tentacles from the bodies. Peel away the purplish skin from the bodies and pull out the transparent spine and discard the innards. Cut the tentacles from the head and wash well. Discard the heads. Cut the bodies into small rings.

Heat the oil and fry the onion and garlic until soft. Add the rice and cook, stirring, until transparent. Add the red pepper and squid rings and tentacles. Stir well, then stir in the wine and bring to the boil. Stir in half the fish stock, cover and simmer for 5 minutes. Strain the inky liquid through fine muslin and add to the risotto with the tomato purée. Stir well then add the remaining stock. Simmer for a further 10 minutes or until the liquid has been absorbed and the rice is tender. Adjust the seasoning and stir in the lemon juice.

Sprinkle with chopped parsley and serve at once.

SOLE WITH MUSSELS IN TARRAGON CREAM SAUCE

Seafood lovers will delight in this special combination of sole and mussels. Serve on a bed of rice with a lightly steamed green vegetable.

Serves 4

INGREDIENTS

1.2 litres (2 pints) mussels in their shells
100 ml (4 fl oz) dry white wine
1 shallot, finely chopped
sprig of fresh thyme
3 parsley sprigs
4 sole fillets, skinned
salt and white pepper
5 ml (1 tsp) finely chopped tarragon
150 ml (¼ pint) double cream
small tarragon sprigs and lemon slices, to garnish

Scrub the mussels under cold running water and discard any that do not close when sharply tapped. Remove the beards.

Heat 60 ml (4 tbsp) of the wine with the shallot, thyme and parsley. Add the mussels, cover and cook over a high heat for 4–5 minutes, shaking the pan frequently. Remove the mussels from their shells discarding any that have not opened. Strain the juice from the mussels with the cooking liquid and return to the rinsed-out pan.

Season the sole fillets, lay them in the liquid and poach gently for 4–5 minutes, or until the flesh is just opaque. Transfer the sole to a warmed plate, add the mussels, cover and keep hot. Stir the remaining wine into the cooking liquid with half the tarragon. Boil until reduced to about 30 ml (2 tbsp). Stir in the cream and simmer until thickened. Add the remaining tarragon and reheat gently. Season and coat the base of warmed serving plates with the sauce.

Carefully place the sole on the sauce. Place some of the mussels along the length of the sole and arrange the remainder around the side. Garnish with tarragon and lemon.

CHINESE EGG NOODLES
WITH SHRIMPS AND GOLDEN THREADS

*Egg noodles tossed in a piquant sauce are quick to cook and require very
little preparation. Serve as a lunch dish or for a light supper
with steamed broccoli or beans.*

Serves 4

Heat the water in a large saucepan and cook the noodles according to the packet instructions. Drain and set aside. Heat a wok, then add the groundnut oil. The oil is hot enough to stir-fry when a small piece of ginger floats to the top of the oil.

Stir in the white spring onion, garlic and ginger, and stir-fry for 30 seconds. Add the mushrooms, green onion shoots and shrimps. Stir-fry for a further 30 seconds. Pour in the cornflour mixture and add the sugar. Stir-fry for 1 minute, then add the bean shoots.

Add the drained noodles, stirring and tossing them until they are coated in the sauce. Sprinkle over the sesame oil and stir-fry for 30 seconds. Serve immediately.

INGREDIENTS

2.3 litres (4 pints) water
225 g (8 oz) Chinese egg noodles
45 ml (3 tbsp) ground nut or
    sunflower oil
4 cm (1½ inch) piece fresh root
    ginger, cut into thin strips
3 spring onions, white part finely
    chopped and the green shoots
    cut into 2.5 cm (1 inch) pieces
1 large garlic clove, finely
    chopped
100 g (4 oz) button mushrooms,
    sliced
225 g (8 oz) peeled shrimps or
    prawns
15 ml (1 tbsp) cornflour,
    mixed with 45 ml (3 tbsp) light
    soy sauce, and 75 ml (5 tbsp)
    medium dry sherry
2.5 ml (½ tsp) sugar
225 g (8 oz) bean shoots
5 ml (1 tsp) sesame oil

CHINESE EGG NOODLES WITH
SHRIMPS AND GOLDEN THREADS

PAUPIETTES OF SOLE WITH SALMON MOUSSELINE

*Fillets of sole, filled with a delicate salmon mousse and poached in vermouth,
make an elegant and delectable dish to serve for a special dinner party.*

Serves 4

INGREDIENTS

4 sole fillets, cut in half
   lengthways and skinned

25 g (1 oz) butter

salt and pepper

90 ml (6 tbsp) dry white vermouth

60 ml (4 tbsp) water

225 ml (8 fl oz) single cream

7.5 ml (1½ tsp) chopped fresh dill

10 ml (2 tsp) lemon juice

fresh dill sprigs, to garnish

MOUSSELINE

225 g (8 oz) salmon fillet, skinned,
   boned, shredded and chilled

1 egg white, chilled

90 ml (6 tbsp) double cream,
   chilled

5 ml (1 tsp) chopped fresh dill

7.5 ml (1½ tsp) lemon juice

For the mousseline, mix the salmon in a food processor until smooth, then add the egg white and mix again. Gradually add the double cream, mixing after each addition. Add the dill, lemon juice, salt and pepper.

Divide the mousseline between the 12 sole fillets. Roll up and secure each one with a wooden cocktail stick.

Grease an ovenproof dish with the 25 g (1 oz) butter and arrange the sole in a single layer. Season well, then pour in the vermouth and water. Cover with aluminium foil and bake at 190°C (375°F) mark 5 for 20 minutes until the fish is white and the mousseline firm. Transfer to a serving plate and keep hot.

Strain the juices into a saucepan and boil rapidly until reduced by half. Stir in the cream, chopped dill, lemon juice and seasoning. Simmer gently to reduce slightly. Do not boil. Remove the cocktail sticks from the sole and serve garnished with dill sprigs and the sauce.

LANGOUSTINE THERMIDOR WITH RICE PILAF

If using cooked langoustines, remove the meat from the shells and use
300 ml ($\frac{1}{2}$ pint) fish stock (see page 246) made with the langoustine shells added,
then strained.

Serves 4

Place the wine, onion, carrot, celery, parsley, bay leaf, peppercorns, thyme and tarragon in a very large saucepan with the water. Bring to the boil, cover and simmer gently for 15 minutes. Return to the boil and add about one-quarter of the langoustines. They must be completely immersed in liquid, so do not add too many at one time. Bring back to the boil, then simmer for 2 minutes. Remove the langoustines from the pan. Repeat this process until all the langoustines are cooked. Allow to cool then remove the shells. To do this, separate the head from the body and, using scissors, cut down the underside of the body. The tail meat can easily be removed. Reserve a few langoustine heads for garnish if wished.

Strain the cooking liquid then boil rapidly until reduced to 300 ml ($\frac{1}{2}$ pint).

Meanwhile make the rice pilaf. Heat the oil and fry the onion until soft. Stir in the rice and fry until transparent. Add stock, bring to the boil, cover and simmer for 15–20 minutes or until the stock has been absorbed. Adjust the seasoning, stir in the chopped parsley and keep hot.

Melt 25 g (1 oz) of the butter and fry the mushrooms for 3 minutes. Add the lemon juice and set aside. Melt 25 g (1 oz) of the remaining butter and fry the langoustine meat for 1 minute. Pour over the brandy and boil until reduced to 15 ml (1 tbsp).

Melt the remaining butter and stir in the flour and the mustard. Cook, stirring, for 1 minute. Remove from the heat and gradually stir in the reduced stock. Bring to the boil, stirring, then simmer for 5 minutes. Mix the cream and egg yolks together and stir into the sauce over gentle heat. Cook, stirring, until thickened slightly.

Stir in the mushrooms and their juices, and the langoustines with their juices. Stir in the cayenne and adjust the seasoning. Transfer the mixture to a flameproof dish, sprinkle with the cheese and cook under a hot grill until golden. Garnish with langoustine heads and serve at once with the rice pilaf.

INGREDIENTS
750 ml (1$\frac{1}{4}$ pints) dry white wine
1 large onion, sliced
1 medium carrot, sliced
1 celery stalk, sliced
6 parsley sprigs
1 bay leaf
6 peppercorns
1.25 ml ($\frac{1}{4}$ tsp) thyme
15 ml (1 tbsp) chopped fresh
   tarragon
900 ml (1$\frac{1}{2}$ pints) water
1.8 kg (4 lb) medium-sized
   langoustines (about 36–40),
   preferably alive
75 g (3 oz) butter
175 g (6 oz) button mushrooms,
   sliced
20 ml (4 tsp) lemon juice
60 ml (4 tbsp) brandy
15 ml (1 tbsp) flour
2.5 ml ($\frac{1}{2}$ tsp) mustard powder
150 ml ($\frac{1}{4}$ pint) double cream
2 egg yolks
pinch of cayenne pepper
salt and pepper
25 g (1 oz) freshly grated
   Parmesan cheese
RICE PILAF
30 ml (2 tbsp) olive oil
1 medium onion, chopped
225 g (8 oz) long-grain rice
500 ml (18 fl oz) fish stock
   (see page 246)
salt and pepper
15 ml (1 tbsp) chopped fresh
   parsley

PAUPIETTES OF SOLE WITH SALMON MOUSSELINE

SUSHI

Sushi is a Japanese snack food of seasoned rice mixed with a variety of ingredients and served in decorative, edible packages. These recipes are to serve with the seasoned rice on a large platter or individual plates with soy sauce for dipping.

Serves 4

BASIC RECIPES

INGREDIENTS
SEASONED SUSHI RICE (SHARI)
*150 g (5 oz) short-grain rice,
    preferably Japanese, rinsed and
    drained*
200 ml (7 fl oz) water
*7.5 cm (3 inch) piece konbu
    seaweed*
20 ml (4 tsp) rice vinegar

Put the rice, water and konbu in a saucepan and leave to soak for 15 minutes. Cover the pan, bring to the boil and simmer for 10 minutes or until tender. Leave to cool. Do not remove the lid during this time. Remove the konbu and stir in the rice vinegar.

THIN EGG CRÊPES
(USU YAKI TAMAGO)
2 eggs (size 4)
15 ml (1 tbsp) sake or mirin
7.5 ml (1½ tsp) sugar
1.25 ml (¼ tsp) salt
7.5 ml (1½ tsp) water
vegetable oil, for frying

Mix the eggs, sake, sugar, salt and water together until evenly blended. Allow the foam to settle. Lightly oil a 20 cm (8 inch) frying pan and place over gentle heat. Pour in half of the egg mixture and swirl it to evenly coat the base of the pan. Cook until the edges of the pancake begin to dry out. Remove from the heat and allow to cool slightly until you can turn it over. Return to the heat and cook the other side for about 30 seconds. Remove from the pan and leave to cool. Repeat for second crêpe.

Using a sharp knife cut each crêpe into a rectangle. Reserve trimmings to use, shredded, in other sushi.

TIED GOLDEN ROLLS
¼ quantity Seasoned Sushi Rice
5 ml (1 tsp) toasted sesame seeds
*2.5 ml (½ tsp) grated fresh root
    ginger*
5 ml (1 tsp) rice vinegar
5 ml (1 tsp) sugar
*2 Thin Egg Crêpes, trimmed to
    rectangles*
*100 g (4 oz) smoked salmon, cut
    into long strips*

Mix the rice, sesame seeds, ginger, vinegar and sugar together. Shape into 2 even rolls, the same length as the egg crêpes, with wetted hands or by rolling up in a damp clean tea towel, or piece of muslin.

Place each roll on an egg crêpe and roll up carefully. Tie 4 strips of smoked salmon along the length of each roll at regular intervals. Chill until required, then cut each roll in 4 pieces between the smoked salmon.

CRAB AND AVOCADO ROLLS
*½ ripe medium avocado, about
    100 g (4 oz), peeled and mashed*
2.5 ml (½ tsp) wasabi powder
10 ml (2 tsp) mayonnaise
salt
lemon juice
5 crab sticks
¼ quantity Seasoned Sushi Rice
2 sheets nori seaweed

Mix the avocado with the wasabi and mayonnaise. Season to taste with salt and lemon juice. Sprinkle the crab sticks with lemon juice.

Roll the rice into 2 even rolls the length of the nori seaweed. Place a sheet of nori on a work surface, preferably on a sudare mat. Arrange a roll of rice at one end, spread half the avocado mixture along the length of the rice and then arrange 2½ crab sticks along the length of the nori. Roll up carefully, using the sudare mat. Chill until required. Cut each roll into 6 pieces.
Note
Wasabi is a pungent horseradish spread which is available from speciality stores as a powder.

Lay the pieces of nori seaweed on a work surface. Divide the rice between each, placing it on the top corner of the nori. Top each with a piece of salmon, cucumber, dill and wasabi. Sprinkle with lemon juice. Fold up the opposite bottom corner of the seaweed to half cover the filling.

Roll the seaweed into a cone shape, damping the edge if necessary to seal. Chill until required.

SALMON AND DILL HAND ROLLS
2 sheets nori seaweed, each cut into
    4 squares
¼ quantity Seasoned Sushi Rice
    (opposite)
50 g (2 oz) smoked salmon, cut in
    8 pieces
8 slices cucumber or mangetout,
    cut in julienne strips
8 sprigs fresh dill
5 ml (1 tsp) wasabi powder mixed
    with 5 ml (1 tsp) water
lemon juice

Shape the sushi rice into 4 ovals. Sprinkle with a little wasabi and top each with a prawn. Chill until required.

PRAWN SUSHI
¼ quantity of Seasoned Sushi Rice
    (opposite)
2.5 ml (½ tsp) wasabi powder
    mixed with 2.5 ml (½ tsp) water
4 large cooked prawns, peeled

PRAWN AND COCONUT CURRY

This curry is very easy to prepare and quick to cook. The coconut milk is made by grating the white flesh, adding boiling water and leaving it to soak for 20 minutes.

Serves 4

Pour boiling water over the grated coconut and leave to soak for 20 minutes. Place a piece of double muslin in a sieve, over a bowl. Pour the coconut with all of the water into the cloth, pull the ends of the cloth together and squeeze out as much liquid as possible. Set the liquid aside.

Melt the ghee in a pan and fry the onion until soft. Add the garlic, chillies, mustard seed, turmeric and coriander.

Mix the ground rice with the coconut milk and stir it into the onion mixture. Add the lemon juice and salt, and simmer gently for 10 minutes, stirring occasionally. Add the prawns and simmer for a further 5 minutes. Serve hot with rice.

INGREDIENTS
225 g (8 oz) white coconut flesh,
    all brown husk removed,
    finely grated
300 ml (½ pint) boiling water
50 g (2 oz) ghee or clarified butter
1 small onion, finely chopped
1 garlic clove, crushed
2 dried chillies
2.5 g (½ tsp) black mustard seed,
    ground
2.5 g (½ tsp) ground turmeric
5 ml (1 tsp) ground coriander
15 ml (1 tbsp) ground rice
juice of ½ lemon
salt
750 g (1½ lb) peeled prawns

POULTRY
AND GAME

POULTRY AND GAME

·◆·

*Every morning, an astounding variety of seasonal game and fresh poultry
is bought at Smithfield market; the remainder is sent overnight from
private suppliers. With such a wide choice you can be adventurous
with your cooking. Stay traditional with such recipes as Jugged Hare,
or take your inspiration from the East with Stir-Fried Chicken with
Ginger and Mangetout.*

CHICKEN EN PAPILLOTE

*Cooking 'en papillote' (in paper parcels) ensures that the contents retain their moisture.
Serve with the sauce accompanied by thinly sliced sautéed mushrooms and a
julienne of celery and potato.*

Serves 4

INGREDIENTS

*4 chicken breasts, skinned and
    boned*

15 g ($\frac{1}{2}$ oz) butter

1 shallot, finely chopped

*100 g (4 oz) mushrooms, finely
    chopped*

*50 g (2 oz) hazelnuts, blanched and
    finely chopped*

1 egg white, lightly beaten

15 ml (1 tbsp) double cream

salt and pepper

10 ml (2 tsp) medium dry sherry

SAUCE

25 g (1 oz) butter

30 ml (2 tbsp) flour

*300 ml ($\frac{1}{2}$ pint) chicken stock
    (see page 247)*

2 egg yolks

100 ml (4 fl oz) single cream

15 ml (1 tbsp) medium dry sherry

Cut a slit in each chicken breast to make a pocket to hold the stuffing. Melt the
butter and fry the shallot until soft. Add the mushrooms, and cook gently for 2–3
minutes. Allow to cool slightly. Add the hazelnuts, egg white and cream to the
shallots and mushrooms, and season.

Place each chicken breast on a buttered circle of greaseproof paper, large
enough to enclose it. Fill each one with the stuffing mixture. Sprinkle 2.5 ml ($\frac{1}{2}$ tsp)
sherry over each piece of chicken and seal the parcels. Place on a baking tray and
bake at 180°C (350°F) mark 4 for 40 minutes.

Meanwhile, make the sauce. Melt the butter and stir in the flour. Cook the
flour for 1 minute. Remove the pan from the heat and gradually stir in the stock.
Bring to the boil and simmer for 5 minutes, stirring occasionally. Mix the egg
yolks with the cream. Remove the pan from the heat and stir a little of the stock
into the egg mixture. Stir the egg mixture into the sauce and heat. Adjust the
seasoning and stir in the sherry. Serve with the chicken breasts.

PERSIAN-STYLE CHICKEN

*The substantial stuffing for this chicken is fragrant and spicy. Serve garnished
with lemon slices, walnut halves and fresh coriander.*

Serves 4—6

Wipe the chicken inside and out and pour half the lemon juice inside the cavity.
Boil the rice in lightly salted, boiling water for 7—8 minutes, then drain
thoroughly. Melt 50 g (2 oz) of the butter and fry the onion until golden. Stir in
the raisins, walnuts, turmeric and cumin. Remove from the heat and add the
drained rice. Mix the ingredients well and season to taste.

Stuff the chicken with the rice mixture and place it in a roasting tin. Pour the
remaining lemon juice over the chicken and sprinkle with salt. Spread the
remaining butter over the breast. Roast at 190°C (375°F) mark 5, for 1½ hours,
basting occasionally. Serve at once.

INGREDIENTS
1.8 kg (4 lb) chicken
juice of 1 lemon
75 g (3 oz) rice
salt and pepper
90 g (3½ oz) butter
1 onion, finely chopped
75 g (3 oz) raisins
50 g (2 oz) walnuts, coarsely
    chopped
2.5 ml (½ tsp) turmeric
2.5 ml (½ tsp) ground cumin
    seeds

ROAST TURKEY WITH LEMON AND ALMOND STUFFING

*Turkeys are available throughout the year and make an ideal choice for a
large dinner party. Serve with this delectable stuffing.*

Serves 8—10

For the stuffing, melt the butter and fry the shallots and celery until soft. Add the
turkey liver and cook for 2 minutes. Mix all the remaining ingredients together in
a large bowl and add the liver mixture.

Stuff the neck end of the turkey. Truss, and place the turkey on a rack in a
roasting tin. Roll any remaining stuffing into balls. Mix the melted butter, lemon
juice and wine together and pour over. Roast for 30 minutes at 220°C (425°F)
mark 7, then continue roasting at 180°C (350°F) mark 4 for a further 3—3½ hours.
Baste occasionally during roasting. One hour before the end of cooking, cook
any remaining stuffing in a roasting tin.

For the giblet gravy, place the giblets and water in a pan, bring to the boil,
then simmer for 1½—2 hours while the turkey is cooking. Strain. When the turkey
is cooked, spoon off most of the fat from the roasting tin. Sprinkle the flour over
the pan juices. Brown over high heat stirring, for 1 minute, then gradually stir in
the giblet stock. Season to taste and simmer, stirring, for 10 minutes. Strain into a
gravy boat and serve with the turkey.

INGREDIENTS
3.5—4.5 kg (8—10 lb)
    oven-ready turkey
100 g (4 oz) butter, melted
juice of ½ lemon
60 ml (4 tbsp) white wine
LEMON AND ALMOND STUFFING
40 g (1½ oz) butter
100 g (4 oz) shallots or onion,
    finely chopped
2 celery stalks, finely chopped
the turkey liver, finely chopped
500 g (1 lb) pork sausagemeat
finely grated rind of 2 lemons
100 g (4 oz) fresh breadcrumbs
75 g (3 oz) almonds, finely chopped
30 ml (2 tbsp) finely chopped fresh
    parsley
2.5 ml (½ tsp) dried thyme
salt and pepper
GIBLET GRAVY
turkey giblets, minus the liver
1.2 litres (2 pints) water
15 ml (1 tbsp) flour

CHICKEN BREASTS WITH PARMA HAM AND MOZZARELLA

*This succulent dish is both quick and easy to prepare. Serve with new
potatoes and a green vegetable, or a crisp green salad.*

Serves 4

INGREDIENTS

*4 chicken breasts, skinned and
   boned*
8 fresh sage leaves
salt and pepper
25 g (1 oz) butter
*4 thin slices Parma ham, about
   50 g (2 oz)*
*200–225 g (7–8 oz) mozzarella
   cheese, sliced*
fresh sage leaves, to garnish

Cut a slit horizontally along each chicken breast to make a pocket. Insert 2 sage leaves into each and season lightly.

Melt the butter and fry the chicken for 15–20 minutes or until tender. Place the chicken breasts in an ovenproof dish and pour over the pan juices. Place a slice of prosciutto over each, then cover with the mozzarella. Grill for 5 minutes, or until the cheese begins to melt and turn golden. Garnish each of the chicken breasts with fresh sage leaves and serve.

CHICKEN ENCHILADAS

*To give the enchilada sauce the correct Mexican 'heat', be sure to use small
hot green chillies. Double the amount of tortillas if using commercially prepared ones.*

Serves 4–6

INGREDIENTS
TORTILLAS
275 g (10 oz) plain flour
7.5 ml (1½ tsp) salt
50 g (2 oz) lard, cubed
150 ml (¼ pint) warm water
150 ml (¼ pint) vegetable oil
ENCHILADA SAUCE
45 ml (3 tbsp) vegetable oil
1 onion, finely chopped
45 ml (3 tbsp) tomato purée
*1.2 kg (1 lb 10 oz) canned
   tomatoes*
2.5 ml (½ tsp) sugar
7.5 ml (1½ tsp) salt
*3 small fresh green chillies,
   seeded and finely chopped*
CHICKEN FILLING
30 ml (2 tbsp) vegetable oil
1 onion, finely chopped
*225 g (8 oz) green pepper, seeded
   and roughly chopped*
*3 chicken breasts, skinned and cut
   into 2.5 cm (1 inch) cubes*
2.5 ml (½ tsp) salt
75 g (3 oz) black olives, chopped
*275 g (10 oz) Cheddar cheese,
   grated*
*Lime slices and chillies,
   to garnish*

To make the tortillas, sift the flour and salt into a bowl and rub in the lard until the mixture resembles breadcrumbs. Gradually add the water, mixing lightly with a knife. Knead the dough on a lightly floured surface and divide it into 8 even-sized balls. Place them in a bowl and cover with a damp cloth. Roll out each ball into a 23 cm (9 inch) circle. Heat a large, ungreased frying pan or a griddle over moderate heat. Cook the tortillas on both sides, until the dough puffs slightly and light brown flecks appear on the surface.

To make the enchilada sauce, heat the vegetable oil and fry the onion until soft. Add the tomato purée and fry for 1 minute. Place the tomatoes, with their juice, in a blender or food processor and blend until smooth. Add to the pan with the sugar, salt and chillies. Bring to the boil and simmer for 15 minutes.

To make the chicken filling, heat the oil and fry the onion until soft. Add the green pepper and chicken, and fry for 5 minutes, stirring occasionally. Add the salt and 300 ml (½ pint) of the enchilada sauce. Bring to the boil, cover the pan, reduce the heat and simmer for 15 minutes. Add the olives and 50 g (2 oz) of the cheese and simmer for 5 minutes.

To assemble the enchiladas, heat the 150 ml (¼ pint) vegetable oil in a frying pan. Dip each tortilla into the hot oil for about 10 seconds, until it becomes pliable. Drain slightly, then dip it into the warm enchilada sauce for 1–2 seconds. Fill each 'dipped' tortilla by spooning some of the chicken filling across the middle, rolling it up and placing it seam side down in a baking dish.

Pour the remaining sauce over the top and sprinkle with the remaining cheese. Bake at 180°C (350°F) mark 4 for 20 minutes. Serve garnished with lime slices and chillies.

JUGGED HARE

Order the hare ready jointed if possible and ask for the blood to be included in the order.

Serves 6

Wash the hare and pat dry with kitchen paper. Place the bacon in a large heavy-based pan and cook gently until the fat runs. Add 50 g (2 oz) of the butter and fry the hare until evenly browned all over.

Add the onion, carrots, celery, seasoning, bouquet garni and lemon rind. Add the stock and bring it gently to the boil. Reduce the heat, cover the pan tightly and simmer gently for $2\frac{1}{2}$–3 hours or until the hare is tender. Blend the remaining butter with the flour to a smooth paste. Whisk it into the liquid, a little at a time, and cook for 5 minutes, stirring, until thickened. Season to taste.

Mix the blood and port together.

Just before serving, remove the pan from the heat and gradually stir in the port and blood mixture. Serve immediately.

INGREDIENTS

1 hare, jointed

3 slices streaky bacon, rinded and diced

75 g (3 oz) unsalted butter

1 large onion, chopped

2 carrots, chopped

2 celery stalks, chopped

salt and pepper

bouquet garni

finely grated rind of 1 lemon

900 ml ($1\frac{1}{2}$ pints) chicken stock (see page 247)

25 g (1 oz) flour

45 ml (3 tbsp) port

DUCKLING WITH COGNAC AND NECTARINES

*Nectarines are a perfect accompaniment to duck. Peaches may be used if
nectarines are unavailable.*

Serves 4

INGREDIENTS

75 g (3 oz) dried nectarines
boiling water
30 ml (2 tbsp) Cognac or brandy
30 ml (2 tbsp) port
25 g (1 oz) butter
1.8 kg (4 lb) oven-ready duckling
¼ orange
salt and pepper
300 ml (½ pint) cold water
4 fresh nectarines, stoned and cut
   into slices

Place the dried nectarines in a bowl and cover with boiling water. Leave until
lukewarm then stir in the Cognac and port. Leave to soak overnight.

Place the nectarines, soaking liquid and the butter in a small pan. Cover and
simmer very gently for about 20 minutes, adding more water if the mixture
seems too dry. Purée the fruit and reserve.

Prick the duck all over with a fork and place the orange inside the cavity. Place
it on a rack in a roasting tin. Season and pour half the cold water into the tin.
Roast at 180°C (350°F) mark 4 for 30 minutes per 500 g (1 lb), increasing the
temperature to 220°C (425°F) mark 7 for the last 15 minutes.

Remove the duckling from the oven and discard the orange. Carefully tip the
duckling up so that the cavity juices run into the tin, then transfer it to a plate and
keep hot. Pour off the fat from the pan juices and stir in the remaining water and
nectarine purée. Simmer over moderate heat for about 10 minutes.

Warm the sliced nectarines in the oven for 2 minutes. Carve the duck into
slices and arrange on a warmed serving plate with the nectarine slices. Spoon
over the sauce and serve at once.

PIGEONS IN HONEY SAUCE WITH FRESH FIGS

*This rich and fruity dish is excellent for entertaining. The pigeons are cooked
in a casserole flavoured with honey, brandy and wine, with fresh figs added
to the sauce just before serving.*

Serves 4

Heat the oil in a large casserole, add the pigeons and cook until browned all over.
Remove from the pan. Fry the onion and garlic in the oil until soft, then stir in the
brandy and wine. Increase the heat and bring to the boil.

Return the pigeons to the casserole, then add the stock, honey, dried figs,
lemon juice and bouquet garni. Cover and simmer over low heat for about $1\frac{1}{2}$
hours. The pigeons are cooked when the juices run clear after a skewer has been
inserted into the leg. Remove the pigeons from the pan and keep hot.

Strain the cooking liquid into a clean pan. Mash the butter and flour together
and whisk into the sauce, a little at a time. Simmer gently for 5 minutes then
adjust the seasoning. Add the fresh figs and simmer for 1–2 minutes or until
heated through.

Using meat scissors, cut each pigeon in half and arrange on a warmed serving
platter. Spoon the sauce and figs carefully over them and serve at once.

INGREDIENTS
30 ml (2 tbsp) olive oil
4 pigeons, prepared
1 medium onion, chopped
2 garlic cloves, crushed
15 ml (1 tbsp) brandy
150 ml ($\frac{1}{4}$ pint) dry white wine
300 ml ($\frac{1}{2}$ pint) chicken stock
  (see page 247)
60 ml (4 tbsp) clear honey
50 g (2 oz) dried figs, chopped
20 ml (4 tsp) lemon juice
bouquet garni
15 g ($\frac{1}{2}$ oz) butter, softened
15 ml (1 tbsp) flour
salt and pepper
4 fresh figs, quartered

73

ROAST GOOSE WITH SAGE, ONION AND APPLE STUFFING

Sage and onion stuffing is traditionally English and is used for poultry, pork and lamb recipes. The addition of apple and Calvados makes it an ideal accompaniment to roast goose.

Serves 6–8

INGREDIENTS

3.5–4.5 kg (8–10 lb) goose,
*   trussed weight*
salt and pepper
SAGE, ONION AND APPLE
STUFFING
50 g (2 oz) butter
1 large onion, finely chopped
the goose liver, finely chopped
225 g (8 oz) fresh breadcrumbs
175 g (6 oz) sausagemeat
finely grated rind of 1 lemon
5 ml (1 tsp) chopped fresh sage or
*   2.5 ml (½ tsp) dried sage*
225 g (8 oz) cooking apples, peeled
*   and coarsely chopped*
30 ml (2 tbsp) Calvados or brandy

Wipe the goose inside and out, remove any lumps of fat from the inside and dry thoroughly. Season well.

Melt the butter and fry the onion until soft. Add the goose liver and fry until it changes colour. Cool the mixture slightly before adding it to the remaining ingredients. Mix well then stuff the body cavity loosely with the mixture.

Truss the goose neatly and place it on a rack in a roasting tin. Prick the lower legs, breast and sides of the bird. Roast, breast side up, for 20 minutes at 200°C (400°F) mark 6.

Remove the goose from the oven and turn it over on to the breast. Reduce the temperature to 170°C (325°F) mark 3 and roast for 1 hour. Turn the goose on to its back and roast for a further 1–1¼ hours. The bird is cooked when a skewer is inserted into the leg and the juices run clear. Pour off the fat several times during cooking.

When the goose is cooked, leave it in a warm place for 15 minutes before carving.

Serve with giblet gravy, see page 69. A little Calvados may be added if wished.

QUAIL CASSEROLE

These delicate birds are cooked with orange and flavoured with thyme and brandy. Serve for supper with new potatoes and mangetout.

Serves 4

INGREDIENTS

40 g (1½ oz) butter
100 g (4 oz) unsmoked bacon,
*   rinded and chopped*
4 quail
2 oranges, peeled and roughly
*   chopped*
1 garlic clove, crushed
6 shallots, finely chopped
300 ml (½ pint) hot chicken stock
*   (see page 247)*
sprig of fresh thyme
salt and pepper
15 ml (1 tbsp) brandy
croûtons, watercress and strips of
*   orange rind, to garnish*

Melt 25 g (1 oz) of the butter in a large casserole and fry the bacon until lightly coloured. Add the quail and cook on all sides until evenly browned. Stir in the orange flesh, garlic, shallots, stock, thyme and seasoning. Cover the casserole and cook at 180°C (350°F) mark 4 for 35–45 minutes or until the quail are tender. Transfer the quail to a warmed serving dish and keep hot.

Skim off any excess fat from the cooking liquid, then strain. Stir in the brandy, then boil rapidly until the liquid has reduced and is slightly thickened. Remove from the heat and stir in the remaining butter. Pour the sauce over the quail and serve garnished with croûtons, watercress sprigs and strips of orange rind.

Stir-Fried Chicken with Ginger and Mangetout

The secret of success when stir-frying is organization. Having all the ingredients prepared and close at hand is essential, as the actual cooking time is surprisingly quick. Mangetout add colour and a crunchy texture to this delicious Chinese dish.

Serves 4

INGREDIENTS

3 chicken breasts, skinned and cut
    into 2.5 cm (1 inch) squares
300 ml (½ pint) groundnut oil
10 ml (2 tsp) finely chopped fresh
    root ginger
2 spring onions, finely chopped
1 large clove garlic, finely chopped
175 g (6 oz) mushrooms, sliced
175 g (6 oz) mangetout
spring onion curls, to garnish
MARINADE
1 egg white, beaten
15 ml (1 tbsp) cornflour
10 ml (2 tsp) light soy sauce
10 ml (2 tsp) shaohsing wine or
    medium dry sherry
SAUCE
30 ml (2 tbsp) light soy sauce
45 ml (3 tbsp) shaohsing wine or
    medium dry sherry
5 ml (1 tsp) sugar
5 ml (1 tsp) cornflour

Mix the marinade ingredients together and pour over the chicken. Marinate for 30 minutes. Mix all the sauce ingredients together and set aside. Heat a wok over high heat and add the groundnut oil. When the oil is smoking hot, stir-fry the chicken for 2 minutes. Place a sieve over a bowl and pour the chicken and all of the oil into it.

Return 45 ml (3 tbsp) of the oil to the wok, and stir-fry the ginger, spring onions and garlic for 30 seconds. Add the mushrooms and stir-fry for 30 seconds. Add the mangetout and sauce and stir. Return the drained chicken to the wok and stir-fry for a further 1 minute. Garnish and serve at once.

GUINEA FOWL CASSEROLE

The guinea fowl has grey feathers speckled with white, and is a native of Africa. Reared commercially, it is in season throughout the year. Similar in taste to pheasant, it can be cooked in any way suitable for chicken, although guinea fowl tends to be dry. If roasting, cover the breast with streaky bacon.

Serves 3–4

Place the onions in a pan of cold water, bring to the boil, and drain immediately. Melt the butter in a round flameproof casserole over gentle heat. Add the onions and the guinea fowl, and slowly brown the bird on all sides, taking care not to burn the butter.

Pour over the cream and season. Cover and simmer gently, for 1 hour, or until the bird is cooked, basting occasionally.

Remove the bird from the casserole, and keep hot. Add the lemon juice and jelly to the sauce, stir until well blended, and adjust the seasoning. Divide the guinea fowl into portions, arrange on a serving plate, and pour over the sauce.

INGREDIENTS
8 small button onions
40 g (1½ oz) butter
1.2–1.5 kg (2½–3 lb) guinea fowl, cleaned and trussed
300 ml (½ pint) single cream
salt and pepper
15 ml (1 tbsp) lemon juice
15 ml (1 tbsp) rowanberry or redcurrant jelly

ROAST VENISON WITH FRUITY WINE SAUCE

This richly marinated venison is roasted with its tangy citrus sauce and is an ideal dish for any special occasion.

Serves 8

Wipe the meat with kitchen paper and trim off any excess fat. Place the onion, carrot, celery, garlic, bouquet garni, peppercorns, wine and 150 ml (¼ pint) oil in a large dish. Add the venison and baste with the marinade. Cover the dish with cling film and leave to marinate in the fridge for 48 hours.

Drain the venison and reserve the marinade. Brush the meat with oil and wrap in aluminium foil. Roast at 170°C (325°F) mark 3 for 25 minutes per 500 g (1 lb). About 30 minutes before the end of the cooking time, remove the aluminium foil, sprinkle the meat with flour and baste with the pan juices.

Meanwhile, place the marinade in a pan and cook, uncovered, for about 20 minutes, until reduced by half. Strain and reserve.

Cut the citrus rind into thin strips and simmer in 150 ml (¼ pint) water for 5 minutes. Drain and reserve. Place the citrus juices and redcurrant jelly in a pan. Stir over low heat until the jelly has dissolved, then add the port and strained marinade. Simmer for 10 minutes. Blend the cornflour to a smooth paste with 30 ml (2 tbsp) water. Add to the pan, stirring until thickened and clear. Add the citrus rind and wine vinegar and simmer for a further 5 minutes.

Place the venison on a warmed serving plate and sprinkle with chopped parsley. Serve with the hot sauce.

INGREDIENTS
1 haunch venison, about 2.5 kg (5½ lb)
1 large onion, chopped
1 carrot, chopped
1 celery stalk, chopped
2 garlic cloves, crushed
bouquet garni
6 black peppercorns
750 ml (1¼ pints) red wine
olive oil
flour, for dredging
thinly pared rind and juice of 1 orange
thinly pared rind and juice of 1 lemon
water
60 ml (4 tbsp) redcurrant jelly
60 ml (4 tbsp) port
15 ml (1 tbsp) cornflour
15 ml (1 tbsp) red wine vinegar
chopped fresh parsley, to garnish

STIR-FRIED CHICKEN WITH GINGER AND MANGETOUT

ROAST DUCK AND
POMEGRANATES IN NUT SAUCE

*This dish, which is of Persian origin, may also be made with pheasant, goose,
chicken, or small lamb meatballs. Garnish with rosy pomegranate seeds,
fresh limes and walnuts. Serve with boiled rice or tagliatelle.*

Serves 4—6

INGREDIENTS

2.3 kg (5 lb) duckling, giblets
    reserved
600 ml (1 pint) water
salt and pepper
1 small, whole onion
fresh pomegranate, lime slices and
    walnuts, to garnish

SAUCE

50 g (2 oz) butter
1 onion, finely chopped
175 g (6 oz) ground walnuts
225 ml (8 fl oz) fresh pomegranate
    juice
5 ml (1 tsp) sugar
30—45 ml (2—3 tbsp) fresh lime
    juice

ROAST DUCK AND
POMEGRANATES IN NUT SAUCE

Place the duckling giblets (except the liver) and neck in a small saucepan, with
the water. Bring it to the boil, skim any scum from the surface, cover and simmer
gently for 45 minutes.

Wipe the duckling inside and out. Season the cavity and place the whole onion
inside. Truss, prick the skin, and rub all over with salt. Place upside down on a
rack in a roasting tin and pour in 45 ml (3 tbsp) of water. Roast the duckling for 45
minutes at 190°C (375°F) mark 5 then turn it over and roast for a further 50
minutes. It is cooked when the juices run clear after a skewer has been inserted
into the thigh.

Meanwhile, prepare the sauce. Melt the butter and fry the onion until golden.
Remove the pan from the heat and stir in the walnuts. Return the pan to the heat
and add the pomegranate juice. Strain the giblet stock and add it to the sauce,
with the sugar and lime juice. Cover and simmer gently for 30 minutes or until
the sauce has thickened.

Remove the duckling from the oven. Pour off the fat and add the juices from
the duck cavity to the pan juices. Add both to the sauce. Taste and adjust the
seasoning. Simmer the sauce, stirring, for 3 minutes.

Joint the duckling, garnish and serve with the sauce.

Note Do not be tempted to use an electric juicer for the pomegranates, as the
bitter pith will be included. A manual juice squeezer is perfectly adequate.

WILD DUCK WITH ANCHOVIES AND CAPERS

The combination of anchovies and capers gives a tart taste that blends well with the richness of the wild ducks. Serve with wild rice.

Serves 4

Blend the wine, oil, tarragon, marjoram, peppercorns and salt together. Pour over the ducks, cover and leave in a cool place for 12 hours. Turn the birds every 2 hours on to a different side until all sides have been marinated.

Remove the ducks from the marinade and dry them well. Insert a piece of lemon in the cavity of each bird, season then put a slice of bacon over each breast. Place in a roasting tin and cook at 200°C (400°F) mark 6 for 30–35 minutes. The birds are cooked when the juices run clear after a skewer has been inserted into the leg.

Meanwhile, strain the marinade into a jug and skim off the fat from the surface. Heat 15 ml (1 tbsp) of this fat and fry the onion until soft. Stir in the strained marinade and the anchovies, and boil until reduced by half. Purée the sauce in a blender or food processor then return to the rinsed pan. Stir in the capers.

Remove the trussing string from the ducks, place them on a warmed plate, cover and keep hot. Remove the excess fat from the pan juices then pour the juices and cream into the anchovy and caper sauce. Reheat and simmer until reduced to a slightly syrupy consistency. Spoon some of the sauce over the ducks and serve the rest separately in a warmed sauceboat.

INGREDIENTS
300 ml (½ pint) full-bodied dry white wine
30 ml (2 tbsp) olive oil
sprig of fresh tarragon
sprig of fresh marjoram
6 black peppercorns, crushed
salt and pepper
2 wild ducks, about 1.2 kg (2½ lb) each, plucked and trussed
½ lemon, cut in half
2 slices bacon
1 onion, finely chopped
10 anchovy fillets, soaked in milk then drained
30 ml (2 tbsp) chopped capers
30 ml (2 tbsp) double cream

ROAST DUCK WITH PECAN AND ORANGE STUFFING

This rich and fragrant stuffing perfectly complements the flavour of duck.

Serves 4

To make the stuffing, soak the dried apricots in half the orange juice for 1 hour, then drain and finely chop. Melt the butter and fry the onion and celery until soft. Add the duck liver and cook for 2 minutes. Mix all the remaining ingredients together in a large bowl then add the liver mixture. Allow to cool slightly. Wash the duck and dry it completely with absorbent paper. Spoon the stuffing into the neck end of the duck and truss.

Put the duck on a wire rack in a roasting tin and sprinkle the breast liberally with salt and pepper. Rub the seasoning thoroughly into the skin. Prick the skin all over with a fork or skewer to allow the fat to escape. Roast at 190°C (375°F) mark 5, allowing 20 minutes per 500 g (1 lb), basting occasionally with the fat in the tin. While the duck is cooking, bring the stock to the boil in a saucepan and boil rapidly until reduced to about 300 ml (½ pint). Cool and skim the fat off the surface of the liquid.

The duck is cooked, when a skewer pushed into the thigh releases clear, not pink juices. Transfer to a warm dish, remove the trussing string and keep hot.

Drain the fat from the roasting tin and stir the flour into the remaining juices. Bring to the boil, stirring constantly to prevent it sticking. Gradually stir in the reduced stock and the remaining orange juice. Cook the gravy for about 10 minutes, stirring, until smooth and thickened. Season to taste and serve with the duck.

INGREDIENTS
2 kg (4 lb) duck
15 ml (1 tbsp) plain flour
600 ml (1 pint) duck stock
PECAN AND ORANGE STUFFING
75 g (3 oz) dried apricots, chopped
100 ml (4 fl oz) fresh orange juice
40 g (1½ oz) butter
1 small onion, finely chopped
1 celery stalk, chopped
the duck liver, chopped
225 g (8 oz) pork sausagemeat
50 g (2 oz) fresh breadcrumbs
75 g (3 oz) pecan nuts, chopped
1 egg
finely grated rind of 1 orange
15 ml (1 tbsp) brandy
15 ml (1 tbsp) chopped parsley
1.25 ml (¼ tsp) dried thyme

BRAISED VENISON WITH RED WINE

*Serve with small potatoes steamed in their skins, braised fennel or celery
and glazed carrots.*

Serves 6

INGREDIENTS

*6 venison steaks, about
225 g (8 oz) each, cut from the
shoulder
75 g (3 oz) unsalted butter
30 ml (2 tbsp) oil
225 g (8 oz) belly of pork, rinded
and diced
2 onions, chopped
3 carrots, chopped
3 celery stalks, chopped
2 small turnips, chopped
salt and pepper
25 g (1 oz) flour
30 ml (2 tbsp) redcurrant jelly*
MARINADE
*1 small onion, finely chopped
6 black peppercorns
sprig of thyme
1 celery stalk, chopped
1 garlic clove, crushed
600 ml (1 pint) red wine
60 ml (4 tbsp) oil*

To make the marinade, place the onion, peppercorns, thyme, celery, garlic, red wine and oil in a large shallow bowl. Add the steaks and coat with the marinade. Marinate, turning occasionally, for up to 2 days.

When ready to cook, remove the meat from the marinade and dry with kitchen paper.

Melt half the butter with the oil in a large flameproof casserole. Add the venison and fry until evenly browned. Remove from the pan and set aside. Add the belly of pork to the pan and fry until lightly coloured. Add the onions, carrots, celery and turnips and fry until soft.

Place the venison steaks on the bed of sautéed vegetables. Strain over the marinade and season. Cover the pan tightly and simmer for 2–2½ hours or until the meat is tender. Alternatively, cook in the oven at 170°C (325°F) mark 3 for 2½–3 hours.

Place the meat on a serving plate and keep hot. Strain the cooking liquid into a clean pan. Blend the remaining butter with the flour to a paste, then whisk it into the liquid, a little at a time. Cook, stirring, until the sauce thickens. Stir in the redcurrant jelly and simmer until it has melted. Taste and adjust the seasoning.

Pour a little sauce over the meat and serve the remainder separately.

PEKING DUCK

INGREDIENTS

*1.8 kg (4 lb) oven-ready duck
15 ml (1 tbsp) brandy
12 spring onions*
PANCAKES
*500 g (1 lb) plain flour
450 ml (15 fl oz) boiling water
30 ml (2 tbsp) sesame oil*
BASTING SAUCE
*30 ml (2 tbsp) clear honey
30 ml (2 tbsp) dark soy sauce
150 ml (¼ pint) cold water*
PLUM SAUCE
*60 ml (4 tbsp) hoisin sauce
1.25 ml (¼ tsp) sesame oil
5 ml (1 tsp) clear honey*

This delicious Chinese dish first appeared in Europe and America towards the end of the last century. Originally, only the skin was eaten in the pancakes, while the meat was served with another dish. To dry the duck, rub the skin with the brandy and hang it up overnight to dry. This ensures the skin will be crispy.

Serves 4–6

Wash and dry the duck thoroughly. Rub the brandy all over the skin. Tie a piece of string under each wing and hang the duck in a cool, dry, airy place overnight.

To make spring onion tassels for the garnish, trim the root ends and all but 5 cm (2 inches) of the leaves from two spring onions. Skin the onions and cut the green leaves two or three times lengthways. Drop them into iced water and leave for 2 hours, or until the ends open and curl up. Slice the white part only of the remaining spring onions lengthways into thin strips. Wrap until needed.

To make the pancakes, sift the flour into a bowl and stir in the boiling water. Mix to a dough. Knead in the bowl or on a lightly floured surface for 3 minutes. Cover with clingfilm or a clean tea towel and rest for 30 minutes.

Meanwhile, mix all the basting sauce ingredients together. Place the duck on a rack in a roasting tin half filled with cold water. Pour some of the basting sauce over the breast. Roast, breast side up at 200°C (400°F) mark 6 for 35 minutes, basting every 10 minutes or so with the sauce. Using two wooden spoons, turn

the duck over on to its breast and baste with more sauce. The wooden spoons
prevent the skin from being pierced and the juices escaping. Roast for a further 30
minutes, basting frequently. Turn the duck over on to its back, and cook for a
further 10 minutes, basting with the sauce.

While the duck is roasting, make the pancakes. Knead the dough briefly.
Divide in half and keep one half covered. Roll the first half into a sausage shape
about 40 cm (16 inches) long and cut it into 16 equal pieces. Flatten each piece
into a 6.5 cm (2½ inch) round. Brush half the circles with sesame oil, then press the
remaining circles on top of them, making 8 pairs. Make more pancakes with the
remaining dough in the same way, to give 16 pairs. Roll out the circles until they
measure 15 cm (6 inches) in diameter. Heat a heavy-based frying pan and cook
the pancakes in the dry pan for 2 minutes on each side. When ready, the pancake
will look dry on the underside and have brown flecks. The pancake will puff when
turned over. Remove from the pan, and while still hot, peel the two pieces apart.
Keep hot wrapped in a cloth.

Mix all the plum sauce ingredients together. Remove the skin from the duck in
one piece and cut into 5 cm (2 inch) squares. Using 2 forks, pull the meat into
shreds. Arrange the meat on a serving platter and garnish with the onion tassels.

To serve, spread a little plum sauce over a pancake. Top with duck skin and
meat, sprinkle with spring onion strips, and roll up.

ROAST GROUSE WITH BREAD SAUCE, GAME CHIPS AND CHESTNUTS

The best time to eat grouse is from August to October. Serve with the traditional accompaniments of bread sauce and game chips.

Serves 4

INGREDIENTS

4 young grouse
juice of 1 lemon, strained
salt and pepper
16 slices unsmoked streaky bacon
50 g (2 oz) butter
5 ml (1 tsp) flour
BREAD SAUCE
450 ml (¾ pint) milk
2 cloves
1 small onion, sliced
salt and pepper
pinch of grated nutmeg
75 g (3 oz) fresh white
  breadcrumbs
30 ml (2 tbsp) single cream
GAME CHIP BASKETS
350 g (12 oz) potatoes
oil, for deep-frying
50 g (2 oz) butter
550 g (1¼ lb) canned whole
  unsweetened chestnuts, drained
25 g (1 oz) pine kernels
small bunch white grapes, to
  garnish (optional)

Remove the giblets from the grouse and use for the gravy. Cover the giblets with water, bring to the boil and simmer for 30 minutes. Set aside.

Wipe the birds inside and out and truss. Sprinkle with lemon juice and season. Bard with the bacon and place the birds in a roasting tin with the butter. Roast at 230°C (450°F) mark 8 for 15 minutes. Remove the bacon and return the grouse to the oven for a further 5 minutes to brown the breasts. Remove from the pan and keep hot. Skim off the excess fat from the pan juices. Stir in the flour then strain in the giblet stock. Bring to the boil and boil until well reduced. Season and strain. Remove the trussing string from the grouse.

To make the bread sauce, bring the milk, cloves, onion, seasoning and nutmeg to the boil. Reduce the heat and barely simmer for 10 minutes. Cool and strain. Return the infused liquid to the pan and stir in the breadcrumbs and cream. Simmer for 10 minutes, stirring often to prevent it from sticking. Adjust the seasoning before serving.

To make the game chip baskets, slice the potatoes finely on a mandoline, or slice very thinly with a sharp knife. Dip a double wire mesh basket into the hot oil, remove, then line the bottom of the basket with overlapping potato slices. Push the top basket into place and plunge into the hot oil. Deep-fry until crisp and golden. Make 3 more baskets in the same way. Drain on kitchen paper, sprinkle with salt and keep hot. Melt the butter in a saucepan and add the chestnuts and pine kernels. Stir until they are heated through, then use to fill the baskets. Serve.

GRILLED POUSSINS WITH GARLIC AND LIMES

A poussin is a very young chicken weighing about 500–600 g (1–1¼ lb). In this recipe the birds are halved and grilled.

Serves 4

INGREDIENTS

2 poussins
juice of 3 limes
100 ml (4 fl oz) olive oil
4 garlic cloves, quartered
salt and pepper
1.25 ml (¼ tsp) turmeric

Split the birds in half by cutting down one side of the breastbone. Open the birds out, turn them over and cut through the other side close to the backbone. Cut the backbone out completely.

Place the jointed birds in a bowl. Mix all of the remaining ingredients together, using the juice of 2 limes only, and pour it over. Leave to marinate for 1½–2 hours, turning occasionally. Remove from the marinade.

Cook the poussins over charcoal, or under a hot grill. If cooking over charcoal, baste the birds during cooking with the marinade. To grill, place the portions in a shallow heatproof dish or grill pan. Pour the remaining lime juice over the poussins, tuck the garlic pieces under the joints and grill for 20–25 minutes, turning and basting occasionally with the marinade. Serve with the pan juices poured over the birds.

ROAST GROUSE WITH BREAD SAUCE, GAME CHIPS AND CHESTNUTS

PHEASANT WITH CALVADOS AND APPLES

The cock pheasant is a beautiful bird with long speckled tail feathers.
The hen, although smaller, is fatter, with succulent flesh. Young pheasants
may be roasted but older birds should be casseroled.
This recipe combines the rich flavours of the pheasant, Calvados (apple brandy)
and cream. Serve with sautéed apple rings.

Serves 2—3

INGREDIENTS

1 pheasant, about 1 kg (2 lb)
*   trussed weight*
salt and pepper
40 g (1½ oz) clarified butter
2 shallots, finely chopped
90 ml (6 tbsp) Calvados or brandy
300 ml (½ pint) jellied chicken or
*   chicken stock (see page 247)*
bouquet garni
1.25 ml (¼ tsp) arrowroot
15 ml (1 tbsp) water
150 ml (¼ pint) double cream
25 g (1 oz) butter
3 Cox's apples, peeled and cut into
*   1 cm (½ inch) thick rings*
watercress, to garnish

Wipe the pheasant and season well. Heat the clarified butter in a casserole and brown the bird on all sides. Add the shallots and fry until golden. Add the Calvados, stock and bouquet garni, and bring to the boil. Reduce the heat, cover and cook gently for 1 hour.

Remove the pheasant from the pan, divide into portions and keep hot. Strain the pan juices, skimming off the fat. Return the juices to the pan. Mix the arrowroot with the water to a smooth paste, and add it to the pan juices. Stir over a gentle heat for 1 minute then add the cream. Cook gently, stirring, for 5 minutes. Season to taste.

Melt the butter in a frying pan and cook the apples for 5 minutes or until golden but still firm. Arrange the apple rings around the edge of a serving dish. Place the pheasant in the centre and pour over the sauce. Garnish with watercress.

PHEASANT WITH CALVADOS
AND APPLES

SPICED SALMIS OF GUINEA FOWL WITH CAPERS

Coriander and cumin flavour this dish of jointed guinea fowl.

Serves 4

Cover the breast of each guinea fowl with 2 slices of bacon and secure with fine string or cotton. Put 2 lemon quarters inside each bird. Place in a roasting tin and roast at 220°C (425°F) mark 7 for 30 minutes, basting occasionally. Remove from the pan and allow to cool slightly.

Remove the legs from each guinea fowl and carefully remove each breast. Roughly chop the carcasses. Remove and discard the skin from each portion.

Add the butter to the juices in the roasting tin and fry the onion until soft. Stir in the coriander and cumin and cook, stirring, for 2 minutes. Add the stock and bring to the boil. Transfer to a large saucepan. Add the carcasses, cover and simmer for 30 minutes. Strain.

Add the lemon juice to the stock then boil rapidly until reduced to about 450 ml (¾ pint). Stir in the capers and adjust the seasoning.

Arrange the guinea fowl joints in a single layer in a flameproof dish. Pour over the sauce and simmer gently for 15–20 minutes or until the guinea fowl is tender. Transfer to a heated serving dish and serve.

INGREDIENTS

*2 guinea fowl, about 1 kg (2 lb)
   each*
4 slices streaky bacon, rinded
1 lemon, quartered
25 g (1 oz) butter
1 medium onion, chopped
15 ml (1 tbsp) ground coriander
10 ml (2 tsp) ground cumin
*600 ml (1 pint) chicken stock
   (see page 247)*
30 ml (2 tbsp) lemon juice
25 ml (1½ tsp) capers, drained
salt and pepper

RABBIT WITH TARRAGON CIDER SAUCE

*The combination of the tarragon and cider in this sauce provides a sharp,
piquant contrast to the rich game flavour of the rabbit.*

Serves 4

Grease the base of a roasting tin with 15 g (½ oz) butter. Add the chopped onion. Wrap a slice of bacon around each piece of rabbit and secure with a wooden cocktail stick. Place the rabbit on top of the onion. Roast at 230°C (450°F) mark 8 for 15 minutes.

Mix the cider, chopped tarragon, honey and mustard together and pour it over the rabbit. Cover and continue cooking at 170°C (325°F) mark 3 for 1 hour.

Melt the remaining butter and fry the apple until golden brown. Remove the rabbit from the roasting tin and keep hot. Remove the cocktail sticks. Pour the pan juices over the apples. Dissolve the cornflour in the water and stir it into the pan. Simmer gently, stirring, until thickened. Stir in the tomato purée and season to taste.

Pour the sauce over the rabbit and garnish with the tarragon sprigs.

INGREDIENTS

40 g (1½ oz) butter
1 onion, finely chopped
*4 slices streaky bacon, or thin
   slices of salt pork, rinded*
*4 rabbit portions, each about
   225 g (8 oz)*
300 ml (½ pint) dry cider
*15 ml (1 tbsp) chopped fresh
   tarragon or 5 ml (1 tsp) dried
   tarragon*
30 ml (2 tbsp) clear honey
15 ml (1 tbsp) Dijon mustard
*2 dessert apples, peeled, cored
   and cut into 8 pieces*
15 ml (1 tbsp) cornflour
30 ml (2 tbsp) water
5 ml (1 tsp) tomato purée
salt and pepper
fresh tarragon sprigs, to garnish

PARTRIDGE WITH APRICOTS
UNDER A PUFF PASTRY CRUST
(SHOWN HERE IN AN
INDIVIDUAL SERVING DISH)

PARTRIDGE WITH APRICOTS
UNDER A PUFF PASTRY CRUST

These individual pies can be served as a luncheon dish. For a dinner party,
serve with glazed carrot and steamed broccoli.

Serves 4

INGREDIENTS

4 partridges
60 ml (4 tbsp) olive oil
4 shallots, chopped
1 carrot, diced
1 celery stalk, diced
1 bay leaf
9 sprigs of fresh thyme
sprig of fresh parsley
150 ml ($\frac{1}{4}$ pint) dry white wine
300 ml ($\frac{1}{2}$ pint) chicken
* stock (see page 247)*
50 g (2 oz) butter
25 g (1 oz) pine kernels
30 ml (2 tbsp) dry sherry
15 ml (1 tbsp) cornflour
salt and pepper
squeeze of lemon juice
8 fresh apricots, skinned, halved
* and stoned*
puff pastry, made with 225 g
* (8 oz) flour (see page 248)*
beaten egg, to glaze

Using a sharp knife, carefully remove the legs from each partridge. Cut a line down the length of each leg bone and carefully ease the flesh away from the bone. Discard the skin. Ease the breasts from the carcasses and discard the skin. Roughly chop the meat and then all the carcasses and bones. Heat half the oil in a heavy-based casserole and brown the bones well. Remove from the pan.

Add half the shallot, carrot and celery to the pan and fry until golden. Add the bay leaf, 1 sprig of thyme and the parsley, and return the bones to the pan. Pour over the white wine and bring to the boil. Add the stock, then cover and simmer for 45 minutes. Strain and reserve the stock. There should be about 300 ml ($\frac{1}{2}$ pint).

Melt the butter and fry the partridge until golden all over. Season the meat and divide it between 4 individual pie dishes.

Add the remaining oil to the pan and fry the remaining shallot and pine kernels until golden. Stir in the sherry and bring to the boil. Add the reserved stock. Mix the cornflour with 30 ml (2 tbsp) water and stir it into the sauce. Simmer until thickened. Adjust the seasoning and stir in the lemon juice. Cool.

Finely chop remaining thyme sprigs. Divide the apricots and thyme between the 4 dishes. Pour the cooled sauce on top.

Roll out the pastry on a lightly floured surface and use to cover the pies. Brush with beaten egg. Re-roll the trimmings and cut out leaves. Arrange on the pies and brush with beaten egg. Bake at 230°C (450°F) mark 8 for 20–25 minutes or until crisp and golden.

WIDGEON WITH RED WINE AND ORANGE

*Widgeon is a wild duck and is in season from September 1st to February 20th.
It is a small bird, weighing about 750 g (1½ lb), and may be found along the
coast and in marshy areas. The flesh of the widgeon is rather oily with a slightly
fishy flavour. Serve garnished with orange segments and watercress.*

Serves 4

Wipe the widgeon, season and place half a slice of orange in the cavity of each
bird. Bard with the bacon and truss neatly. Smear the surfaces with butter, place in
a roasting tin and roast at 200°C (400°F) mark 6 for 45 minutes, basting
occasionally.

Meanwhile, make the demi-glace sauce. Heat the oil and gently fry the onion,
celery and carrot for 15 minutes. Stir in the flour and cook, stirring, until
browned, scraping the crusty sediment from the base of the pan. Add 450 ml
(¾ pint) of the beef stock, mushroom peelings, tomato purée and the bouquet
garni. Bring to the boil, reduce the heat, partially cover the pan, and simmer for
30 minutes.

Add half the remaining stock, return the sauce to the boil and skim constantly
as the fat rises to the surface. Repeat with the remaining stock to give the sauce a
glossy appearance. Strain the sauce and adjust the seasoning. This makes 300 ml
(½ pint) demi-glace sauce.

To make the red wine sauce, melt the butter and fry the shallots until soft. Add
the red wine and the bay leaf, and simmer until reduced slightly. Add
300 ml (½ pint) of the demi-glace sauce with the orange rind and juice. Bring to the
boil and simmer for about 5–8 minutes.

When cooked, remove the widgeon from the oven cut it into serving portions
and keep hot. Add the pan juices to the sauce, then strain it and skim any fat from
the surface. Return to the pan and stir in the redcurrant jelly and season to taste.
Simmer, stirring, to reheat. Place the widgeon on a serving plate, pour the sauce
around it and garnish with orange segments and watercress.

INGREDIENTS
*2 widgeon, about 500 g (1 lb)
    trussed weight*
salt and pepper
1 thick orange slice, halved
4 slices streaky bacon
25 g (1 oz) butter
DEMI-GLACE SAUCE
30 ml (2 tbsp) oil
½ onion, finely chopped
½ celery stalk, finely chopped
1 small carrot, finely chopped
15 ml (1 tbsp) flour
*600 ml (1 pint) beef stock
    (see page 246)*
few mushroom peelings
5 ml (1 tsp) tomato purée
bouquet garni
RED WINE SAUCE
15 g (½ oz) butter
2 shallots, finely chopped
90 ml (3½ fl oz) red wine
bay leaf
pared rind of ½ orange
juice of 1 orange
5 ml (1 tsp) redcurrant jelly

ROAST TEAL WITH ORANGE BUTTER

*Teal or wild duck make a succulent and tasty meal. Roast and serve
dripping with orange butter on a bed of watercress.*

Serves 4

First, make the orange butter. Beat the butter with the orange rind and juice,
mustard and seasoning until evenly mixed. Form into a roll on a piece of
aluminium foil, then wrap and chill until hard.

Season the teal, then wrap a bacon slice over each breast. Place in a roasting tin
and cook at 220°C (425°F) mark 7 for 8–10 minutes. Remove the bacon and cook
for a further 5 minutes.

Remove the trussing string from the teal, then transfer the birds to warmed
serving plates. Arrange the watercress around the birds. Cut the orange butter
into 4 slices and place a slice on each bird. Spoon over the cooking juices and
serve at once.

INGREDIENTS
salt and pepper
*4 young teal, about 350 g (12 oz)
    each, plucked, drawn and
    trussed*
4 slices bacon
8 sprigs of watercress
ORANGE BUTTER
100 g (4 oz) butter, softened
finely grated rind of 2 oranges
juice of 1 orange
2.5 ml (½ tsp) Dijon mustard

TURKEY AND CHESTNUT PIE

*A delicious pie made with hot water crust pastry which is perfect for picnics
or buffets. A good jellied stock is essential—stock cubes simply won't do. If there
is not any good stock to hand, make the required amount by covering 4 chicken
wings with cold water, bringing it to the boil and simmering for 2 hours.
Boil it until reduced to the required amount of stock. When cold it jellies beautifully.*

Serves 6–8

Roll out two-thirds of the pastry to a 1 cm ($\frac{1}{2}$ inch) thickness and use it to line a
lightly greased 18 cm (7 inch) round cake tin with a removable base.

Mix the turkey, bacon, parsley and half the chestnuts together and season.
Spoon half the mixture into the lined cake tin. Arrange the remaining chestnuts in
a layer over the filling. Spoon the remaining turkey mixture over the top and
sprinkle with brandy.

Roll out the remaining pastry to an 18 cm (7 inch) circle. The top should be
slightly thinner than the base. Cover the pie, seal the edges and crimp. Re-roll the
trimmings and cut into leaves. Cut a cross in the centre of the pie and turn back
the pastry. Insert a small funnel of aluminium foil into the hole. Brush the pie top
with the beaten egg. Position the leaves and brush with beaten egg.

Bake at 230°C (450°F) mark 8 for 20 minutes. Reduce the temperature to
170°C (325°F) mark 3, cover the pie with aluminium foil and cook for a further 2
hours. Remove the aluminium foil and cook the pie for 20 minutes more or until
the pastry is a rich golden brown. Heat the stock gently until it is just liquid.
Remove it from the heat and sprinkle the gelatine over the surface. Leave for a
few minutes to soften, then return the pan to the heat and stir until it dissolves
completely. Pour it into the middle of the pie and allow it to cool completely.
Remove the funnel and transfer the pie to a serving dish.

INGREDIENTS

*hot water crust pastry, made with
500 g (1 lb) plain flour (see
page 249)*

600 g (1¼ lb) turkey meat, diced

*225 g (8 oz) unsmoked streaky
bacon, rinded and diced*

*30 ml (2 tbsp) chopped fresh
parsley*

*500 g (1 lb) canned whole
unsweetened chestnuts, drained*

salt and pepper

45 ml (3 tbsp) brandy

1 egg, beaten

*300 ml (½ pint) jellied turkey or
chicken stock (see page 247)*

15 ml (1 tbsp) powdered gelatine

PARTRIDGES WRAPPED IN VINE LEAVES

*Partridges belong to the same family as pheasants and quail and are in season from
September 1st to February 1st. The stuffing in this recipe is made with mushrooms,
breadcrumbs, ham and cream and is pre-cooked as the roasting time
for partridge is so brief. The bird should be served slightly pink.*

Serves 4

Wipe the partridges, season and set aside. Melt half the butter and fry the onion
until soft. Add the mushrooms and cook for 3 minutes or until the moisture has
evaporated. Remove from the heat, place in a bowl, and allow to cool slightly.
Stir in the breadcrumbs, ham, parsley and cream, and season to taste. Stuff the
partridges with the mixture. Smear the breasts with the remaining butter.

If canned vine leaves are used, rinse well in cold water and dry them.
Remove the stems and cover each breast with a leaf. Place 3 slices of bacon over
each bird and tie loosely in place with string.

Place the birds in an ovenproof dish and roast at 230°C (450°F) mark 8 for 15
minutes. Remove the birds from the oven, discard the bacon and vine leaves, and
return the partridges to the oven for 5–10 minutes, or until the breasts have
browned.

Serve with the pan juices and game chips. Garnish with extra vine leaves and
lamb's lettuce.

PARTRIDGE WRAPPED IN VINE LEAVES

INGREDIENTS

4 young partridges

salt and pepper

50 g (2 oz) butter

1 medium onion, finely chopped

75 g (3 oz) mushrooms, chopped

25 g (1 oz) fresh breadcrumbs

25 g (1 oz) ham, finely chopped

*15 ml (1 tbsp) chopped fresh
parsley*

15 ml (1 tbsp) double cream

4 large vine leaves

12 slices unsmoked streaky bacon

*extra vine leaves and lamb's
lettuce, to garnish*

RAISED GAME PIE

A favourite recipe for lunchtime snacks or picnics. The game is flavoured with wine, juniper berries, herbs and spices to make a tasty pie.

Serves 8

INGREDIENTS

1 pheasant, about 800 g (1¾ lb)

1 wild duck, about 1 kg (2 lb)

1 grouse, about 500 g (1 lb)

1 partridge, about 500 g (1 lb)

225 g (8 oz) belly of pork, rinded

1 medium onion

salt and pepper

hot water crust pastry made
   with 500 g (1 lb) flour (see page
   249)

1 egg, beaten, to glaze

MARINADE

200 ml (7 fl oz) red wine

100 ml (4 fl oz) olive oil

100 ml (4 fl oz) wine vinegar

8 juniper berries, crushed

1 medium onion, sliced

few sprigs of parsley

few sprigs of thyme

2 bay leaves

1 garlic clove, crushed

pinch of grated nutmeg

15 ml (1 tbsp) sugar

5 ml (1 tsp) salt

1.25 ml (¼ tsp) Tabasco sauce

STOCK

1 onion, chopped

1 carrot, chopped

1 celery stalk

1 bay leaf

sprig of fresh thyme

sprig of fresh rosemary

few sprigs of parsley

4 juniper berries

150 ml (¼ pint) white wine

450 ml (¾ pint) chicken stock
   (see page 247)

10 ml (2 tsp) powdered gelatine

First bone the game birds. Carefully remove the breasts from each bird with a sharp knife, cutting away the meat from the legs. Remove all the skin, tendons and fat, and cut the meat in to 1.5 cm (½ inch) strips. Roughly chop the carcasses and discard any skin and fat. Place the bones in a roasting tin.

Mix together all the ingredients for the marinade. Add the game meat, cover and leave in the refrigerator to marinate overnight, or up to 24 hours.

For the stock, roast the bones at 220°C (425°F) mark 7 for 20 minutes. Add the onion, carrot and celery and roast for a further 10 minutes. Transfer to a large saucepan. Add the herbs, juniper berries, white wine and stock, and bring to the boil. Cover and simmer for 1½ hours. Leave to cool, then strain. Boil the stock rapidly until reduced to 450 ml (¾ pint). Strain through fine muslin then chill. Remove the surface fat.

The following day, remove the strips of meat from the marinade and dry them well. Discard the marinade. Coarsely mince the belly of pork and onion, and combine with the game. Season generously.

Reserve a scant one-third of the pastry and wrap in clingfilm Roll out the remaining pastry on a lightly floured surface and use to line the base and sides of a 23 cm (9 inch) long raised pie mould, allowing the pastry to overlap the rim a little. Spoon the filling into the pastry case, pressing it down gently. Brush the edges of the pastry with water. Roll out the remaining pastry and cover the top of the pie. Press the edges well to seal them, then trim off the excess pastry. Crimp the edges. Re-roll the pastry trimmings and use to make leaves. Make a 2.5 cm (1 inch) hole in the top of the pie and insert a small funnel of aluminium foil in the hole. Brush with beaten egg. Arrange the pastry leaves on top and brush with beaten egg.

Bake at 190°C (375°F) mark 5 for 45 minutes. Remove the sides of the mould, brush the sides of the pie with beaten egg and return to the oven for 15 minutes. Brush the pie all over with beaten egg and return to the oven for a further 15 minutes. To check if the filling is cooked, insert a skewer into the centre of the pie. Leave for 10 seconds then remove the skewer; it should be hot. If not, brush the pie with more beaten egg and return it to the oven for a further 15 minutes. When cooked, leave the pie until cold.

Sprinkle the gelatine over the stock and leave it to soften for 2 minutes. Stir over gentle heat until the gelatine has dissolved completely. Leave until cool then pour into the pie. Chill the pie until required. Serve at room temperature.

CHICKEN AND HAM PIE

*A raised pie is ideal for a picnic, as the filling is set in a rich firm jelly
and encased in a thick pastry crust, so it is easy to pack and carry.*

Serves 8

Lightly grease a deep 18 cm (7 inch) cake tin with a removable base. Alternatively, if the base is not removable, line the base and sides of the tin with greaseproof paper. Roll out two-thirds of the pastry to 6 mm ($\frac{1}{4}$ inch) thick and use to line the cake tin. Mix the chicken, gammon, bacon, herbs and seasoning together. Spoon the filling into the lined tin. Pour over the wine and dot with butter. Roll the remaining pastry into an 18 cm (7 inch) circle. Re-roll the pastry trimmings and cut into leaves. Brush the edges of the pie with some of the beaten egg and cover with the circle of pastry. Crimp the edges to seal.

Glaze the top of the pie with beaten egg, cut a cross in the centre and turn the pastry back. Insert a small aluminium foil funnel into the hole. Arrange the pastry leaves on top and brush with beaten egg. Bake at 230°C (450°F) mark 8 for 20 minutes. Reduce the temperature to 170°C (325°F) mark 3, cover with aluminium foil and bake for 2 hours. Remove the aluminium foil and cook the pie for a further 20 minutes.

Meanwhile, heat the stock gently until it is just liquid. Remove from the heat. Sprinkle over the gelatine and leave to soften for 2 minutes. Place over gentle heat until it has dissolved completely then pour it into the pie. Cool the pie in the tin then chill until required. Remove the aluminium foil funnel and remove the pie from the tin before serving.

INGREDIENTS

hot water crust pastry, made with
    500 g (1 lb) plain flour (see
    page 249)

750 g (1½ lb) chicken breast,
    skinned and diced

500 g (1 lb) cooked gammon,
    diced

100 g (4 oz) unsmoked streaky
    bacon, rinded and finely
    chopped

60 ml (4 tbsp) chopped parsley

2.5 ml (½ tsp) chopped thyme

pinch of grated nutmeg

salt and pepper

45 ml (3 tbsp) dry white wine

25 g (1 oz) butter

1 egg, beaten, to glaze

300 ml (½ pint) jellied chicken stock
    (see page 247)

15 ml (1 tbsp) powdered gelatine

91

CHEESE AND DAIRY

CREAM OF STILTON SOUP

*The Stilton is not actually cooked, but melts as it is stirred into the hot soup.
It is a very rich soup, so this quantity will easily serve 4 as a starter.
Turkey or veal stock, if you have them, can also be used in place of the
chicken stock.*

Serves 4

INGREDIENTS
300 ml (½ pint) milk
1 bay leaf
½ small onion, sliced
25 g (1 oz) butter
30 ml (2 tbsp) flour
*450 ml (¾ pint) chicken stock
(see page 247)*
*100 g (4 oz) Stilton cheese,
crumbled*
salt and pepper

Bring the milk, bay leaf and onion to the boil, remove from the heat, cover and
leave to infuse for 10 minutes. Strain.

In a heavy-based pan, melt the butter, stir in the flour, and cook, stirring, for 1
minute. Remove the pan from the heat and gradually pour in the milk, stirring
constantly. Return the pan to the heat and cook, stirring, for 1 minute, then add
the stock. Bring the soup to the boil then let it simmer for 5 minutes.

Remove the pan from the heat and immediately add the cheese. Stir until the
cheese melts, then season. Serve hot with crusty bread.

CAMEMBERT CROQUETTES

This simple cheese dish makes a delicious starter served with gooseberry or plum sauce.

Serves 4

INGREDIENTS
*1 round Camembert, about
225 g (8 oz)*
seasoned flour
1 egg, beaten
salt and pepper
75 g (3 oz) fresh breadcrumbs
oil, for deep-frying

Cut the Camembert into eight wedges and toss in seasoned flour. Place the egg
on a plate and season. Dip the cheese in the egg, then coat in the breadcrumbs.
Coat a second time if necessary. Chill the cheese for 30 minutes.

Heat the oil in a deep-fat fryer to 180°C (350°F). Fry the Camembert in two
batches for 1–2 minutes or until the coating is golden brown. Drain on kitchen
paper and serve piping hot.

94

BLUE BRIE TARTLETS

*These little tartlets are perfect for cocktails, as the pastry cases can be made
in advance. Serve immediately, puffed and golden from the oven.*

Makes 18

Roll out the pastry on a lightly floured board, to a 3 mm ($\frac{1}{8}$ inch) thickness.
Cut out 18 circles and use to line the pastry tins. Prick the bases with a fork, cover
the base of each tin with a small circle of greaseproof paper and fill with baking
beans. Bake blind at 220°C (425°F) mark 7, for 10 minutes. Remove from
the oven, leave for 2 minutes, then remove the beans and paper.

To make the filling, chop the brie into small pieces, and place in the top of a
double boiler, or in a bowl set over a pan of simmering water. Add the cream and
stir for 3–4 minutes or until the cheese melts. Remove from the heat and allow
the cheese mixture to cool slightly. Stir in the beaten egg.

Pour about 7.5 ml ($1\frac{1}{2}$ tsp) of the mixture into each pastry case. Bake at 180°C
(350°F) mark 4, for 15–18 minutes, or until puffed and golden.

INGREDIENTS
*shortcrust pastry, made with
    250 g (9 oz) flour (see page 247)*
*350 g (12 oz) blue brie, rind
    removed*
45 ml (3 tbsp) single cream
3 eggs, lightly beaten

CAMEMBERT AND BROCCOLI SOUP

A rich cheese soup which combines beautifully with the flavour of broccoli.

Serves 4

Melt the butter in a large saucepan and fry the shallots until soft. Peel the broccoli
stalks to remove the coarse skin, then chop. Add to the pan and fry gently for 5
minutes. Add the stock and wine. Cover and simmer for 10–15 minutes, or until
the broccoli is tender.

Combine the potato flour with the milk and stir it into the soup. Bring to the
boil then simmer gently for 2–3 minutes. Add the cheese and heat gently until
melted, stirring frequently.

Purée the soup, return it to the rinsed-out saucepan and adjust the seasoning.
Ladle into individual soup bowls.

For the garnish, fry the tiny broccoli florets in the butter until tender but still
crisp. Arrange on the soup with the basil leaves and paprika.

INGREDIENTS
25 g (1 oz) butter
*50 g (2 oz) shallots, or spring
    onion, chopped*
225 g (8 oz) broccoli florets
*300 ml ($\frac{1}{2}$ pint) chicken stock
    (see page 247)*
300 ml ($\frac{1}{2}$ pint) dry white wine
*10 ml (2 tsp) potato flour, or
    cornflour*
150 ml ($\frac{1}{4}$ pint) milk
*225 g (8 oz) Camembert cheese,
    rind removed and cubed*
salt and pepper
GARNISH
8 tiny broccoli florets
15 g ($\frac{1}{2}$ oz) butter
fresh basil leaves
paprika

DILL AND WALNUT YOGURT

*This yogurt may be served as a starter with pitta bread
or as an accompaniment to spicy rice dishes.*

Serve 4—6

Place the cucumber in a colander and sprinkle with salt, then leave to drain for 30 minutes.

Do not rinse the cucumber but pat dry with absorbent paper.

Place the yogurt in a bowl and beat for a few moments until smooth. Add the remaining ingredients and mix well. Pour into a serving bowl. Garnish with fresh dill and walnut halves. Chill until required.

INGREDIENTS
1 large cucumber, peeled and diced
2.5 ml (½ tsp) salt
600 ml (1 pint) natural yogurt
20 ml (4 tsp) finely chopped fresh dill
1 small green chilli, seeded and finely chopped
50 g (2 oz) walnuts, roughly chopped
25 g (1 oz) sultanas
sprigs of fresh dill and walnut halves to garnish (optional)

ROQUEFORT MILLE-FEUILLE

*This savoury pastry slice filled with creamy Roquefort cheese may be cut into
small squares for a cocktail party, or cut into larger portions for a first course
or a snack.*

Serves 4—6

Roll out the pastry on a lightly floured board to a 51 × 22 cm (20 × 8½ inch) rectangle. Cut in half widthways to make 2 rectangles 25 × 22 cm (10 × 8½ inch).

Crumble the cheese into a bowl. Add the butter and mix until well blended, soft and creamy. Stir in the egg and the paprika.

Place half the pastry on a dampened baking sheet (the moisture helps the pastry to rise while cooking). Make sure that the baking sheet is a thick one, as some thinner sheets tend to buckle.

Spread the mixture on to the pastry, leaving at least 2.5 cm (1 inch) of pastry uncovered around the edges. Moisten the edge of the pastry with a little cold water and top with the second piece of pastry. Press the edges together gently to seal. Using a sharp knife, trim the edges evenly and knock up. Brush with the egg glaze—the salt gives a rich golden colour.

Bake at 220—230°C (425—450°F) mark 7—8, for 15—20 minutes or until the pastry is a rich golden brown. Serve immediately.

INGREDIENTS
puff pastry, made with 100 g (4 oz) flour (see page 248)
150 g (5 oz) Roquefort cheese
25 g (1 oz) butter
1 egg, lightly beaten
1.25 ml (¼ tsp) paprika
1 egg, beaten with a pinch of salt, to glaze

NESTLED EGGS

*Filo pastry 'nests' make an attractive serving container for these poached eggs.
They are served with a white wine sauce and garnished with caviar.*

Serves 4

INGREDIENTS

100 g (4 oz) unsalted butter

4 sheets of filo pastry

*50 g (2 oz) carrot, cut into julienne
strips*

*50 g (2 oz) white part of leek, cut
into julienne strips*

90 ml (6 tbsp) dry white wine

1 shallot, chopped

1 egg yolk

salt and pepper

4 eggs, poached

*10 ml (2 tsp) salmon caviar or red
lumpfish roe, to garnish*

*mustard and cress, or 4 parsley
sprigs, to garnish*

Melt 25 g (1 oz) of the butter and brush the inside of 4 individual 10 cm (4 inch) flan tins, or a tray of 4 Yorkshire pudding patty tins.

Cut each sheet of pastry into 4 pieces. Line each tin with 4 pieces of pastry, brushing with melted butter between each layer. The pastry should be roughly pressed in to look like a 'nest'. Bake at 220°C (425°F) mark 7 for 7–8 minutes until crisp and golden. Keep warm.

Melt 25 g (1 oz) of the remaining butter and fry the carrot and leek for 1–2 minutes or until just tender. Add 30 ml (2 tbsp) of the white wine. Reserve.

Place the shallot and remaining white wine in a saucepan. Boil over moderate heat until reduced to 15 ml (1 tbsp). Strain into a small bowl and add the egg yolk.

Place the bowl over a pan of simmering water and whisk until the mixture just holds the trail of the whisk. Remove the pan from the heat. Dice the remaining butter and whisk it into the egg mixture a little at a time. Season to taste. Keep warm over the water.

Place the pastry cases on serving plates. Warm the vegetable julienne, then spoon it around the edges of the pastry cases. Arrange a poached egg in the centre of each, and spoon a little of the sauce over.

Garnish with a little caviar and a tiny bunch of mustard and cress, or parsley sprigs.

QUAILS' EGGS IN A BASKET

*These quails' eggs served in baskets of choux pastry make a delicious
and attractive first course.*

Serves 4

INGREDIENTS

*choux pastry, made with 90 g
(3½ oz) flour (see page 249)*

*15 ml (1 tbsp) finely grated
Parmesan cheese*

FILLING

*75 g (3 oz) Swiss chard leaves,
or lettuce, trimmed weight*

25 g (1 oz) butter

90 ml (6 tbsp) double cream

grated nutmeg

paprika

salt and pepper

8 quails' eggs

Spoon the choux pastry into 4 equal portions on a dampened baking sheet. Spread out slightly into 6 cm (2½ inch) rounds. Sprinkle with Parmesan cheese and bake at 220°C (425°F) mark 7 for 20 minutes. With a small sharp knife, remove the top third of the 'baskets' and place on the baking sheet. Return to the oven for 5 minutes to crisp.

To make the filling, slice the chard into very fine strips. Melt the butter in a frying pan and fry the leaves until just tender. Stir in the cream and season well with nutmeg, paprika, salt and pepper.

Boil the eggs for 2 minutes, drain and dip in cold water. Drain and remove the shells. Using an egg slice, slice almost through the eggs to make a fan shape. Remove carefully.

Warm the chard gently and pile it into the pastry 'baskets'. Arrange 2 eggs on top of each one, sprinkle with paprika and top with the lid.

YOGURT CHEESE BALLS MARINATED IN HERBS

*These walnut-sized balls of thick yogurt cheese look very pretty in their
jar of golden olive oil. Eat with salads, using the flavoured oil as a salad dressing.
Make sure that the remaining balls are still immersed in oil.*

Makes 16 balls

INGREDIENTS

*225 ml (8 fl oz) thick natural
yogurt or Greek yogurt*
600 ml (1 pint) olive oil
*3 large sprigs fresh herbs such as
rosemary, thyme or marjoram*

Stir the yogurt until smooth, then place it in the centre of a large square of muslin. Tie in a bundle and secure with string. Place the bundle in a deep saucepan or casserole (it must not touch the base), position a wooden spoon across the top and tie the bundle to it. Leave to drain overnight, or longer if possible.

Unwrap the drained yogurt cheese and with your fingers, shape it into walnut-sized balls. Pour the olive oil into a glass jar and carefully drop the cheeses, one by one, into the oil. Tuck the herbs down the sides of the jar, cover and leave for at least 2 days before eating.

PHYLLO CHEESE PIE

*Phyllo, or filo, is a wafer thin pastry used to make sweet and savoury pies.
When using this pastry, always keep it under a damp cloth, working with one sheet
at a time as it dries very quickly and becomes impossible to use.*

Serves 6—8

Melt 75 g (3 oz) of the butter in a frying pan and fry the onion until golden. Wash the spinach and cook in the water that clings to the leaves for 5 minutes. Drain thoroughly, then add it to the onion and cook, stirring for 5 minutes. Remove from the heat, add the parsley, seasoning and nutmeg. Leave to cool. Add the feta cheese and eggs and mix well.

Melt the remaining butter. Place one sheet of pastry in a greased 36 × 21.5 cm (14 × 8½ inch) shallow tin. Brush with the melted butter. Tuck in the edges neatly. Continue to make layers with half the pastry, brushing each one with butter.

Spread the spinach and cheese filling over the pastry, then use the remaining sheets, brushed with butter, to cover the filling. When the last sheet of pastry is in place, brush it well with butter, and using a sharp knife, score the top into a diamond pattern.

Bake at 190°C (375°F) mark 5 for 40 minutes or until golden brown. Cool in the tin for 10 minutes, then serve.

INGREDIENTS
200 g (7 oz) butter
1 large onion, finely chopped
*1 kg (2 lb) fresh spinach, central
    core removed*
*30 ml (2 tbsp) finely chopped
    fresh parsley*
salt and pepper
1.25 ml (¼ tsp) grated nutmeg
225 g (8 oz) feta cheese, crumbled
3 eggs, lightly beaten
400 g (14 oz) phyllo pastry

CREAMY SCRAMBLED EGGS WITH CAVIAR

*This will serve four as a first course or two as a light luncheon dish.
Serve with melba toast.*

Serves 4

Lightly grease a frying pan with the butter and place over gentle heat. Pour in the eggs, add the remaining butter and crème fraîche, and season.

Cook, stirring with a wooden spoon, until the eggs begin to set. Remove the pan from the heat and continue stirring until the eggs are thick and creamy. Taste and adjust the seasoning.

Spoon the eggs on to individual serving plates and sprinkle over the caviar. Arrange triangles of melba toast around the dish. Serve immediately.

INGREDIENTS
100 g (4 oz) butter
8 eggs, lightly beaten
45 ml (3 tbsp) crème fraîche
salt and pepper
*60 ml (4 tbsp) caviar, or black
    lumpfish roe*
melba toast, to serve (see page 47)

YOGURT CHEESE BALLS MARINATED IN HERBS

CHICKEN AND MUSHROOM CREPES WITH CRAB SAUCE

The unusual combination of flavours in this recipe blend together very well.
Serve with a crisp salad for lunch, or as a light supper.

Serves 6

INGREDIENTS

25 g (1 oz) butter

1 small shallot, finely chopped

350 g (12 oz) chicken breast,
* skinned and cut into*
* 1 cm (½ inch) cubes*

75 g (3 oz) mushrooms, roughly
* chopped*

salt and pepper

150 ml (¼ pint) single cream

225 g (8 oz) white crabmeat

30 ml (2 tbsp) medium dry sherry

CREPES

50 g (2 oz) plain flour

salt

1 large egg, beaten

75 ml (3 fl oz) milk

50 ml (2 fl oz) water

15 ml (1 tbsp) melted butter

oil, for greasing

To make the crêpes, sift the flour and salt into a bowl. Make a well in the centre and add the egg. Gradually beat in the milk and water until smooth. Stir in the melted butter.

Heat an 18 cm (7 inch) crêpe pan over moderate heat. Pour in a little oil and when hot, add 30–45 ml (2–3 tbsp) of the batter. Cook the crêpes, for 1 minute on each side. Keep warm on a plate, set over a pan of simmering water, with greaseproof paper between each crêpe. This amount of batter should make 6 crêpes.

To make the filling, melt the butter in a heavy-based pan and fry the shallot for 2 minutes. Add the chicken and cook, stirring, until the chicken changes colour. Stir in the mushrooms, cover the pan and cook for 3 minutes. Remove the lid, season and stir in 30 ml (2 tbsp) of the cream. Simmer until the liquid in the pan reduces and thickens slightly.

Meanwhile, make the sauce; blend the crabmeat and sherry together in a blender or food processor, then blend in the remaining cream. Pour into a pan and heat gently.

Spoon the chicken filling on to each crêpe, fold over the edges and place, seam side down, on a serving dish. Spoon the sauce around each crêpe. Serve hot.

SPRINGTIME QUICHE

This quiche combines the fresh flavour of young vegetables with mint.
It is preferable to use a metal flan tin rather than a white ceramic one,
as metal conducts more heat and will produce a better pastry base.

Serves 6

INGREDIENTS

wholemeal pastry, made with
* 200 g (10 oz) wholemeal flour*
* (see page 249)*

25 g (1 oz) butter

100 g (4 oz) spring onions, chopped

100 g (4 oz) lettuce, shredded

100 g (4 oz) peas

salt and pepper

7.5 ml (1½ tsp) chopped fresh mint

100 g (4 oz) Cheddar cheese,
* grated*

1 whole egg

1 egg yolk

150 ml (¼ pint) single cream

150 ml (¼ pint) milk

Roll out the pastry on a lightly floured surface and use to line a 25 cm (10 inch) fluted flan tin with a removable base.

Melt the butter in a pan and fry the spring onions, lettuce and peas over gentle heat for 5 minutes. Season, remove from the heat and stir in the mint.

Sprinkle the cheese evenly over the base of the flan then spread the vegetables over the cheese. Beat the egg with the egg yolk, cream and milk. Pour carefully over the vegetables. Bake at 190°C (375°F) mark 5 for 40 minutes or until the quiche is set and golden brown.

HOT GOAT'S CHEESE SALAD WITH SAGE DRESSING

This recipe will make a light starter for four, or a light luncheon dish for two.

Serves 4

Cut the cheese widthways into 4 equal slices. Pour the olive oil into a bowl, add the sage leaves and immerse the cheese slices carefully. Cover the bowl and leave overnight.

Make the dressing the day before to allow the flavours to blend. Pour all the dressing ingredients into a screw-top jar. Place the top on the jar and shake well to blend.

Drain the cheese, leaving the leaves in the oil. Place the breadcrumbs in a shallow dish and stir in the dried sage. Coat the cheese slices in the breadcrumbs and place on a greased baking sheet. Bake at 200°C (400°F) mark 6, for 10–12 minutes, or until the breadcrumbs are light golden. Leave the cheese on the baking sheet for 2 minutes.

Arrange the lettuce leaves and chicory spears on individual serving plates. Carefully transfer the cheese slices to each plate. Shake the dressing and spoon a little over the leaves. Serve hot.

INGREDIENTS
1 goat's cheese,
weighing 225 g (8 oz)
225 ml (8 fl oz) olive oil
12 sage fresh leaves
25 g (1 oz) fine fresh
breadcrumbs
pinch of dried sage
12 green lettuce leaves
12 spears chicory
DRESSING
25 ml (1½ tbsp) white wine
vinegar
1 garlic clove, quartered
1.25 ml (¼ tsp) Dijon mustard
2 sage leaves
salt
45 ml (3 tbsp) olive oil

GOLDEN RICE MOULD
WITH DUCK EGGS AND YOGURT

Do not use a casserole with raised handles as the edge of the pan needs to be placed
directly on the serving dish when it is turned over to prevent the rice from cracking.
A ring mould may be used, or any mould with a 2.3 litre (4 pint) capacity.

Serves 6

Place the breasts, cold water and seasoning in a saucepan and bring to the boil. Reduce the heat, cover and cook for 30 minutes or until tender. Remove the skin from the breasts and cut the meat into small pieces. Strain the cooking liquid and reserve 75 ml (3 fl oz). In a large bowl, stir the egg yolks, yogurt and oil together.

Mix the saffron with the hot water and leave to infuse for 5 minutes. Stir it into the yogurt mixture with the cooled cooking liquid. Wash the rice in cold water and drain, discarding any husks or discoloured grains. Bring a large saucepan of salted water to the boil. Add the rice, stir and return to the boil. Cook for 3–4 minutes, drain immediately and rinse in cold water. Drain again.

Pour the melted butter into the base of the mould and rotate it to coat the sides well. Dip the chicken pieces in the yogurt mixture. Mix half of the rice with the remaining yogurt mixture. Reserve half of the rice and spread the remainder over the base. Sprinkle 50 g (2 oz) of the currants and the cumin on top, then spread half of the plain rice over the currants and cumin. Top with some of the chicken pieces. Make another layer of white rice, the remaining currants and cumin and top with the yogurt-coated rice. Press the mixture down and cover with aluminium foil. Bake at 190°C (375°F) mark 5 for 1 hour. Plunge the base into cold water for 1 minute. Unmould and serve with extra butter and yogurt.

INGREDIENTS
2 large duck or chicken breasts,
about 225 g (8 oz) each
300 ml (½ pint) cold water
salt and pepper
2 duck egg yolks
225 ml (8 fl oz) natural yogurt
15 ml (1 tbsp) vegetable oil
2.5 ml (½ tsp) saffron powder
15 ml (1 tbsp) hot water
600 g (1¼ lb) basmati rice
75 g (3 oz) butter, melted
100 g (4 oz) currants
2.5 ml (½ tsp) ground cumin

PERSIAN OMELETTE WITH FRESH HERBS

*A baked omelette which can be served hot or cold, with natural yogurt for
breakfast, lunch or a light snack.*

Serves 4–6

INGREDIENTS

6 eggs
50 g (2 oz) fresh coriander,
 finely chopped
50 g (2 oz) fresh parsley,
 finely chopped
15 g (½ oz) chives, finely chopped
green tops of 2 spring onions,
 finely chopped
15 ml (1 tbsp) finely chopped
 fresh dill
pinch of saffron powder
salt and pepper
50 g (2 oz) butter

Lightly beat the eggs in a large bowl. Add all of the remaining ingredients, except the butter and beat together lightly.

Place the butter in a shallow round ovenproof dish.

Melt the butter in the oven at 180°C (350°F) mark 4. Pour the omelette mixture into the hot dish, cover with aluminium foil and bake for 30 minutes. Remove the aluminium foil and return to the oven for a further 15 minutes. Turn the omelette out on to a serving dish, cut into 4–6 wedges, and serve.

FETTUCCINI WITH GORGONZOLA SAUCE

*This rich creamy sauce combines the delicious Italian flavour of
Gorgonzola and basil. Fresh parsley, sage and oregano also go well in this sauce.
Serve with a bottle of Italian red wine.*

Serves 4

INGREDIENTS

25 g (1 oz) butter
175 g (6 oz) Gorgonzola cheese
150 ml (¼ pint) double cream
30 ml (2 tbsp) dry white wine
15 ml (1 tbsp) chopped fresh basil
salt and pepper
500 g (1 lb) fettuccini

Melt the butter in a saucepan. Crumble in the Gorgonzola cheese, then stir over gentle heat for 2–3 minutes, until melted. Pour in the cream and wine, whisking vigorously. Mix in the basil, salt and pepper and cook, stirring, until the sauce thickens. Remove the pan from the heat.

Cook the fettuccini in a large pan of boiling, salted water until al dente. Drain thoroughly.

Gently reheat the Gorgonzola sauce, whisking vigorously all the time. Taste and adjust the seasoning. Turn the pasta into 1 large or 4 individual serving bowls and pour over the sauce. Serve at once.

FRIED BRIE WITH CRANBERRY SAUCE

*The brie for this recipe should not be over-ripe. Serve as a starter or light luncheon dish,
with a crisp green salad.*

Serves 6

First make the cranberry sauce. Place the cranberries and water in a saucepan and
bring to the boil. Cover and simmer for 5 minutes. Remove from the heat and stir
in the sugar. Return the pan to the heat and simmer for 5 minutes more. Pour into
a serving bowl and keep hot.

Sift the flour on to a plate and coat the cheese on all sides. Dip into the beaten
egg, then coat with the breadcrumbs. Heat the oil in a deep fat fryer to 180°C
(350°F). Deep-fry the brie for 1½–2 minutes on either side, or until the
breadcrumbs are golden. Drain well on kitchen paper. Serve hot accompanied by
the cranberry sauce.

INGREDIENTS
30 ml (2 tbsp) flour
*750 g (1½ lb) brie, cut into
    6 wedges*
1 egg, lightly beaten
75 g (3 oz) fresh breadcrumbs
300 ml (½ pint) vegetable oil
CRANBERRY SAUCE
*175 g (6 oz) cranberries,
    fresh or frozen*
75 ml (3 fl oz) water
75 g (3 oz) sugar

CHARCUTERIE AND OFFAL

CHARCUTERIE AND OFFAL

◆

Over 60 different salamis deck the charcuterie counter, as well as
40 types of sausage, including Harrods own hand-made variety.
There are 40 different pâtés and Scottish haggis is also a popular
purchase. Sizzling Farmhouse Sausages make a delicious and simple meal
and the richer Salade de Foie Gras Chaude is the ideal dish
for a special occasion.

PRESSED OX TONGUE IN ASPIC

Tongue pressed and set in aspic, is unmoulded on to a serving plate
and accompanied by Cumberland Sauce.

Serves 6–8

INGREDIENTS
1 salted ox tongue, about
 1.4 kg (3 lb)
6 black peppercorns
2 celery stalks, roughly chopped
2 bay leaves
2 small onions, quartered
2 carrots, roughly chopped
450 ml (¾ pint) jellied chicken stock
 (see page 247) or commercial
 aspic
cranberries, to garnish
lemon slices, to garnish
sprigs of chervil or dill, to garnish
CUMBERLAND SAUCE
pared rind and juice of 1 orange
pared rind and juice of 1 lemon
60 ml (4 tbsp) redcurrant jelly
60 ml (4 tbsp) port
10 ml (2 tsp) arrowroot
10 ml (2 tsp) water

Soak the tongue in cold water for 4–6 hours. Drain and place in a large saucepan with the peppercorns, celery, bay leaves, onions and carrots. Cover with cold water. Bring slowly to the boil, skimming off any scum with a slotted spoon. Cover and simmer for 2½–3 hours or until the tongue is tender when pierced with a fine skewer.

Remove the tongue from the liquid and remove the skin and root, and any small bones.

Pour a little aspic into the base of a 20.5 cm (8 inch) deep round cake tin. Chill until set. Arrange the cranberries, lemon slices and sprigs of chervil or dill in a decorative pattern over the aspic. Cover with a thin layer of aspic and leave to set.

Curl the tongue tightly into the tin and pour the remaining aspic over the top. Place a plate, which just fits inside the tin, over the tongue with a heavy weight on top. Chill overnight.

For the Cumberland sauce, simmer the pared citrus rind for 5 minutes. Drain. In a pan, dissolve the redcurrant jelly in the citrus juices over gentle heat then stir in the port. Blend the arrowroot with the water and stir in. Cook until thickened then stir in the citrus rind.

To serve, dip the tin quickly into hot water to loosen the aspic, then turn out on to a serving plate. Serve with the Cumberland sauce.

SALADE DE FOIE GRAS CHAUDE

This salad is ideal to serve as a luncheon dish or a starter for a dinner party.
The warm dressing blends well with the crisp lettuce and tomatoes.
Radicchio leaves add a splash of colour.

Serves 4

Wash and dry all the salad leaves and tear into bite-sized pieces. Place in a large bowl with the herbs, beans and tomatoes.

Melt the butter with the oil in a frying pan and fry the onion rings until golden. Add the mushrooms and toss quickly in the fat. Add to the salad ingredients.

Put all the dressing ingredients into the pan and whisk over gentle heat until warmed through. Season generously.

Add to the salad and toss quickly, coating the leaves evenly with the dressing. Serve at once, topped with slices of pâté de foie gras.

INGREDIENTS
350 g (12 oz) mixed salad leaves—watercress, curly endive, radicchio, oakleaf lettuce, purslane, etc
30 ml (2 tbsp) chopped fresh herbs—parsley, chives, tarragon, basil, etc
100 g (4 oz) French beans, trimmed and blanched for 2 minutes
2 firm tomatoes, skinned, seeded and cut into 8
15 g (½ oz) butter
15 ml (1 tbsp) olive oil
1 small red onion, cut in rings
50 g (2 oz) button mushrooms, sliced
100 g (4 oz) pâté de foie gras aux truffes, cut into 12 slices
DRESSING
45 ml (3 tbsp) olive or walnut oil
30 ml (2 tbsp) raspberry vinegar
5 ml (1 tsp) green peppercorns
5 ml (1 tsp) Dijon or Meaux mustard
5 ml (1 tsp) sugar
salt and pepper

SALADE DE FOIE GRAS CHAUDE

CERVELLES BOURGUIGNONNE

*Poached in stock and served in an onion and mushroom sauce,
brains make an appetising first course.*

Serves 4

INGREDIENTS

*2 sets of calves' brains, or
4 sets of lambs' brains*

45 ml (3 tbsp) vinegar

40 g (1½ oz) butter

1 carrot, diced

1 onion, diced

1 leek, diced

1 celery stalk, diced

2 garlic cloves, chopped

few parsley sprigs

few thyme sprigs

1 bay leaf

*300 ml (½ pint) Burgundy, or other
red wine*

*300 ml (½ pint) chicken stock
(see page 247)*

*4 slices smoked streaky bacon,
rinded, rinds reserved*

24 button onions

100 g (4 oz) button mushrooms

15 ml (1 tbsp) plain flour

15 ml (1 tbsp) tomato purée

salt and pepper

chopped fresh parsley, to garnish

Soak the brains in several changes of lightly vinegared water (about 15 ml (1 tbsp) to every 1 litre (2 pints) water), for a total of 2 hours. Carefully remove the blood vessels and membrane.

In a heavy-based pan, melt 15 g (½ oz) of the butter and fry the carrot, onion, leek, celery, garlic, parsley and thyme sprigs, and bay leaf for 5 minutes. Add the wine and stock, and bring to the boil. Reduce the heat, then add the brains. Cover and simmer for 30 minutes (lambs' brains may be ready in 20 minutes).

Place the bacon rind in a frying pan. Add 15 g (½ oz) of the remaining butter and fry the button onions gently for about 10 minutes or until golden. Discard the rind.

Carefully remove the brains from the cooking liquid. Strain the liquid and return it to the rinsed-out pan with the onions. Boil rapidly for about 5 minutes until the liquid has reduced by one-third.

Meanwhile, cut the bacon into strips and fry in the pan juices until crisp. Remove from the pan, add the mushrooms and fry for 1–2 minutes.

Combine the remaining butter with the flour and work it to a smooth paste. Whisk it into the onion sauce with the tomato purée and simmer gently until thickened. Adjust the seasoning to taste. Add the brains, cut into even-sized pieces, with the bacon and mushrooms, and simmer very gently until heated through. Serve at once sprinkled with chopped parsley.

RILLETTES DE CANARD

Serve with hot toast or French bread.

Serves 4

INGREDIENTS

225 g (8 oz) raw duck breast

*225 g (8 oz) belly of pork, boned
and rinded weight*

225 g (8 oz) pork fat

1 garlic clove, chopped

1 bay leaf

few sprigs of fresh thyme

salt and pepper

50 ml (2 fl oz) water

Cut the duck and belly of pork into 2.5 × 5 cm (1 × 2 inch) strips and dice the pork fat. Place all the ingredients in an ovenproof casserole with a tight-fitting lid. If wished, cover securely with aluminium foil to prevent evaporation. Cook at 140°C (275°F) mark 1 for 4 hours, shaking the dish from time to time to prevent sticking.

Strain the contents of the dish through a metal sieve, discarding the bay leaf and thyme. Place the meat in a bowl, and using two forks, pull it into shreds. Adjust the seasoning. Press the meat into 4 ramekin dishes and pour the strained fat over. Cool, then chill until set.

Note

For a classic pure pork rillettes use all belly of pork. Rillettes d'oie may be made by replacing the duck breast with goose.

JAMBON PERSILLE DE BOURGOGNE

*Serve this dish as a light lunch or first course, or take on a picnic,
accompanied by crusty French bread.*

Serves 6

Place the bacon, veal and trotters in a large pan and cover with water. Bring slowly to the boil, then simmer for 10 minutes. Drain and discard the water.

Cut the bacon into 5 cm (2 inch) cubes and return it to the pan with the veal and trotters. Add the bouquet garni, peppercorns and onion. Add the wine and sufficient water to cover the meat. Bring to the boil, cover and simmer gently, for 3 hours. Do not allow the liquid to boil.

Remove the pieces of bacon from the stock with a slotted spoon. Flake the meat with a fork. Strain the stock through muslin or a clean tea towel then stir in the vinegar.

Pack the flaked meat into a glass serving dish. When the stock begins to set, stir in the parsley. Pour the stock over the meat to cover it completely and leave to set. Chill for 24 hours before serving.

INGREDIENTS

*1.5 kg (3 lb) mild cured bacon or
   gammon joint*
1 veal knuckle, chopped
2 pig's trotters
*bouquet garni, made with parsley
   sprigs, 2 bay leaves, tarragon
   and thyme*
12 black peppercorns
1 small onion, quartered
1 litre (1¾ pints) dry white wine
20 ml (4 tsp) tarragon vinegar
25 g (1 oz) parsley, finely chopped

PORK AND WALNUT PATE

*This tasty pâté, made with brandy, juniper berries and orange rind,
can be served as a first course or for a picnic lunch.*

Serves 8

Mince the liver, belly of pork and bacon together. Place in a mixing bowl and stir in the brandy, wine, eggs, juniper berries, mace, orange rind and seasoning.

Line a 1 kg (2 lb) terrine dish or loaf tin with some of the pork fat. Press one-third of the mixture into the dish and sprinkle half the walnuts over the top. Press half the remaining mixture over the walnuts. Arrange the remaining walnuts over the top and spread with the remaining pâté mixture. Smooth over the top and cover with the remaining pork fat.

Cover with aluminium foil and place in a roasting tin. Add enough boiling water to come halfway up the side of the dish. Bake at 170°C (325°F) mark 3 for 1½–2 hours depending on the depth of the dish. When cooked, the pâté will have shrunk from the sides of the dish and the juices will run clear. Put a plate on top of the pâté and place a heavy weight on top. Cool, then chill until required.

INGREDIENTS

225 g (8 oz) pig's liver
*750 g (1½ lb) lean belly of pork,
   rinded and boned*
225 g (8 oz) streaky bacon, rinded
30 ml (2 tbsp) brandy
75 ml (3 fl oz) dry white wine
2 eggs, beaten
*15 ml (1 tbsp) juniper berries,
   crushed*
pinch of ground mace
5 ml (1 tsp) grated orange rind
salt and pepper
225 g (8 oz) pork fat slices
*75 g (3 oz) walnuts, roughly
   chopped*

DUCK PATE WITH GREEN PEPPERCORNS

Green peppercorns are a perfect foil for the rich flavour of duck.

Serves 6–8

INGREDIENTS

2 kg (4½ lb) duck, boned
45 ml (3 tbsp) brandy
10 ml (2 tsp) dried thyme
salt and pepper
225 g (8 oz) lean veal
2 duck livers
2 shallots, finely chopped
pinch of ground allspice
2 eggs, lightly beaten
225 g (8 oz) streaky bacon, rinded
30 ml (2 tbsp) green peppercorns
bay leaf
endive and lamb's lettuce,
    to garnish

Remove the skin and trim off the excess fat from the duck. Cut the larger pieces into long strips about 5 mm (¼ inch) wide. Place them in a bowl with the brandy, half the thyme and seasoning.

Mince the remaining duck with the veal and livers. Stir in the shallots, remaining thyme, allspice and eggs. Season and mix well.

Line a 1 kg (2 lb) terrine or loaf tin with the bacon. Remove the duck strips from the marinade and stir the marinade into the minced mixture. Spread one-third of the minced mixture over the base of the terrine, cover with half the duck strips and sprinkle with half the green peppercorns. Spread half the remaining minced mixture over the duck, then cover with the remaining duck strips and peppercorns. Spread the remaining minced mixture over the top. Cover with bacon rashers and the bay leaf.

Cover with aluminium foil and place in a roasting tin. Pour in enough boiling water to come halfway up the sides of the dish. Bake at 180°C (350°F) mark 4 for 1¾–2 hours until the pâté has shrunk from the sides of the dish. Drain off the excess liquid. Cover with aluminium foil and place heavy weights on top of the pâté. Leave until cold. If using a loaf tin, turn the pâté out on to a serving plate. If using a terrine, serve from the dish.

FOIE GRAS SAUTE

The foie gras should be firm and a creamy white, tinged with pink.
A few diced truffles tossed in melted butter may be used to garnish
this dish if wished.

Serves 4

INGREDIENTS

1 fresh duck foie gras, about
    450 g (15 oz), trimmed and cut
    into 12 slices
1 egg, lightly beaten
50 g (2 oz) fresh breadcrumbs
salt and pepper
50 g (2 oz) clarified butter
30 ml (2 tbsp) Madeira
175 ml (6 fl oz) jellied veal stock
15 ml (1 tbsp) orange juice
2 large oranges, segmented,
    to garnish

Dip the foie gras slices into the egg, then in the breadcrumbs. Season. Melt the butter in a sauté pan and fry the foie gras for 1 minute on each side. Remove from the pan and keep hot.

Stir the Madeira into the pan, then add the veal stock and orange juice. Boil for 3–4 minutes until reduced. Adjust the seasoning, strain, and pour it around the foie gras. Garnish with the orange segments and serve immediately.

Note

Both goose or duck liver can be used in this recipe.

BOUDIN BLANC

CHICKEN LIVER MOUSSELINE
WITH CRANBERRY SAUCE

The rich fruity flavour of cranberries marries well with this light liver mousseline.
Serve as a starter with croûtes of toast.

Serves 4

INGREDIENTS

40 g (1½ oz) butter

25 g (1 oz) shallots, finely chopped

1 small garlic clove, chopped

100 g (4 oz) chicken livers

50 g (2 oz) raw chicken breast

25 g (1 oz) fresh white breadcrumbs

1 egg

75 ml (3 fl oz) double cream

salt and pepper

parsley or chervil sprigs, to garnish

SAUCE

50 g (2 oz) cranberries

15 ml (1 tbsp) sugar

30 ml (2 tbsp) Madeira

225 ml (8 fl oz) chicken stock
  (see page 247)

40 g (1½ oz) butter, chilled

Melt the butter in a saucepan and use a little to grease the inside of 4 individual 75 ml (3 fl oz) dariole moulds.

Fry the shallots and garlic until soft, cool slightly, then place them in a food processor with the chicken livers, chicken breast, breadcrumbs, egg, cream and seasoning. Blend to a smooth purée.

Spoon the purée into the dariole moulds and cover each one with aluminium foil. Place in a small roasting tin, and pour in enough boiling water to come three-quarters of the way up the sides of the moulds. Cook at 180°C (350°F) mark 4 for about 25 minutes or until firm to the touch. Remove from the water.

Meanwhile, make the sauce. Place the cranberries, sugar and Madeira in a saucepan, and boil until the liquid has reduced to 15 ml (1 tbsp). Add the stock and boil rapidly for about 5 minutes until the sauce is of a light syrupy consistency. Remove from the heat, adjust the seasoning and whisk in the butter.

Unmould the mousses on to individual plates, spoon the sauce around and garnish with parsley. If wished, serve with small croûtes of toast or fried bread.

BOUDIN BLANC

Boudin blanc are sausages made with chicken and veal and are traditionally served with creamed potatoes and apple slices sautéed in butter and sugar. Accompany with the piquant mustard and Calvados sauce.

Makes 8 sausages

Soak the sausage casings in water in the refrigerator for about 4–5 hours. Scald the cream and stir in the breadcrumbs, seasoning, allspice and nutmeg, and leave until cold. Melt the butter and fry the onion until soft. Leave to cool.

Roughly chop the chicken, veal and belly of pork and pass through a mincer twice, or mince in a food processor. Add the breadcrumb mixture, the cooked onion and egg whites. Pass through the mincer again or process in the food processor.

Attach the sausage casings to the end of the cold water tap or a funnel and pass water through them. Put the sausage mixture into a large piping bag fitted with a large plain nozzle, and pipe the mixture into the soaked sausage casings. Each sausage should be about 15 cm (6 inches) in length, so either twist the skin at intervals or tie with fine string. Prick the sausages with a sterilized pin to prevent them bursting during cooking.

For the cooking liquid, pour the water into a roasting tin, and bring slowly to a simmer. Add the herbs and vegetables, then add the sausages. They must be covered with liquid, so add extra if necessary. Simmer gently for 20 minutes. Do not allow the liquid to boil as the sausages may burst. Remove from the heat and cool in the liquid. Drain and dry on kitchen paper.

To finish cooking, melt the butter in a pan and fry the sausages for 8–10 minutes or until brown. Alternatively, brush with melted butter and brown under a moderate grill.

For the mustard sauce, melt the butter in a frying pan and fry the shallot until soft. Stir in the flour and cook for 1–2 minutes, stirring continuously. Slowly add the stock and cream, then stir in the mustard and simmer, covered, for 5 minutes. Stir in the Calvados and lemon juice and adjust the seasoning.

INGREDIENTS
about 2 m (6 ft) sausage casings
100 ml (4 fl oz) double cream
100 g (4 oz) fresh breadcrumbs
salt and pepper
1.5 ml ($\frac{1}{4}$ tsp) allspice
1.5 ml ($\frac{1}{4}$ tsp) grated nutmeg
25 g (1 oz) butter
1 medium onion, finely chopped
225 g (8 oz) raw chicken breast
225 g (8 oz) lean stewing veal
225 g (8 oz) belly of pork, rinded
2 egg whites
25 g (1 oz) butter
COOKING LIQUID
about 2 litres (3 pints) water
few parsley sprigs
2 bay leaves
1 carrot, diced
1 celery stalk, diced
1 small leek, diced
MUSTARD SAUCE
25 g (1 oz) butter
25 g (1 oz) shallots, chopped
30 ml (2 tbsp) plain flour
175 ml (6 fl oz) chicken
   stock (see page 247)
100 ml (4 fl oz) single cream
30 ml (2 tbsp) Meaux mustard
15 ml (1 tbsp) Calvados
5 ml (1 tsp) lemon juice
salt and pepper

CHICKEN LIVER PATE

This quick pâté involves the minimum of cooking. Serve as a first course or snack.

Makes about 600 g (1$\frac{1}{4}$ lb)

Melt 50 g (2 oz) of the butter gently and fry the garlic and chicken livers for 5 minutes. Place them in a blender or food processor, but do not blend. Stir the brandy into the pan juices then add it to the liver and garlic. Blend until smooth.

Melt 75 g (3 oz) of the remaining butter and fry the mushrooms for 5 minutes. Drain the mushrooms and reserve. Stir the butter into the chicken livers, cool slightly and season to taste with mace, salt and pepper. Stir in the cream and mix well. Pour the pâté mixture into a 600 ml (1 pint) mould or individual ramekins. Arrange the mushrooms on top. Melt the remaining butter, skim off the scum and pour it over the mushrooms. Cool, then chill until set.

INGREDIENTS
200 g (7 oz) butter
2 garlic cloves, crushed
225 g (8 oz) chicken livers
30 ml (2 tbsp) brandy or Cognac
50 g (2 oz) mushrooms, sliced
1.25 ml ($\frac{1}{4}$ tsp) ground mace
salt and pepper
30 ml (2 tbsp) double cream

FARMHOUSE SAUSAGES

This is a tasty recipe for making herb-flavoured sausages. Serve sizzling hot with mustard and creamed potatoes, for a traditional country-style meal.

Makes 8 sausages

INGREDIENTS

750 g (1½ lb) belly of pork, rinded

45 ml (3 tbsp) chopped fresh parsley

7.5 ml (1½ tsp) chopped fresh thyme

7.5 ml (1½ tsp) chopped fresh marjoram

4 ml (¾ tsp) chopped fresh sage

salt and pepper

2.5 ml (½ tsp) paprika

1.5 ml (¼ tsp) ground mace

15 ml (1 tbsp) brandy

about 1.3 m (4 ft) sausage casings

butter, for frying

Roughly chop the pork and pass it through a mincer twice. Alternatively, use a food processor. Combine the pork with the parsley, thyme, marjoram, sage, seasoning, paprika, mace and brandy and mix well. Cover and leave for up to 24 hours in the refrigerator, for the flavours to develop.

Soak the sausage casings in water in the refrigerator for about 4–5 hours. Attach them to the end of the cold water tap or a funnel and pass water through them.

Spoon the sausage mixture into a large piping bag fitted with a large plain nozzle and carefully pipe the mixture into the sausage casings. Twist into 8 even-sized links. Alternatively, cut the casings into four even lengths and make two sausages at a time. Twist the ends well, or tie with strings at intervals.

Fry or grill the sausages with a little extra butter for 10–15 minutes until well browned.

CRUMBED TRIPE WITH WHITE WINE SAUCE

Strips of tripe simmered with vegetables and then deep fried, are served in a white wine sauce.

Serves 4

INGREDIENTS

1 kg (2 lb) dressed tripe

1 onion, roughly chopped

1 carrot, roughly chopped

1 celery stalk, roughly chopped

½ lemon, sliced

bouquet garni

flour

salt and pepper

3–4 eggs, beaten

6–8 garlic cloves, crushed

175 g (6 oz) fresh white breadcrumbs

oil, for deep-frying

SAUCE

1 shallot, finely chopped

75 ml (3 fl oz) dry white wine

75 ml (3 fl oz) white wine vinegar

175 g (6 oz) butter, diced

30 ml (2 tbsp) chopped fresh parsley

Place the tripe in a large saucepan with the onion, carrot, celery, lemon and bouquet garni. Add sufficient boiling water to cover it, and simmer gently for 15 minutes or until tender. Drain well and dry on kitchen paper. Leave until cold. Trim off any skin then cut the tripe into 1.5 cm (½ inch) strips.

Evenly coat the strips of tripe in flour seasoned with salt and pepper. Mix the eggs, garlic and seasoning together. Dip the tripe into the beaten egg and then in breadcrumbs to coat. Leave to one side whilst making the sauce.

Place the shallot, wine and wine vinegar in a saucepan and boil until reduced to 30 ml (2 tbsp). Remove from the heat and whisk in the butter a little at a time, until each amount turns creamy, but not oily, before adding the next amount. Pass the pan over the heat from time to time if necessary, to just warm the mixture. When all the butter has been added, stir in the parsley and adjust the seasoning. Keep the sauce just warm.

In a deep frying pan heat the oil to 190°C (375°F) and deep-fry the tripe in batches until crisp and golden. Drain on kitchen paper and serve at once, with the sauce.

PIG'S TROTTERS WITH CABBAGE AND REDCURRANTS

The casserole may be boiled rapidly for about 5 minutes to reduce the liquid with the cabbage, before serving, if wished.

Serves 4

Singe the trotters over a gas flame or candle. Scrub well, then tie each one tightly in cheesecloth so that it keeps its shape during cooking. Place them in a large pan or pressure cooker and add the carrots, onions, leeks, celery, bay leaves, bouquet garni, peppercorns, wine, wine vinegar and enough stock to just cover. If using a pressure cooker add 300 ml ($\frac{1}{2}$ pint) stock.

Bring to the boil, then reduce the heat, cover and simmer for up to 6 hours or until the trotters are tender when tested with a skewer. If using a pressure cooker, follow manufacturer's instructions and allow about 50 minutes. Remove the trotters from the pan and leave until cool enough to handle. Strain the stock and boil rapidly until reduced to about 300 ml ($\frac{1}{2}$ pint).

Place the cabbage in a large saucepan, cover with boiling water and bring back to the boil. Drain well. Heat the oil in a large flameproof casserole and fry the onion until soft. Add the apple, juniper berries, redcurrants and cabbage. Pour the reduced stock over and season generously.

Remove the trotters from the cheesecloth and split through the centre lengthways without completely cutting them in half. Arrange, skin-side up, on top of the cabbage. Bring to the boil, then transfer the casserole to the oven and cook at 200°C (400°F) mark 6 for about 45 minutes.

Sprinkle with parsley and serve at once.

INGREDIENTS
4 pig's trotters
2 carrots, sliced
2 onions, stuck with 4 cloves each
2 leeks, sliced
2 celery stalks, sliced
2 bay leaves
bouquet garni
20 peppercorns
150 ml ($\frac{1}{4}$ pint) dry white wine
50 ml (2 fl oz) white wine vinegar
600–850 ml (1–1$\frac{1}{2}$ pints) chicken stock (see page 247)
1 kg (2 lb) red or white cabbage, shredded
30 ml (2 tbsp) oil
1 onion, chopped
225 g (8 oz) cooking apples, peeled and chopped
12 juniper berries, crushed
50 g (2 oz) redcurrants, fresh or frozen
salt and pepper
chopped fresh parsley, to garnish

HAGGIS

Haggis, a stuffed sheep's stomach, is a popular and traditional Scottish dish served with 'tatties' (potatoes), 'neeps' (swedes) and a glass of Scotch whisky.

Serves 10–12

Place the stomach bag in cold water in the fridge until required. Do not keep longer than 4 days. Cover the pluck in cold water, bring to the boil, cover the pan and simmer for 2 hours.

Meanwhile, spread the oatmeal on a baking sheet and toast at 200°C (400°F) mark 6 for 10 minutes.

When the pluck is cooked, strain and reserve the stock. Finely chop the heart, liver, and about one-third of the lungs. Place in a bowl with the oatmeal, suet, seasoning, cayenne, nutmeg and onions. Add 450 ml ($\frac{3}{4}$ pint) of the reserved stock. Drain the stomach bag thoroughly and fill just over half full with the stuffing mixture. Sew up the bag with cotton thread and prick in a few places.

Place a trivet in the base of a large pan of boiling water. Lower the haggis into the boiling water, reduce the heat, cover and simmer for 3 hours, pricking the skin occasionally, to prevent the haggis from bursting.

To serve, drain the haggis, place it on a serving dish, slit the skin and spoon out the filling from the bag.

INGREDIENTS
1 sheep's stomach bag
1 sheep's pluck (liver, heart and lungs)
275 g (10 oz) medium oatmeal
175 g (6 oz) grated beef suet
salt and pepper
1.25 ml ($\frac{1}{4}$ tsp) cayenne pepper
large pinch of grated nutmeg
2 onions, finely chopped

SPINACH-WRAPPED SWEETBREADS IN CREAM SAUCE

Buttered rice or creamed potatoes go well with this dish.

Serves 4

INGREDIENTS

500 g (1 lb) calves' sweetbreads
slice of lemon
25 g (1 oz) butter, chilled
1 carrot, diced
1 celery stalk, diced
1 shallot, diced
1 leek, diced
1 bay leaf
few parsley sprigs
sprig of rosemary
pared rind of $\frac{1}{4}$ lemon
450 ml ($\frac{3}{4}$ pint) chicken stock
  (see page 247)
150 ml ($\frac{1}{4}$ pint) dry white wine
12 large spinach leaves
100 ml (4 fl oz) double cream
5 ml (1 tsp) Meaux mustard
salt and pepper

Wash the sweetbreads well, and place them in a saucepan of cold water, with the slice of lemon. Bring to the boil, then simmer for 3 minutes. Drain, cool, then carefully remove any skin. Melt half the butter and fry the carrot, celery, shallots and leek until soft. Add the bay leaf, parsley sprigs, rosemary and lemon rind. Arrange the sweetbreads on the bed of vegetables, pour over the stock and bring to a simmer. Cover and simmer gently for about 20 minutes until firm and tender. Carefully remove the sweetbreads from the pan. Strain the cooking liquid and return it to the rinsed-out pan. Add the wine and boil rapidly for 10–15 minutes or until the liquid has reduced by half.

Meanwhile, blanch the spinach leaves in boiling water. Drain and plunge into iced water. Drain and dry on kitchen paper. Cut away the coarse stalks. Cut the sweetbreads into 12 even pieces and wrap each one in a spinach leaf.

Add the cream and mustard to the reduced stock and adjust the seasoning. Place the spinach-wrapped sweetbreads in the sauce and simmer gently for 5 minutes.

To serve, remove the sweetbreads from the pan and arrange them on a serving plate or on 4 individual plates. Whisk the remaining chilled butter into the sauce, then spoon a little sauce over the sweetbreads.

CHARLOTTE D'AUBERGINES AUX ROGNONS

This aubergine charlotte, filled with kidneys in tomato and basil sauce is an attractive dish to serve at the table. Accompany with steamed rice.

Serves 4

First, make the sauce. Heat the olive oil and fry the onion until soft. Add the carrot, celery and garlic and fry, stirring occasionally, for 5 minutes. Add the tomatoes and seasoning, and simmer gently, uncovered for about 45 minutes, stirring occasionally. Stir in the basil leaves.

Meanwhile, slice the aubergines fairly thinly. Sprinkle with salt and leave for 30 minutes. Wash and dry well. Heat a little of the oil in a frying pan and fry a few slices of aubergine at a time. Keep adding a little more oil to the pan and continue frying until all the aubergine slices are cooked.

Melt the butter and fry the kidneys until browned. Using a slotted spoon, remove them from the pan and add to the tomato sauce. Boil the kidney juices rapidly until reduced to 15 ml (1 tbsp), then add it to the tomato sauce. Adjust the seasoning.

Brush the inside of a 20 cm (8 inch) deep cake tin with butter or oil. Coat the base and sides with some of the breadcrumbs, then line the base and sides of the tin with three-quarters of the aubergine slices. Sprinkle over one-third of the remaining breadcrumbs. Spoon the kidney and tomato sauce into the tin, and sprinkle with half the remaining breadcrumbs. Top with the remaining aubergine slices and remaining breadcrumbs. Press down gently. Bake, uncovered, at 200°C (400°F) mark 6 for 40 minutes. Unmould on to a serving plate, and garnish with fresh basil leaves.

INGREDIENTS
*2 medium aubergines, about
    500 g (1 lb)*
salt and pepper
100–150 ml (4–5 fl oz) olive oil
25 g (1 oz) butter
*8 lambs' kidneys, cored and
    chopped*
50 g (2 oz) toasted breadcrumbs
fresh basil leaves, to garnish
TOMATO SAUCE
60 ml (4 tbsp) olive oil
1 onion, finely chopped
1 carrot, finely chopped
1 celery stalk, finely chopped
2 garlic cloves, chopped
*400 g (14 oz) fresh or canned
    tomatoes*
salt and pepper
12 fresh basil leaves, shredded

VEAL SWEETBREADS WITH RED AND YELLOW PEPPERS

The fresh taste of the peppers contrasts well with the smooth texture of the sweetbreads and the cream sauce in this dish.

Serves 4

Wash the sweetbreads well then place them in a saucepan of cold water with the slice of lemon. Bring to the boil, then simmer for 3 minutes. Drain and cool, then carefully remove any skin.

Melt 15 g ($\frac{1}{2}$ oz) of the butter in a saucepan and fry the carrot, celery, leek and garlic until soft. Add the bay leaf, thyme and parsley sprigs, and arrange the sweetbreads on top of the bed of vegetables. Pour over the stock. Bring to a simmer, then cover and cook for about 20 minutes or until firm and tender. Carefully remove the sweetbreads from the pan.

Strain the stock and return it to the rinsed-out pan. Add the brandy and boil rapidly for about 2 minutes until the sauce is slightly syrupy. Return the sweetbreads to the pan and simmer very gently to warm through.

Stir-fry the peppers in the oil for 2 minutes. Season to taste.

Spoon the peppers on to a serving plate. Cut the sweetbreads into thick slices and arrange on top of the peppers. Whisk the remaining butter into the sauce. Stir in the chopped parsley and chives and adjust the seasoning. Pour over the sweetbreads and serve at once.

INGREDIENTS
500 g (1 lb) calves' sweetbreads
slice of lemon
40 g (1$\frac{1}{2}$ oz) butter, chilled
1 carrot, diced
1 celery stalk, diced
1 leek, diced
2 garlic cloves, chopped
1 bay leaf
sprig of fresh thyme
few parsley sprigs
*150 ml ($\frac{1}{4}$ pint) chicken stock
    (see page 247)*
15 ml (1 tbsp) brandy
*1 red pepper, seeded and cut into
    julienne strips*
*1 yellow pepper, seeded and cut
    into julienne strips*
5 ml (1 tsp) oil
salt and pepper
5 ml (1 tsp) chopped fresh parsley
5 ml (1 tsp) chopped fresh chives

VEAL SWEETBREADS WITH RED AND YELLOW PEPPERS

THE FRUIT AND VEGETABLE HALL

VEGETABLES

◆ • ◆

*Regardless of the season, Harrods can always boast a profusion of
excellent quality vegetables: strings of garlic and onions, mangetout,
asparagus and shiny black aubergines. Ideal for warming winter soups,
vegetables also make the perfect accompaniment to a main course dish—
Pommes de Terre à la Lyonnaise, Broccoli Mornay, or as a meal in itself—
Wild Mushroom Ravioli.*

SPINACH AND TANGERINE SOUP

*The combination of spinach mixed with tangerine makes a nourishing and
refreshing soup. This is ideal for serving before a rich course or combined
with pitta bread for a light lunch.*

Serves 4—6

INGREDIENTS

*2 litres (3 pints) chicken stock
(see page 247)*

*75 g (3 oz) yellow split peas,
soaked for 4 hours*

25 g (1 oz) butter

*100 g (4 oz) spring onions, the
white and green parts
chopped separately*

5 ml (1 tsp) turmeric

*50 g (2 oz) fresh coriander,
finely chopped*

*175 g (6 oz) spinach,
finely chopped*

*30 ml (2 tbsp) finely chopped
fresh parsley*

*finely grated rind and juice of 1
tangerine*

*finely grated rind and juice of 2
lemons*

30 ml (2 tbsp) ground rice

150 ml (¼ pint) cold water

225 ml (8 fl oz) natural yogurt

coriander sprigs, to garnish

Bring the chicken stock to the boil, add the yellow split peas and simmer for 15 minutes. Melt the butter in a small pan and gently fry the white spring onion for 5 minutes. Stir in the turmeric and then stir it into the stock and peas. Add the green spring onion, coriander, spinach, parsley and citrus rind and juice. Cover the pan and simmer for 30 minutes.

Mix the ground rice with the cold water and stir it into the soup. Cover the pan and simmer for a further 15 minutes, stirring occasionally.

To serve, swirl some yogurt into each bowl of soup, and garnish with coriander.

WILD MUSHROOM RAVIOLI

*This is a generously seasoned Italian dish containing a wild mushroom filling
and served with a creamy sauce.*

Serves 4

For the filling, if using dried mushrooms cover with boiling water and leave to soak for at least 1 hour. Drain, squeeze out the excess moisture and reserve the liquid. Finely chop the mushrooms.

Melt the butter in a saucepan and fry the shallots and bacon until the shallots are transparent and the bacon golden. Add the mushrooms and fry for 1 minute. Cool slightly, then add the ricotta, parsley, thyme, lemon juice, nutmeg, cayenne and seasoning.

Divide the pasta dough in half. Roll out each piece of dough to a 4 × 30 cm (16 × 12 inch) rectangle on a lightly floured surface.

Either spoon the filling into a piping bag fitted with large plain nozzle, or use a teaspoon. Starting 2.5 cm (1 inch) in from the edge of the dough, place small rounds of the wild mushroom filling at 5 cm (2 inch) intervals, to give 48 piles. Do not use too much filling or the ravioli will split during cooking. Brush in between the piles of filling with water. Carefully place the second piece of dough on top and using a long knife or kitchen ruler, mark lines between each pile of filling to seal the dough.

Using a serrated pastry wheel or sharp knife cut between each parcel to make 48 ravioli. Leave on a lightly floured board covered with a clean cloth. Cook the ravioli in boiling salted water for 5 minutes. Drain well.

For the sauce, scald the cream (if using dried mushrooms, use 175 ml (6 fl oz) cream and 50 ml (2 fl oz) of the reserved mushroom liquid). Remove from the heat and whisk in the egg yolks and nutmeg. Season generously.

Spoon the ravioli into a gratin dish. Pour over the sauce and sprinkle with Parmesan cheese. Cook under a hot grill until golden.

INGREDIENTS
*175 g (6 oz) wild mushrooms or
  75 g (3 oz) dried wild
  mushrooms and 75 g (3 oz) field
  mushrooms*
25 g (1 oz) butter
2 shallots, finely chopped
*50 g (2 oz) bacon, rinded and
  finely chopped*
50 g (2 oz) ricotta or cream cheese
*45 ml (3 tbsp) chopped fresh
  parsley*
2.5 ml (½ tsp) chopped fresh thyme
5 ml (1 tsp) lemon juice
large pinch of grated nutmeg
pinch of cayenne pepper
salt and pepper
*450 g (1 lb) pasta dough
  (see page 251)*
SAUCE
225 ml (8 fl oz) single cream
2 egg yolks
pinch of grated nutmeg
*60 ml (4 tbsp) freshly grated
  Parmesan cheese*

CARROT AND ORANGE SOUP

*This refreshing, bright orange soup may be served hot or cold,
accompanied by thin slices of melba toast.*

Serves 4

Bring the chicken stock to the boil in a large saucepan, add the carrots, seasoning, orange peel and coriander. Reduce the heat, cover the pan and simmer for 10–15 minutes, or until the carrots are cooked.

Remove the strip of orange peel and purée the soup.

Add the orange juice and bring the soup back to the boil. Remove from the heat, stir in the sour cream, adjust the seasoning and pour into bowls. Sprinkle with chopped mint and serve immediately.

INGREDIENTS
*600 ml (1 pint) jellied chicken
  stock (see page 247)*
500 g (1 lb) carrots, finely grated
salt and pepper
pared strip of orange peel
2.5 ml (½ tsp) ground coriander
150 ml (¼ pint) fresh orange juice
150 ml (¼ pint) sour cream
10 ml (2 tsp) chopped fresh mint

FRENCH ONION SOUP WITH COGNAC

*This classic soup seems to possess restorative powers and is ideal to serve for
lunch or light supper.
A good beef stock is essential when making this recipe, and cannot be
substituted with stock cubes.*

Serves 4–6

INGREDIENTS

65 g (2½ oz) butter
850 g (1¾ lb) onions, sliced
5 ml (1 tsp) sugar
*1.4 litres (2½ pints) beef stock
  (see page 246)*
150 ml (¼ pint) dry white wine
salt and pepper
45 ml (3 tbsp) Cognac
1 loaf French bread
225 g (8 oz) Gruyère cheese, grated

Melt the butter in a saucepan and gently fry the onions for 20 minutes until soft. Sprinkle over the sugar and continue to cook, stirring occasionally, until golden brown.

Add the stock and white wine and bring it to the boil. Reduce the heat, cover and simmer gently for 1 hour. Season to taste and stir in the Cognac.

About 10 minutes before the soup is ready, cut 6 slices of bread 2.5 cm (1 inch) thick and toast.

Place the slices of toasted bread in individual ovenproof bowls, or a soup tureen. Pour the soup over the bread, and when the bread floats to the surface, place the cheese on top. Grill under a hot grill for 2 minutes or until the cheese is bubbling. Serve immediately with the remaining French bread.

FENNEL AND SALAMI WITH BLACK OLIVES

*Fennel has a refreshing aniseed flavour and may be eaten raw or cooked.
This recipe makes an ideal starter, or a luncheon dish for two, served with warm
crusty bread.*

Serves 4

Place two radicchio leaves on each plate and fill them with the shredded fennel.
Arrange the slices of salami around one side of each plate and place a fan of olives
on top of the salami.

Mix the lemon juice, walnut and olive oil together, and season to taste. Pour
the dressing over the fennel and serve.

INGREDIENTS
8 large radicchio leaves
*3 heads of fennel, trimmed and
    finely shredded*
16 slices salami, about 150 g (5 oz)
*12 black olives, stoned and
    quartered lengthways*
juice of ½ lemon
5 ml (1 tsp) walnut oil
15 ml (1 tbsp) olive oil
salt and pepper

TIMBALES DE COURGETTE

*A lightly poached purée of courgette which can be served as an attractive
side dish with meat, poultry or fish.*

Serves 4–8

Steam the courgettes until tender then blend to a purée. Grease 8 individual
timbale moulds and coat with 25 g (1 oz) of the breadcrumbs. Melt 25 g (1 oz)
of the butter in a small pan and fry the onion for 5 minutes or until soft. Cool
then transfer to a bowl. Add the nutmeg and cheese and season. Beat in the eggs.
Heat the milk gently with the remaining butter until it has melted, then pour it
into the egg mixture in a steady stream beating constantly. Fold in the courgette
purée.

Evenly divide the mixture between the prepared moulds. Place in a roasting tin
half filled with hot water. Bake at 170°C (325°F) mark 3 for about 25–30 minutes
or until the custard is lightly set. Cool for 5 minutes, then loosen the edge of each
mould with the point of a knife. Carefully turn out on to a warm serving dish and
pour a little hot tomato sauce over or around each. Garnish with chervil or parsley.

INGREDIENTS
500 g (1 lb) courgettes, sliced
75 g (3 oz) toasted breadcrumbs
75 g (3 oz) butter
1 small onion, finely chopped
pinch of grated nutmeg
*50 g (2 oz) Gruyère cheese,
    finely grated*
salt and pepper
4 large eggs, lightly beaten
300 ml (½ pint) milk
tomato sauce (see page 251)
*chervil or parsley sprigs,
    to garnish*

FRENCH ONION SOUP WITH COGNAC

CELERY CREAM WITH TOASTED ALMONDS

A delicately flavoured dish which is excellent served with white meat and poultry.

Serves 4

INGREDIENTS

40 g (1½ oz) butter

40 g (1½ oz) flaked almonds

2 shallots, finely chopped

500 g (1 lb) celery, trimmed and cut into julienne strips

salt and pepper

150 ml (¼ pint) jellied chicken stock (see page 247)

5 ml (1 tsp) chopped fresh parsley

100 ml (4 fl oz) single cream

Melt the butter in a pan and fry the almonds for 3 minutes or until golden brown. Remove the almonds from the pan with a slotted spoon and reserve. Add the shallots and celery to the butter in the pan and fry until soft. Season and stir in the stock. Cover the pan, and cook for 15 minutes.

Stir in the parsley and cream, cover and simmer gently for 10 minutes. Serve hot, sprinkled with the toasted almonds.

BAKED FENNEL WITH TOMATO

Fennel is available during the autumn, winter and spring and has an unmistakable flavour of aniseed. To prepare, trim the upper stalks and leaves, and remove the outer leaves as these can be stringy.

Serves 6

INGREDIENTS

75 g (3 oz) butter

1 onion, finely chopped

1 large garlic clove, crushed

3 heads of fennel, halved and thinly sliced

5 ml (1 tsp) tomato purée

350 g (12 oz) ripe tomatoes, skinned and finely chopped

salt and pepper

75 g (3 oz) fresh breadcrumbs

50 g (2 oz) grated Parmesan cheese

Melt the butter in a saucepan and fry the onion and garlic until golden. Add the fennel slices and cook over moderate heat for a further 10 minutes. Stir in the tomato purée and tomatoes. Season to taste and cook for 5 minutes or until reduced slightly. Spoon the mixture into a gratin dish. Mix the breadcrumbs with the Parmesan cheese and sprinkle over the surface. Bake at 200°C (400°F) mark 6 for 15 minutes, or until the breadcrumbs are golden brown. Serve with grilled fish or meat.

PUMPKIN RISOTTO

The rich orange colour and distinctive sweet flavour of the pumpkin is highlighted in this risotto.

Serves 4

Melt 25 g (1 oz) of the butter in a large, heavy-based frying pan and fry the shallots for 2–3 minutes.

Add the pumpkin and cook, stirring occasionally, for 5 minutes. Add the rice and cook for 2 minutes more, stirring. Stir in 75 ml (3 fl oz) of the stock, the orange rind and juice, and the ginger. Simmer, stirring, until all the moisture has evaporated. Add another 75–100 ml (3–4 fl oz) of the stock and cook again until it has evaporated. Continue adding the stock and cooking the rice in the same way until all the stock has been used up. The rice should be tender but firm to the bite and creamy. The pumpkin should also be tender. Season and stir in the remaining butter. Serve hot.

INGREDIENTS
40 g (1½ oz) butter
30 ml (2 tbsp) finely chopped shallots
500 g (1 lb) pumpkin, skinned, seeded and cubed
225 g (8 oz) Arborio rice
600 ml (1 pint) hot chicken stock (see page 247)
finely grated rind and juice of 2 large oranges
25 ml (1½ tbsp) finely chopped fresh root ginger
salt and pepper

CAULIFLOWER WITH CARAWAY SEEDS

Cauliflower may be cooked whole, or broken into florets, the latter being the quicker method. Choose one with a firm white head, without any brown patches.

Serves 4

Cook the cauliflower until tender, either by steaming, or by boiling in salted water. Melt the butter in a frying pan and add the caraway seeds. Heat until the butter foams, then add the lemon juice. Remove from the heat. Drain the cauliflower and place it on a serving dish. Season the butter and pour it over the cauliflower.

INGREDIENTS
1 large cauliflower, trimmed
50 g (2 oz) butter
2.5 ml (½ tsp) caraway seeds
5 ml (1 tsp) lemon juice
salt and pepper

RED CABBAGE WITH APPLES AND CHESTNUTS

This is a very good Christmas vegetable as it is an ideal accompaniment to roast turkey. Quick and easy to prepare, the dish can be made in advance and reheated.

Serves 4–6

Melt the butter in an ovenproof dish and fry the onion until soft. Add the cabbage and stir well to coat in butter. Add the wine, 90 ml (6 tbsp) water and sugar. Stir well, cover the pan and cook at 180°C (350°F) mark 4 for 1 hour.

Season to taste. Add the chestnuts and apples and cook for a further 1 hour. Check occasionally that there is sufficient liquid, adding more water if necessary.

INGREDIENTS
75 g (3 oz) butter
1 onion, finely chopped
1 kg (2 lb) red cabbage, sliced
60 ml (4 tbsp) dry white wine
15 ml (1 tbsp) sugar
salt and pepper
500 g (1 lb) canned, unsweetened chestnuts, drained
175 g (6 oz) cooking apples, peeled, cored and chopped

LETTUCE AND PEA SOUP

This light and delicate cream soup captures the flavour of summer. To thicken and enrich the soup, a liaison of egg yolks and cream is added.

Serves 4

INGREDIENTS
40 g (1½ oz) butter
1 onion, finely chopped
1 large round lettuce, shredded
15 ml (1 tbsp) flour
225 g (8 oz) shelled peas
450 ml (¼ pint) chicken stock
  (see page 247)
450 ml (¾ pint) milk
salt and pepper
2 egg yolks
75 ml (3 fl oz) single cream
mint sprigs, to garnish

Melt the butter in a large saucepan and add the onion and lettuce. Stir, cover the pan and cook over gentle heat for 10 minutes. Stir in the flour, then add the peas. Pour in the stock and milk, season and bring to the boil. Reduce the heat, cover, and simmer for 20 minutes. Press the soup through a sieve or purée in a blender or food processor, and return it to the pan. Mix the egg yolks with the cream and add a little of the warm soup to the mixture. Add the liaison to the soup and heat, but do not allow it to boil. Adjust the seasoning, pour into serving bowls and serve garnished with mint.

TOMATO SORBET WITH A
JULIENNE OF SMOKED SALMON

TOMATO SORBET WITH A JULIENNE
OF SMOKED SALMON

*This is a pretty and refreshing starter to serve at any time of the year.
Alternatively the smoked salmon may be omitted and the sorbet served in
hollowed out tomato shells garnished with thin slices of lemon and sprigs of fresh dill.*

Serves 4

Rub the tomatoes through a sieve into a bowl. Stir in the lemon juice, Worcestershire and Tabasco sauces, salt and sugar. Pour into a shallow container and freeze until frozen around the edges. Turn into a chilled bowl and beat to break up the ice crystals. Return to the container and freeze until hard.

To serve, place spoonfuls of sorbet on to individual serving plates. Arrange the smoked salmon around the sorbet and garnish with a dill sprig and lemon twist.

INGREDIENTS
750 ml (1½ lb) ripe tomatoes,
    skinned and finely chopped
juice of 1 lemon
5 ml (1 tsp) Worcestershire sauce
few drops Tabasco sauce
salt
2.5 ml (½ tsp) sugar
75–100 g (3–4 oz) smoked
    salmon, cut into julienne strips
fresh dill sprigs, to garnish
thin lemon slices, twisted,
    to garnish

129

SUMMER TERRINE

This terrine of layered vegetables wrapped in spinach leaves is very attractive to serve either whole, or sliced and arranged on individual serving plates.

Serves 4

INGREDIENTS

100 g (4 oz) small French beans, trimmed

100 g (4 oz) peas

175 g (6 oz) young carrots, cut in lengthways strips

100 g (4 oz) young spinach leaves

500 g (1 lb) curd or cream cheese

2 eggs, lightly beaten

finely grated rind of ½ lemon

1 garlic clove, crushed

25 g (1 oz) ham, minced

salt and pepper

6 canned artichoke hearts, diced

Boil the beans, peas and carrots separately until just tender, then drain and refresh under cold running water. Blanch the spinach leaves for 30 seconds.

Line a 1 kg (2 lb) loaf tin with the spinach leaves, overlapping the edges. Beat the cheese until softened, then gradually beat in the eggs, lemon rind, garlic, ham and seasoning.

Layer the cheese mixture in the dish alternating with the beans, carrots, artichokes and peas, in that order. Finish with a layer of cheese mixture. Fold the spinach leaves over the filling to enclose it. Cover with aluminium foil and place in a roasting tin. Add boiling water to come halfway up the sides of the dish. Bake at 170°C (325°F) mark 3 for 40 minutes. Remove from the oven and allow to cool completely. Chill for at least 4 hours or overnight. Turn out and garnish with the lemon slices if wished.

SALAD ROQUEFORT

The creamy cheese dressing in this salad is also delicious with home-made hamburgers. It may also be served as a 'dip', served with crudités and is a suitable dressing for most green salads.

Serves 4—6

INGREDIENTS

2 heads of chicory, trimmed and separated into spears

1 crisp green lettuce, shredded

2–3 celery stalks, sliced

1 eating apple, peeled, cored and diced

DRESSING

75 g (3 oz) Roquefort cheese

150 ml (¼ pint) sour cream

5 ml (1 tsp) olive oil

salt and pepper

To make the dressing, mash the cheese with a fork and add the sour cream. Blend thoroughly in a blender or food processor, then add the oil and seasoning.

Arrange the chicory around the edge of a large shallow dish. Place the lettuce in the centre of the dish and sprinkle over the celery and apple. Serve with the dressing.

WINTER SALAD

This salad is an ideal accompaniment to roast game and poultry.

Serves 4

INGREDIENTS

225 g (8 oz) radicchio
100 g (4 oz) lamb's lettuce
1 large head of chicory
30 ml (2 tbsp) raspberry vinegar
salt and pepper
30 ml (2 tbsp) walnut oil
60 ml (4 tbsp) olive oil
walnut halves, chopped

Wash and dry the salad leaves and arrange them on a platter. Pour the raspberry vinegar into a small bowl and season. Pour in the oils and whisk until blended. Dribble the salad dressing over the leaves just before serving, then sprinkle with the walnuts.

DEVILLED ARTICHOKE HEARTS

A light salad to serve for a summer luncheon.

Serves 4

INGREDIENTS

45 ml (3 tbsp) walnut oil
5 ml (1 tsp) Dijon mustard
15 ml (1 tbsp) lemon juice
15 ml (1 tbsp) chopped fresh chervil
salt and pepper
1 lettuce, separated into leaves
175 g (6 oz) peeled prawns
425 g (15 oz) canned artichoke hearts, drained and halved
2 tomatoes, skinned, seeded and chopped

In a bowl, beat the walnut oil with the mustard, then beat in the lemon juice, chervil and seasoning.

Arrange the lettuce on four individual plates. Pile the prawns in the centre. Arrange the artichoke hearts around the prawns and scatter the tomatoes over the artichokes. Spoon the dressing over the artichoke hearts and trickle a little over the lettuce. Serve at once.

ONIONS A LA GRECQUE

This variable recipe can be served as an unusual starter, an accompaniment to boiled ham or roasted meat or poultry.

Serves 8

INGREDIENTS

900 g (2 lb) small pickling onions
75 ml (5 tbsp) olive oil
5 ml (1 tsp) sugar
150 ml (¼ pint) dry white wine
10 ml (2 tsp) tomato purée
salt and pepper
30 ml (2 tbsp) chopped parsley

Blanch the onions in boiling water for 1 minute only, then drain and rinse under cold running water. Remove the onion skins.

Put the onions in a large, heavy-based pan with 300 ml (½ pint) water and the remaining ingredients except the chopped parsley. Add salt and pepper to taste. Bring to the boil, then lower the heat, cover and simmer gently for 30 minutes. Uncover and cook for a further 15 minutes or until onions are tender. Taste and adjust the seasoning, then stir in the chopped parsley. Turn into a warmed serving dish and serve hot.

STUFFED VINE LEAVES

This delightful dish may be made with fresh or preserved vine leaves.
When using fresh leaves, soak them for a few minutes in boiling water, until they become
limp. If canned leaves are used, pour off the brine, place the leaves in a bowl
and cover them with boiling water. Leave them to soak for 20 minutes,
drain and rinse under cold water.

Serves 6—8

Pour boiling water over the rice, soak for 20 minutes, then drain well. Mix the beef, pine kernels, currants, onion, parsley, mint, allspice, cinnamon, tomato purée, salt and pepper together. Add the drained rice.

Select the larger vine leaves for stuffing and use the smaller and torn leaves to line the base and sides of a medium-sized pan. Place one vine leaf at a time, vein side up, on a board, and snip off any stalk that may be left on. Place 15 ml (1 tbsp) of filling, or less, depending on the size of the leaf, near the centre of the stem. Fold the sides over and roll the leaf into a small rectangular parcel. Should some of the leaves be too small, place one leaf on top of another, half way down, and roll as one. Continue this process until all the stuffing mixture has been used. Pack the parcels tightly into the prepared pan, pushing the slivers of garlic in between them. Mix the olive oil, water, lemon juice and sugar together, and pour over the vine leaves. Place a small plate on the top, to prevent them from unravelling during the cooking process. Bring to the boil, reduce the heat, cover the pan and simmer gently for 2 hours.

The vine leaves may be served either hot or cold, accompanied by natural yogurt.

INGREDIENTS

100 g (4 oz) long grain rice
225 g (8 oz) minced beef
25 g (1 oz) pine kernels
25 g (1 oz) currants
150 g (5 oz) spring onions or onion, finely chopped
45 ml (3 tbsp) chopped fresh parsley
15 ml (1 tbsp) dried mint
1.25 ml ($\frac{1}{4}$ tsp) ground allspice
1.25 ml ($\frac{1}{4}$ tsp) ground cinnamon
30 ml (2 tbsp) tomato purée
salt and pepper
500 g (1 lb) vine leaves, prepared
3 large garlic cloves, slivered
150 ml ($\frac{1}{4}$ pint) olive oil
150 ml ($\frac{1}{4}$ pint) water
juice of 2 lemons
5 ml (1 tsp) sugar

STUFFED VINE LEAVES

CABBAGE SAUTEED WITH CUMIN AND BACON

*This dish is a good accompaniment to pork or sausage. Buy whole cumin
seed and grind it in a mortar with a pestle for the best flavour.*

Serves 4

INGREDIENTS
50 g (2 oz) butter
75 g (3 oz) onion, finely chopped
*3 slices smoked back bacon,
    rinded and chopped*
5 ml (1 tsp) ground cumin seed
*750 g (1½ lb) white cabbage, stalks
    removed and shredded*
freshly ground black pepper

Melt the butter and fry the onion until soft. Add the bacon, and cook over gentle heat for a further 10 minutes. Stir in the cumin, then add the cabbage and stir until it is completely covered in butter. Season with black pepper but do not add salt. Cover and cook over gentle heat for 20 minutes, stirring occasionally. Adjust the seasoning and serve hot.

BROAD BEANS BAKED
WITH ALMONDS IN SOUR CREAM

A tasty side dish to serve with gammon.

Serves 4

INGREDIENTS
25 g (1 oz) butter
1 small shallot, finely chopped
*25 g (1 oz) lean unsmoked bacon,
    rinded and finely chopped*
25 g (1 oz) slivered almonds
*225 g (8 oz) broad beans, shelled
    weight*
30 ml (2 tbsp) dry white wine
30 ml (2 tbsp) water
salt and pepper
large pinch of chopped fresh dill
1 egg yolk
*150 ml (¼ pint) sour cream or
    crème fraîche*

Melt the butter in a casserole and gently fry the shallot and bacon for 5 minutes. Stir in the almonds, broad beans, wine, water, seasoning and dill. Cover and simmer for 10 minutes.

Mix the egg yolk with the sour cream.

When the beans are tender, remove the pan from the heat and cool for 2 minutes. Gradually stir the cream mixture into the beans. Cook over gentle heat for 4–5 minutes, stirring, but do not allow the sauce to boil.

Serve hot.

BRAISED CHICORY WITH HAM

Chicory may be cooked or eaten raw. Trim each head and remove the bitter core by inserting a knife into the base and cutting round the inner core. Select even-sized heads of chicory for this dish.

Serves 4

Melt the butter in a pan and add the chicory. Tip the pan to one side and spoon the melted butter over the chicory. Season, then cover the pan and sweat over moderate heat for 20 minutes or until the chicory is tender.

Add the ham and adjust the seasoning. Pour in the lemon juice and cook for a further 2 minutes to let the flavours develop. Serve hot.

INGREDIENTS
75 g (3 oz) butter
8 heads of chicory, trimmed and cored
salt and pepper
100 g (4 oz) ham, chopped
15 ml (1 tbsp) lemon juice

KOHLRABI WITH CREAM SAUCE

Cooked in cream, kohlrabi is a tasty dish to serve with meat, fish or poultry.

Serves 4

Place the kohlrabi in the top part of a steamer or in a colander, cover and cook over simmering water for about 30 minutes or until tender.

Meanwhile, simmer the shallots in the wine in a covered pan for 5 minutes or until tender. Bring to the boil and boil until the wine has reduced to 45 ml (3 tbsp). Stir in the cream and simmer until slightly thickened. Press the sauce through a sieve, return it to the rinsed-out pan and reheat gently. Gradually whisk in the butter, one piece at a time. Stir in the lemon juice. Season and keep warm. Do not allow the sauce to boil or it will curdle.

Remove the kohlrabi from the heat, cool slightly, then rub off the skin. Slice finely and arrange the slices in a warmed serving dish. Spoon over the sauce and garnish with the parsley.

INGREDIENTS
4 small kohlrabi, trimmed
30 ml (2 tbsp) finely chopped shallots
175 ml (6 fl oz) dry white wine
150 ml (¼ pint) double cream
25 g (1 oz) butter, diced
5 ml (1 tsp) lemon juice
salt and pepper
parsley sprigs, to garnish

GLAZED SHALLOTS

The light sugar glaze in this recipe enhances the shallots' mild taste.

Serves 4

Place the shallots in a pan and cover with cold water. Bring to the boil and blanch for 10 minutes. Drain.

Melt the .butter in a saucepan, add the sugar, shallots and salt and pepper. Cover and cook for about 15 minutes, until the shallots are tender and well glazed. Stir occasionally to prevent the sugar from burning. Turn into a warmed serving dish and sprinkle with parsley.

INGREDIENTS
450 g (1 lb) shallots, skinned
50 g (2 oz) butter
10 ml (2 tbsp) sugar
salt and pepper
chopped fresh parsley, to garnish

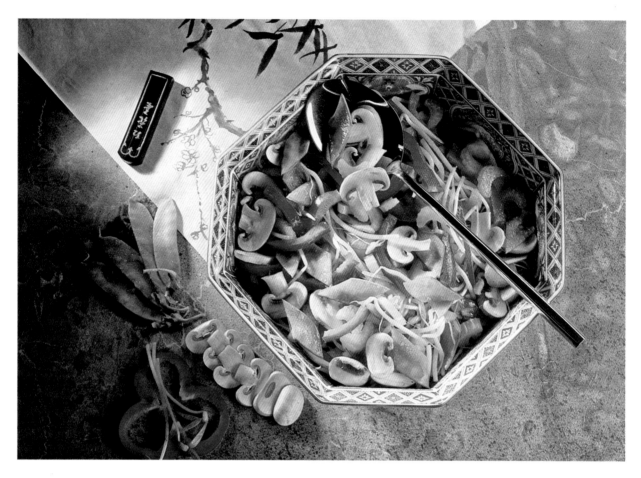

CHINESE SALAD

Some of the vegetables used in Chinese stir-fry dishes are equally good eaten raw in a salad. The dressing consists of some of the flavourings used in hot Chinese dishes.

Serves 6

INGREDIENTS

4 celery stalks

1 small head Chinese cabbage, shredded

75 g (3 oz) beanshoots

75 g (3 oz) mangetout, sliced diagonally into diamond shapes

½ small red pepper, cut into thin rings and seeded

75 g (3 oz) mushrooms, sliced

DRESSING

10 ml (2 tsp) lemon juice

25 ml (1½ tbsp) light soy sauce

4 ml (¾ tsp) sesame oil

60 ml (4 tbsp) sunflower oil

5 ml (1 tsp) caster sugar

1.25 ml (¼ tsp) finely chopped fresh root ginger

Mix all the dressing ingredients together and set aside for the flavours to develop.

Slice the celery into horseshoe shapes by laying each stalk flat and slicing at an angle.

Arrange all the vegetables in a large bowl, add the dressing and toss well before serving.

SPINACH AND RICOTTA RAVIOLI WITH SAGE BUTTER

Spinach and ricotta is a popular combination of flavours in Italian cooking.
If fresh sage is unavailable, do not substitute dried. Instead use parsley or basil.

Serves 4

For the filling, melt the butter and fry the shallots and garlic until soft. Add the spinach and cook over high heat stirring constantly until it has softened and the liquid evaporated. Set aside until cold, then chop finely.

In a bowl, mix the spinach with the cheese, nutmeg, cayenne and seasoning. Divide the pasta dough in half. Roll out each piece of dough on a lightly floured surface to a 40 × 30 cm (16 × 12 inch) rectangle. Either spoon the filling in a piping bag fitted with a large plain nozzle or use a teaspoon. Starting 2.5 cm (1 inch) in from the edge of the dough place small rounds of the spinach filling at 5 cm (2 inch) intervals, to give 48 piles. Do not overfill or the ravioli will burst during cooking. Brush in between the filling with water. Place the second piece of dough carefully on top and using a long kinfe or kitchen ruler, mark lines between each pile of filling to seal the dough.

Using a serrated pastry wheel or sharp knife, cut between each parcel to make 48 ravioli. Cover until required. Cook the ravioli in boiling salted water for 5 minutes. Drain well.

For the sauce, melt the butter and fry the sage leaves until the butter just starts to turn pale gold. Pour over the ravioli, add the Parmesan cheese and plenty of freshly ground black pepper. Toss well and serve at once.

INGREDIENTS
15 g (½ oz) butter
2 shallots, chopped
1 garlic clove, crushed
225 g (8 oz) fresh spinach, trimmed
100 g (4 oz) ricotta cheese
25 g (1 oz) freshly grated
  Parmesan cheese
pinch of freshly grated nutmeg
pinch of cayenne pepper
salt and pepper
500 g (1 lb) pasta dough (see page 251)
SAUCE
125–150 g (4–5 oz) butter
24 large sage leaves, slivered
60 ml (4 tbsp) freshly grated
  Parmesan cheese

BROCCOLI MORNAY

The sauce in this dish may also be served with fish and chicken.

Serves 4

Cook the broccoli until tender, either by steaming, or by boiling in water. Melt the butter in a pan over gentle heat. Stir in the flour and cook for 1 minute. Remove the pan from the heat and gradually stir in the milk. Cook, stirring for 5 minutes, then stir in the grated cheese and seasoning.

Drain the broccoli, place in a serving dish and pour over the sauce.

INGREDIENTS
500 g (1 lb) broccoli, trimmed
25 g (1 oz) butter
25 g (1 oz) flour
350 ml (12 fl oz) milk
50 g (2 oz) Cheddar cheese, grated
salt and pepper

HOT ENDIVE AND SMOKED BACON SALAD

*There is great confusion regarding endive and chicory. In England, endive
is the curly salad plant, a pale yellowy green in the centre,
with darker green outside leaves.*

Serves 4–6

INGREDIENTS

*100 ml (4 fl oz) sunflower or
     olive oil*

*4 slices smoked streaky bacon,
     rinded and diced*

*2 slices white bread, crusts
     removed and diced*

*1 head curly endive, outer leaves
     removed*

30 ml (2 tbsp) white wine vinegar

5 ml (1 tsp) Dijon mustard

salt and pepper

1 large garlic clove, sliced

Heat 15 ml (1 tbsp) of the oil in a pan and fry the bacon until crisp. Remove with a slotted spoon and keep hot. Add the bread to the pan and fry until it is crisp and golden, using more oil if necessary. Remove the croûtons from the pan and keep hot. Arrange the endive in a salad bowl.

To make the hot vinegar dressing, place the vinegar, mustard, salt, pepper and garlic in a small saucepan and stir well. Add the remaining oil and cook until hot but do not let it boil. Remove the garlic. Pour the dressing over the endive, tossing the leaves until they are well coated. Sprinkle over the bacon and croûtons and serve immediately.

FRENCH BEANS WITH CREAMY HAZELNUT DRESSING

*French beans add a crisp sweetness and vivid green colouring to a salad.
Cook them either by steaming, or by plunging them into boiling water.
Whichever method you use, only cook them for a few minutes so that they retain their
crunch and colour.*

Serves 4

Beat the sour cream and mayonnaise together until blended, then gradually beat
in the lemon juice. Add salt to taste.

Place the hazelnuts on a baking tray in a hot oven for a few minutes, or until
golden brown. Do not allow them to become too dark. Rub them in a tea towel
to remove the skins and chop roughly.

Arrange the beans on individual serving dishes. Spoon the dressing over the
beans, sprinkle with hazelnuts and garnish with lemon slices.

INGREDIENTS
150 ml (¼ pint) sour cream
75 ml (3 fl oz) mayonnaise
  (see page 250)
juice of ½ a lemon
salt
75 g (3 oz) hazelnuts
500 g (1 lb) French beans,
  trimmed and cooked
lemon slices, to garnish

AUBERGINE LASAGNE

*This vegetarian version of lasagne makes an interesting change. To remove the
bitter juices, or degorge, the aubergines should be sliced, sprinkled with salt and
placed in a colander for 20 minutes, then rinsed before cooking.*

Serves 6–8

Roll out the pasta and cut it into 15 × 11 cm (6 × 4½ inch) sheets. Bring a large pan
of salted water to the boil with half the olive oil. Cook a few sheets of pasta at a
time. Drain immediately and place in a bowl of cold water.

Heat the remaining oil and butter in a pan and fry the onion until soft. Stir in
the tomato purée and the tomatoes. Season, and add the aubergine, wine and
oregano. Cover the pan and simmer gently for 10 minutes, or until the aubergine
is tender.

Place a layer of drained pasta in the base of a greased shallow ovenproof dish.
Spread some of the aubergine mixture over the pasta, then a layer of the Bel
Paese, mozzarella and the Parmesan cheese, mixed together. Continue to make
layers in this way, ending with a layer of pasta.

To make the sauce, melt the butter in a small saucepan, stir in the flour and
cook for 1 minute. Remove from the heat and gradually stir in the milk. Add the
bay leaf, seasoning and nutmeg, and cook stirring, over gentle heat for 5 minutes.
Spread the sauce evenly over the top of the lasagne and sprinkle with the
Parmesan cheese. Bake at 200°C (400°F) mark 6, for 20–25 minutes, or until the
topping is golden brown.

INGREDIENTS
225 g (8 oz) pasta dough
  (see page 251)
30 ml (2 tbsp) olive oil
salt and pepper
25 g (1 oz) butter
1 onion, finely chopped
30 ml (2 tbsp) tomato purée
500 g (1 lb) ripe tomatoes, peeled
500 g (1 lb) aubergines, degorged
150 ml (¼ pint) dry white wine
5 ml (1 tsp) dried oregano
225 g (8 oz) Bel Paese cheese,
  grated
225 g (8 oz) mozzarella, grated
50 g (2 oz) Parmesan cheese
BECHAMEL SAUCE
25 g (1 oz) butter
25 g (1 oz) plain flour
450 ml (¾ pint) milk
1 bay leaf
a pinch of grated nutmeg
25 g (1 oz) finely grated Parmesan
  cheese

HOT ENDIVE AND SMOKED BACON SALAD

PUMPKIN PANCAKES WITH SAUTEED APPLES

This recipe combines two flavours abundant in the autumn and makes an interesting brunch dish.

Serves 4

To make the pumpkin purée, remove the seeds and stringy membrane from the pumpkin then place it on a lightly greased baking sheet and bake at 180°C (350°F) mark 4 for 45 minutes–1 hour or until tender. Remove the flesh with a large spoon and purée in a blender or food processor.

Sift all the dry ingredients together into a bowl. Make a well in the centre and add the orange rind, egg, pumpkin purée and milk. Beat to a stiff batter.

Melt the butter and fry the apple slices until golden and just softened. Keep hot. Heat a griddle or large frying pan over moderate heat. Brush with melted butter and pour 30–45 ml (2–3 tbsp) of the pumpkin mixture on to the griddle, spreading it slightly. Cook 2 or 3 at one time.

Cook for 1–2 minutes or until bubbles appear at the edges. Carefully turn over and cook for a further 1–2 minutes or until golden brown and just firm to the touch. Keep hot while you make the remaining pancakes. Serve at once, with the sautéed apple slices and maple syrup.

INGREDIENTS
500 g (1 lb) pumpkin
50 g (2 oz) cornmeal
50 g (2 oz) flour
5 ml (1 tsp) baking powder
50 g (2 oz) light brown sugar
2.5 ml (½ tsp) ground cinnamon
1.25 ml (¼ tsp) ground ginger
1.25 ml (¼ tsp) ground mace
salt
5 ml (1 tsp) grated orange or lemon rind
1 egg
about 60 ml (4 tbsp) milk
50 g (2 oz) butter
2 large dessert apples, peeled, cored and sliced
maple syrup, to serve

OKRA WITH RICH TOMATO SAUCE

There are a number of different species belonging to the mallow family, but the best known variety is okra, also known as gumbo and ladies' fingers. Do not cut into the flesh when trimming.

Serves 4

Heat the oil in a casserole and fry the onion until soft. Add the garlic and cook for a further 5 minutes.

Stir in the coriander. Add the okra and gently stir until it is coated in oil. Cook the okra for 2 minutes. Stir in the tomato purée. Add the tomatoes and bring to the boil. Season well then add the water. Return to the boil, cover, reduce the heat and simmer gently for 45–50 minutes, checking that there is sufficient water. Add the lemon juice and cook for a further 10 minutes, or until the okra is tender. Serve either hot or cold.

INGREDIENTS
45 ml (3 tbsp) olive oil
1 large onion, sliced
1 large garlic clove, crushed
5 ml (1 tsp) ground coriander
500 g (1 lb) okra, trimmed of hard stems
25 ml (1½ tbsp) tomato purée
500 g (1 lb) tomatoes, skinned and roughly chopped
salt and pepper
300 ml (½ pint) water
juice of ½ lemon

CELERIAC AND POTATO GRATIN

*Celeriac is a variety of celery with a large edible root. Its flavour combines
well with potato, making this dish an excellent accompaniment to roast meat and game.*

Serves 4

INGREDIENTS

*500 g (1 lb) potatoes, cut into
5 mm (¼ inch) slices
75 g (3 oz) butter
500 g (1 lb) celeriac, cut into
5 mm (¼ inch) slices
salt and pepper*

Rinse the potato slices in cold water and dry thoroughly. Melt the butter in a frying pan and lightly fry half of the potato slices for 1 minute on each side. Arrange them in a gratin dish and season. Fry the celeriac and then the remaining potato slices in the same way. Place the celeriac layer on top of the potatoes, season and place the remaining potatoes on top of them. Pour over any melted butter remaining in the pan. Bake at 190°C (375°F) mark 5, for 1 hour.

LATKES

*Latkes are potato cakes made with grated potatoes and served as a snack.
Do not use new potatoes for this recipe.*

Makes 12

INGREDIENTS

*750 g (1½ lb) potatoes
3 eggs, beaten
30 ml (2 tbsp) flour
1.25 ml (¼ tsp) salt
½ medium onion, grated
75 g (3 oz) butter
45 ml (3 tbsp) oil*

Grate the potatoes and squeeze as much water out of them as possible, by hand, or by placing them in a muslin cloth. You should have about 500 g (1 lb) grated potatoes. Place them in a bowl with the eggs. Sift the flour with the salt and add it to the potato mixture. Stir in the onion and mix well.

Melt 25 g (1 oz) of the butter with 15 ml (1 tbsp) of the oil together in a frying pan. Take spoonfuls of the potato mixture, and make into 7.5 cm (3 inch) wide pancakes. Fry 4 at a time for 5 minutes each side, or until cooked and golden brown. Drain on kitchen paper and keep hot. Cook the remaining latkes in the same way. Serve immediately.

POMMES DE TERRE A LA LYONNAISE

*Pommes de terre à la Lyonnaise is delicious served with a simple main course,
such as grilled meat, poultry or fish.*

Serves 4

INGREDIENTS

*1 kg (2 lb) potatoes, sliced
5 mm (¼ inch) thick
75 g (3 oz) butter
2 medium onions, thinly sliced
salt and pepper
15 ml (1 tbsp) chopped fresh
parsley*

Rinse the potato slices in cold water and dry them thoroughly. Melt 50 g (2 oz) of the butter in a large frying pan and cook the potatoes over moderately low heat for 20 minutes, turning regularly until light golden brown.

Meanwhile, melt the remaining butter in another pan, and cook the onions until golden. Add the onions to the potatoes, season to taste, and cook together for 2 minutes. Make sure the potatoes are cooked through: if not, cook a little longer. Transfer to a serving dish and sprinkle with chopped parsley.

'SEAWEED'

This crunchy, sweet 'seaweed' is served in Chinese restaurants preceding or accompanying the main dishes. However, few people realize that they are in fact eating cabbage, and not seaweed.

Serves 4

To prepare the cabbage, roll 2 leaves together into a tight cigar shape and shred the leaves as finely as possible using a Chinese cleaver or sharp knife. Continue in this way until all the cabbage has been used.

Half fill the wok with oil then heat it over high heat. When the oil is hot, add the cabbage and stir-fry for 2 minutes. Do not allow the cabbage to become too dark or it will taste bitter. Drain on kitchen paper. Place in a serving dish and sprinkle with sugar, salt and almonds. Serve immediately.

INGREDIENTS
175 g (6 oz) dark green cabbage leaves, (the outer leaves of the cabbage), thick stems removed
groundnut oil
5 ml (1 tsp) sugar
pinch of salt
25 g (1 oz) almonds, slivered

FENNEL AND RED ONION SALAD WITH TARRAGON DRESSING

The rich combination of colour and flavour makes this an attractive side dish or salad.

Serves 4

Place the onion and fennel in a bowl.

Mix the wine vinegar with the salt, pepper and the tarragon. Whisk in the olive oil and pour the dressing over the onion and fennel. Leave for 1 hour.

INGREDIENTS
1 large red onion, thinly sliced into rings
4 fennel bulbs, trimmed and thinly sliced
30 ml (2 tbsp) white wine vinegar
salt and pepper
5 ml (1 tsp) chopped fresh tarragon
175 ml (6 fl oz) olive oil

POMMES DE TERRE SOUFFLE

These delicate potatoes are light and fluffy and guaranteed to impress. Serve with roast game birds or fillet of beef.

Serves 4

Peel the potatoes and cut into slices 3 mm ($\frac{1}{8}$ inch) thick. Allow these to soak in a bowl of cold water for at least 1 hour. Drain the potatoes and pat dry with absorbent paper. Heat the oil to 160°C (325°F) and lower half the potato slices into the oil. When the slices rise to the surface, remove them and allow to drain and cool thoroughly on absorbent paper. Repeat with the remaining slices.

Just before serving, heat the oil to 200°C (395°F) and plunge in the first batch of potatoes. They should puff up almost immediately and turn golden brown. Lift them out of the oil, and again drain on absorbent paper. Repeat this process with the second batch of potatoes. Serve immediately.

INGREDIENTS
500 g (1 lb) waxy potatoes, such as Desirée, Vanessa or Maris Piper
vegetable oil for deep frying

PEPPERS WITH PINE NUT STUFFING

*Red, green and yellow peppers are used for this colourful dish. Serve with
a fresh tomato sauce, accompanied by rice.*

Serves 4—6

INGREDIENTS

75 g (3 oz) rice

8 peppers, stalks removed

75 g (3 oz) butter

1 onion, finely chopped

*3 spring onions, the white and
green parts chopped separately*

350 g (12 oz) minced beef

50 g (2 oz) pine kernels

50 g (2 oz) raisins

*45 ml (3 tbsp) finely chopped
fresh parsley*

15 ml (1 tbsp) tomato purée

1.25 ml ($\frac{1}{4}$ tsp) ground allspice

1.25 ml ($\frac{1}{4}$ tsp) ground cinnamon

salt and pepper

*600 ml (1 pint) beef stock
(see page 246)*

Cook the rice in lightly salted boiling water, until just tender. Drain. Slice the tops
off the peppers and reserve them. Scoop out all the seeds and pith, and discard.

Melt the butter in a casserole and fry the onion and the white of the spring
onions until golden.

Mix all the remaining ingredients together in a bowl, except the beef stock,
and add the rice and cooked onions.

Stand the peppers in a baking dish and stuff with the mixture. Replace the tops
and dot with the remaining butter. Pour the stock around the peppers and bake at
180°C (350°F) mark 4 for 1 hour.

MINIATURE ASPARAGUS TARTS

*Asparagus is one of the most delicious vegetables. This elegant recipe
doesn't mask the fresh asparagus taste and is simple to prepare.*

Serves 4

Butter 4 tartlet tins. Roll out the pastry and use to line the tins. Bake blind at
200°C (400°F) mark 6 for 15 minutes. Remove the beans and paper.

Meanwhile, cook the asparagus in boiling salted water for about 10 minutes, or
until just tender. Drain. Bend the asparagus spears around the edge of the pastry
cases, leaving the centres free. Break an egg into the centre of each case. Pour a
little cream over each egg and dot with butter. Season and sprinkle with the
cheese. Bake at 180°C (350°F) mark 4 for 6–8 minutes, or until the egg is just set.
Serve warm.

INGREDIENTS
shortcrust pastry, made with
  175 g (6 oz) flour (see page 247)
175 g (6 oz) thin asparagus spears
4 eggs
60 ml (4 tbsp) single cream
25 g (1 oz) butter
salt and pepper
*10 ml (2 tsp) grated Parmesan
  cheese*

145

RED AND YELLOW PEPPERS WITH SCALLOPS

*This starter may be served hot or cold. The peppers are cooked in their skins,
under a hot grill, or directly over a gas flame.*

Serves 4

INGREDIENTS

1 medium red pepper

1 medium yellow pepper

*12 scallops, with corals, shelled
weight about 500 g (1 lb)*

2 shallots, finely chopped

40 g (1½ oz) butter

salt and pepper

*30 ml (2 tbsp) chopped fresh
parsley*

100 ml (4 fl oz) dry white wine

Place the whole peppers under a hot grill, turning them often, for 20 minutes. When the peppers are soft, remove them from the grill, cut in half and place in a colander. Remove the skins while the peppers are still hot and discard the stalks and seeds. Cut into 0.5 cm (¼ inch) wide strips and arrange on a plate in alternate colours in a 'sun-ray' pattern, leaving a space for the scallops.

Meanwhile, prepare the scallops. If large, cut each of the white parts into three slices, leaving the coral intact. Place them in a pan with the shallots, butter and a little salt and pepper. Add half the parsley and the wine and bring to the boil. Reduce the heat, cover the pan, and simmer for 5 minutes. Strain the contents of the pan, and reserve. Bring the liquid to the boil, and boil for 5–8 minutes, or until reduced. If the dish is to be served hot, return the scallops to the liquid, and heat them through.

Pile the scallops into the centre of the pepper strips, and pour the liquid over them. Garnish with the remaining parsley and serve.

GINGERED BEETROOT

A spicy dish which is the perfect accompaniment for roasted chicken or turkey.

Serves 4

INGREDIENTS

450 g (1 lb) beetroot

25 g (1 oz) butter

*25 g (1 oz) crystallised ginger,
finely chopped*

2 pineapple slices, chopped

45 ml (3 tbsp) white wine vinegar

30 ml (2 tbsp) sugar

salt and pepper

Trim the stalks to within 2.5 cm (1 inch) of the beetroot and leave whole. Cook in boiling salted water for 1–3 hours, according to size. The skin will rub off easily when cooked. Drain well, peel and cut into 0.5 cm (¼ inch) dice.

Melt the butter in a large saucepan, add the beetroot, ginger, pineapple, vinegar, sugar and seasoning. Heat through, stirring, before serving.

THE FRUIT AND VEGETABLE HALL

FRUIT

FRUIT

———— ◆ ————

*Delicious to round off a meal, or to eat alone, fresh fruit can
always be bought at Harrods. Fruits can be used to great advantage
in main course dishes, such as Chicken Breasts with Mangoes and Almonds
or as an exquisite end to a meal—Kumquats Poached in Rose Water or,
for that special occasion, Melon and Strawberries in Champagne.*

RABBIT IN RED WINE SAUCE
WITH PRUNES AND RAISINS

*For a stronger flavour, marinate the rabbit with the wine and vegetables
for up to 48 hours, in the refrigerator in a covered dish. When ready to cook
remove the rabbit and dry well. Drain and dry the vegetables and reserve the marinade.*

Serves 4

INGREDIENTS

1 kg (2 lb) dressed rabbit,
   jointed
30 ml (2 tbsp) flour
salt and pepper
30 ml (2 tbsp) olive oil
15 g (½ oz) butter
1 onion, finely chopped
1 celery stalk, finely chopped
1 carrot, finely chopped
1 garlic clove, chopped
150 ml (¼ pint) red wine
300 ml (½ pint) chicken stock
   (see page 247)
bouquet garni
4 slices streaky bacon,
   rinded and cut into thin strips
12 prunes, stoned
25 g (1 oz) raisins
chopped fresh parsley, to garnish

Coat the rabbit joints in the flour, seasoned with salt and pepper. Heat the oil with the butter in a frying pan and fry the rabbit until golden brown all over. Transfer it to a flameproof casserole.

Add the onion, celery, carrot and garlic to the pan and fry until soft. Add the red wine and bring it to the boil, scraping any sediment from the sides of the pan. Pour the wine and vegetables over the rabbit joints. Add the stock and bouquet garni, cover and simmer for 45 minutes.

Fry the bacon strips without any extra fat, until crisp. Remove the rabbit joints from the casserole. Strain the pan juices, then return them to the rinsed-out pan. Add the rabbit, bacon, prunes and raisins. Cover and simmer for a further 15 minutes. Remove the lid and simmer for a further 15 minutes. Adjust the seasoning. Garnish with chopped parsley.

MELON AND PARMA HAM RISOTTO

MELON AND PARMA HAM RISOTTO

Melon and Parma ham seem universally popular as a cold starter.
In this recipe they are equally delicious combined in a creamy risotto, and
smothered with freshly grated Parmesan cheese. The rice should be 'al dente', retaining
a chewy core, but the risotto will be fairly runny and must be served immediately.

Serves 6

Weigh 275 g (10 oz) of the melon, purée and reserve. Weigh another 225 g (8 oz) and cut it into small cubes. Slice or dice any remaining melon and use it to garnish the finished dish.

Melt the butter over moderate heat in a large saucepan and fry the onion until golden. Add the rice and stir well until all the grains are coated with the melted butter. Add the wine, a little at a time, stirring frequently.

Cook uncovered, stirring until the wine has almost been absorbed by the rice. Increase the heat and add the chicken stock, about 150 ml ($\frac{1}{4}$ pint) at a time. Bring to the boil, then reduce the heat and simmer.

From the moment the rice is added, the risotto will take 20–25 minutes to cook. About 5 minutes before the rice is cooked, add the puréed melon and the cream, stirring constantly.

When the risotto reaches the correct consistency, remove the pan from the heat and season. Add the cubed melon and ham to the risotto. Serve with extra pieces of melon and Parmesan cheese.

INGREDIENTS

*1 large ripe honeydew melon,
   cut into lengthways slices, rind
   removed and seeded*
75 g (3 oz) butter
1 onion, finely chopped
400 g (14 oz) Arborio rice
150 ml ($\frac{1}{4}$ pint) dry white wine
*900 ml–1.2 litres (1$\frac{1}{2}$–2 pints)
   hot chicken stock (see page 247)*
225 ml (8 fl oz) single cream
salt and pepper
*100 g (4 oz) thinly sliced Parma
   ham, diced*
*175 g (6 oz) freshly grated
   Parmesan cheese*

STUFFED PAPAYAS

Papaya or pawpaw, may be used in either sweet or savoury recipes. As the fruit and leaves contain an enzyme that tenderizes meat, it is an ideal fruit to use in savoury dishes. For this dish, choose papayas with mottled green and yellow skins, as they should be slightly under-ripe.

Serves 4

Peel the papayas, cut them in half lengthways and remove the black seeds with a teaspoon. Parboil the fruit in gently boiling, salted water for 10 minutes, then drain them upside down on kitchen paper.

Heat the oil in a large frying pan and fry the onion, garlic and bacon together until the onion is soft. Add the pork and chilli and fry until browned, stirring to break up the meat. Add the tomato purée, and cook, stirring, for 2 minutes. Pour over the white wine and stir in the tomatoes. Bring to the boil, reduce the heat and simmer for 5 minutes. Season to taste, remove from the heat and allow the mixture to cool slightly.

Grease a baking dish just large enough to hold the papaya shells and place them, cavity side up, in the dish. Pile the meat mixture into the centre of each papaya.

Sprinkle with Parmesan cheese and dot with butter. Bake at 180°C (350°F) mark 4 for 30–40 minutes, or until the papaya is tender. Serve with the tomato sauce poured around each papaya.

INGREDIENTS
2 papayas
30 ml (2 tbsp) vegetable oil
1 onion, finely chopped
1 large garlic clove, crushed
1 slice unsmoked streaky bacon, rinded and finely chopped
500 g (1 lb) minced pork
1 small green hot chilli, seeded and finely chopped
15 ml (1 tbsp) tomato purée
75 ml (3 fl oz) dry white wine
175 g (6 oz) ripe tomatoes, peeled and chopped
salt and pepper
45 ml (3 tbsp) freshly grated Parmesan cheese
15 g ($\frac{1}{2}$ oz) butter
450 ml ($\frac{3}{4}$ pint) tomato sauce (see page 251)
parsley, to garnish

LAMB WITH QUINCE

Lamb has an affinity with certain fruits and quince is one of them. The combination of fresh ginger, lemon and quince blends well with the sweetness of the lamb. Serve with plain rice.

Serves 6

Trim the fat from the underside of the lamb. Heat the oil in a large casserole and fry the onion until soft. Add the meat and brown it on all sides. Stir in the ginger. Season, then add the water and saffron. Bring to the boil, cover and simmer for 2 hours.

Add the sliced quinces and lemon juice, and continue to simmer the lamb for 30 minutes or until the quinces are tender.

Adjust the seasoning.

INGREDIENTS
1.8 kg (4 lb) shoulder of lamb
30 ml (2 tbsp) oil
1 small onion, finely chopped
2.5 ml ($\frac{1}{2}$ tsp) finely chopped fresh root ginger
salt and pepper
450 ml ($\frac{3}{4}$ pint) water
1.25 ml ($\frac{1}{4}$ tsp) saffron powder
500 g (1 lb) quinces, cored and sliced
juice of $\frac{1}{2}$ lemon

STUFFED PAPAYAS

GRANNY SMITH'S SALAD

*The name of this salad is derived from the Granny Smith, a particularly
crisp and juicy apple. This cheese and apple salad is an ideal luncheon dish,
served with crusty French bread.*

Serves 4

INGREDIENTS

3 Granny Smith apples

lemon juice

175 g (6 oz) celery, chopped

175 g (6 oz) cheese, Cheddar,
 double Gloucester or Leicester,
 diced

1 small spring onion,
 finely chopped

celery leaves, to garnish

DRESSING

150 ml ($\frac{1}{4}$ pint) natural yogurt

50 ml (2 fl oz) mayonnaise
 (see page 250)

10 ml (2 tsp) lemon juice

salt and pepper

5 ml (1 tsp) chopped fresh parsley

For the dressing, beat the yogurt until smooth then beat in the mayonnaise. Add
the lemon juice, seasoning and parsley.

Core and slice the apples thinly, but do not peel. Sprinkle with lemon juice
to prevent discoloration. Place 2 of the sliced apples in a bowl and add the celery,
cheese and spring onion. Pour over the dressing and toss well. Arrange the
remaining apple slices on a serving dish and place the salad in the centre. Garnish
with celery leaves.

Crunchy Apple Salad

Prepare the salad as above, omitting the spring onion and substituting 50 g (2 oz)
coarsely chopped walnut or toasted blanched almonds. Sprinkle the nuts over the
top of the salad just before serving so they retain their crunchiness.

APRICOT AND MONKFISH KEBABS

*Monkfish is ideal for kebabs, as the flesh is firm and doesn't flake easily.
Serve with hot pitta bread or boiled rice.*

Serves 4

Place the fish in a bowl. Mix the lime juice, olive oil, garlic, onion, turmeric and seasoning together. Pour the marinade over the fish and marinate for at least 1 hour.

Wrap the bacon around the apricots. Thread pieces of fish, peppers, mushrooms and wrapped apricots alternately on to 4 skewers.

Brush the kebabs with the marinade and cook under a hot grill for 15–20 minutes, turning and basting frequently. Serve garnished with lime wedges and red pepper strips.

Orange and Sole Kebabs

Slice 4 skinned sole fillets in half lengthways. Prepare a marinade of the finely grated rind and juice of 1 orange, 150 ml ($\frac{1}{2}$ pint) olive oil, 1 crushed garlic clove and 50 ml (2 tbsp) finely chopped parsley.

Place the fish in a bowl, pour over the marinade and marinate for at least 1 hour.

Meanwhile, peel and segment two large oranges and trim 8 button mushrooms.

Remove the sole from the marinade with a slotted spoon and roll up tightly, starting at the short ends. Thread the fish, orange segments and mushrooms on 4 well-oiled skewers.

Brush with the marinade and cook as above. Serve garnished with orange twists.

INGREDIENTS
750 g (1½ lb) monkfish, skinned,
    boned and cut into
    4 cm (1½ inch) cubes
50 ml (2 fl oz) lime juice
150 ml (¼ pint) olive oil
1 garlic clove, crushed
1 small onion, chopped
1.25 ml (¼ tsp) turmeric
salt and pepper
6 slices unsmoked streaky bacon,
    rinded and halved
12 dried apricots, soaked overnight
    and drained
3 small red, green or yellow
    peppers, seeded and cut into
    squares
8 button mushrooms
lime wedges and red pepper strips
    to garnish

155

VEAL WITH PORT AND FIGS

*The natural sweetness of this sauce goes very well with veal. Garnish the
finished dish with fresh figs: warm them in the oven for a few minutes, cut through the
stem into 6 sections, leaving the base whole, then open them out like a flower.*

Serves 4

INGREDIENTS

6 dried figs, stems removed and
   coarsely chopped

90 ml (6 tbsp) port

100 ml (4 fl oz) water

75 g (3 oz) butter

4 veal escalopes

15 ml (1 tbsp) raspberry vinegar

350 ml (12 fl oz) bone stock
   (see page 246)

salt and pepper

4 fresh figs, to garnish

Place the dried figs in a bowl and pour over the port. Leave to soak for 1 hour
then place in a saucepan with the water and 25 g (1 oz) of the butter. Bring to the
boil, reduce the heat and simmer gently for 15–20 minutes, stirring occasionally.
Do not allow the mixture to stick to the base of the pan.

Remove from the heat and stir in 25 g (1 oz) of the remaining butter. Purée the
mixture then rub it through a sieve, so that no pips remain.

Melt the remaining butter in a pan and fry the veal for 2 minutes on each side.
Remove and keep hot in a serving dish. Deglaze the pan with the vinegar, then
stir in the stock. Bring to the boil and boil rapidly until reduced by a third. Add
the fig purée and boil again until reduced slightly. Season to taste, then strain the
sauce. Serve the veal garnished with fresh figs and the sauce.

PORK WITH PINEAPPLE AND CASHEW NUTS

*This stir-fried dish is an impressive but simple recipe to prepare
when guests arrive unexpectedly. Serve with boiled rice.*

Serves 4

INGREDIENTS

30 ml (2 tbsp) cornflour

5 ml (1 tsp) ground ginger

60 ml (4 tbsp) dry sherry

750 g (1½ lb) pork fillet, cut
   into 2 cm (¾ inch) cubes

oil, for deep-frying

45 ml (3 tbsp) vegetable oil

1 onion, finely chopped

1 garlic clove, finely chopped

100 g (4 oz) pineapple cubes, fresh
   or canned, drained

½ red pepper, seeded, sliced and
   the slices cut in half

100 g (4 oz) cashew nuts, lightly
   toasted

150 ml (¼ pint) chicken stock
   (see page 247)

30 ml (2 tbsp) soy sauce

Mix the cornflour, ginger and sherry together to form a smooth paste. Add the
pork and stir well to coat the meat. Cover and leave at room temperature for 1
hour.

Heat the oil in a deep-fat fryer to 190°C (375°F). Fry the pork in batches for
5 minutes until crisp and golden. Drain on kitchen paper.

Meanwhile, heat the vegetable oil in a large frying pan and fry the onion and
garlic for 2 minutes. Stir in the pineapple and red pepper and cook, stirring, for 1
minute. Stir in the nuts, stock and soy sauce. Add the pork, bring to the boil and
simmer for 1–2 minutes. Serve at once.

ARABIAN RICE

*This rice pilaf combines meat with dried fruits and pulses. Serve with
extra butter and natural yogurt.*

Serves 6

Cook the lentils in boiling water for 20–25 minutes or until tender. Drain. Cover
the rice with cold water, leave to soak for 15 minutes, then drain. Melt 40 g
(1½ oz) butter, and fry half the onion until golden. Set aside.

Mix the beef with the remaining onion, season, and form into small meatballs,
the size of a cherry. Add the meatballs to the cooked onion and fry until
browned. Stir in the dates and currants. Mix the saffron with the hot water and
add to the meat and fruit mixture.

Cook the rice in a large pan of well salted, boiling water for 5 minutes, and
drain thoroughly.

Heat the cold water and 50 g (2 oz) butter in a heavy-based pan over moderate
heat. Spread a layer of the rice over the base of the pan, then a layer of meat and
fruit, then lentils. Continue making layers ending with the rice, then push a
wooden spoon through the layers to make an air-hole. Wrap the pan lid with a
tea towel and steam over moderate heat for 40 minutes. At the end of the
cooking time, stand the base of the saucepan in cold water, to prevent further
cooking. Serve with extra butter.

INGREDIENTS
100 g (4 oz) brown lentils
500 g (1 lb) basmati rice
90 g (3½ oz) butter
1 medium onion, finely chopped
225 g (8 oz) minced beef
salt and pepper
*100 g (4 oz) dates, stoned and
    chopped*
100 g (4 oz) currants
2.5 ml (½ tsp) saffron powder
15 ml (1 tbsp) hot water
60 ml (4 tbsp) cold water

CALF'S LIVER WITH GREEN GRAPES AND MADEIRA

*Seasoned with sage and served with a slightly sweet sauce, calf's liver
is a delicious, light course. Accompany with rice.*

Serves 4

Melt half the butter and fry the onion until golden. Add the stock and Madeira,
season and bring it to the boil. Boil rapidly for about 4–5 minutes until reduced
and of a slightly syrupy consistency. Add the grape halves and warm through
gently. Adjust the seasoning.

Melt the remaining butter in a large frying pan. Season the liver, and fry with
the sliced sage leaves for about 3–5 minutes, turning once.

Remove from the pan and serve at once with the Madeira sauce. Garnish with
sprigs of fresh sage.

Calf's Liver with Sautéed Apples
Thinly slice and core two medium-sized cooking apples. Proceed as in the recipe
above, substituting apple slices for the green grapes and brandy for the Madeira.
If fresh sage is unavailable, substitute parsley.

INGREDIENTS
50 g (2 oz) butter
*50 g (2 oz) onion or shallot,
    finely chopped*
*175 ml (6 fl oz) chicken stock
    (see page 247)*
100 ml (4 fl oz) Madeira
salt and pepper
*24 large green grapes, skinned,
    halved and seeds removed*
*4 slices calf's liver—about
    75–100 g (3–4 oz) each,
    trimmed*
4 fresh sage leaves, thinly sliced
4 sprigs sage leaves, for garnish

CHICKEN BREASTS WITH MANGOES AND ALMONDS

*The flavour of mango is most agreeable with beef and chicken dishes,
both hot and cold, for pickles and chutneys, and a wide range of desserts.*

Serves 4

INGREDIENTS

3 chicken breasts, skinned, boned
    and cut into 2.5 cm (1 inch)
    squares
300 ml (½ pint) groundnut oil
7.5 ml (1½ tsp) chopped fresh root
    ginger
1 large garlic clove, finely
    chopped
2 large spring onions, white
    part finely chopped and green
    part cut into 2.5 cm (1 inch)
    pieces
2 large mangoes, peeled and cut
    lengthways into strips
MARINADE
15 ml (1 tbsp) cornflour
1 egg white, beaten
5 ml (1 tsp) light soy sauce
5 ml (1 tsp) shaohsing wine or
    medium dry sherry
SAUCE
15 ml (1 tbsp) light soy sauce
30 ml (2 tbsp) shaohsing wine or
    medium dry sherry
5 ml (1 tsp) sugar
5 ml (1 tsp) cornflour
50 g (2 oz) slivered almonds,
    toasted
spring onion tassels, to garnish

Mix the ingredients for the marinade together and pour it over the chicken. Cover and marinate in the refrigerator for 30 minutes.

Heat a wok over high heat, then add the oil. When the oil is hot enough for a piece of ginger to sizzle and float to the surface, add the chicken and marinade, and stir-fry for 30 seconds. Place a sieve over a bowl, and pour the chicken and all of the oil into it. Leave to drain thoroughly, then return 30 ml (2 tbsp) of the oil to the wok. Stir-fry the ginger, garlic and white spring onion for 30 seconds. Return the chicken to the wok and stir-fry for 1 minute. Transfer the chicken to a serving dish.

Pour 15 ml (1 tbsp) of the oil into the wok, heat and add the mango. Stir-fry for 30 seconds, then add all the sauce ingredients except the almonds and onion tassels. Cook for a further 30 seconds or until the sauce thickens.

Stir in the green spring onion and the toasted almonds. Pour over the chicken. Garnish with the spring onion tassels.

KUMQUATS POACHED IN ROSE WATER

*Kumquats resemble tiny, olive-shaped oranges. Their skin is sweet,
but the flesh is sharp. This sharpness counteracts the sweetness of the prunes,
apricots and honey in this compôte.*

Serves 6–8

INGREDIENTS
225 g (8 oz) prunes
225 g (8 oz) dried apricots
100 g (4 oz) kumquats, sliced
    with pips removed
juice of 2 oranges
45 ml (3 tbsp) clear honey
15 ml (1 tbsp) rose water

Place the prunes and apricots in a bowl with sufficient water to cover them by 1 cm (½ inch). Leave to soak overnight.

Place the prunes and apricots, with the water they were soaking in, in a saucepan. Bring to the boil and simmer for 10 minutes, then add the kumquats, orange juice and honey. Simmer for a further 10 minutes. Add the rose water, remove the pan from the heat and pour into a serving bowl. Serve hot or cold.

LYCHEE AND MELON BASKET WITH GINGER CREAM

This dessert is attractive without appearing too contrived. The flavours and colours blend beautifully. Should you wish to serve more than 4–6 people, double the recipe but make only one 'basket', slicing the excess fruit and arranging it around the basket.

Serves 4–6

INGREDIENTS

*1 large ripe green-skinned
   honeydew melon*

*225 g (8 oz) fresh lychees, peeled,
   and stoned*

GINGER CREAM

300 ml (½ pint) double cream

*45 ml (3 tbsp) chopped preserved
   ginger*

60 ml (4 tbsp) advocaat

finely grated rind of 1 lemon

Lay the melon on its side. Cut a small slice from the base so that it will sit securely on the dish. Insert a sharp knife just above where the stalk was and cut lengthways, almost to the centre. Leave a space of 2.5 cm (1 inch) of the melon uncut, and continue cutting lengthways to the end of the melon. Repeat on the other side. Make the melon handle by cutting across the melon leaving 2.5 cm (1 inch) uncut across the centre. Remove the two end wedges of melon. Cut away the flesh about 1 cm (½ inch) from the rind, inside the handle. Cut the flesh into cubes or balls and reserve.

Scoop out the flesh of the melon with a melon baller or cut into cubes. Cut the edge of the basket into a scallop pattern.

Pile the melon and lychees into the basket and place on a serving dish.

To make the ginger cream, lightly whip the cream, then gradually stir in the remaining ingredients until they are all well mixed. Spoon into a bowl and serve with the melon basket.

SPARKLING MELON AND LIME SOUP

*A light, refreshing dessert to serve on a hot summer evening. Use either Galia,
Ogen, Honeydew or Charentais melons.*

Serves 4

Dissolve the sugar in the water over gentle heat. Add the lime rind, bring to the boil, then simmer for 2–3 minutes. When cold, strain the syrup into a liquidizer goblet. Add the lime juice and melon and purée until smooth. Chill until required.

Just before serving stir in the champagne and garnish with the prepared fruit and leaves.

INGREDIENTS
50 g (2 oz) granulated sugar
150 ml (¼ pint) water
pared rind and juice of 1 lime
350 g (12 oz) melon flesh, diced
*90 ml (6 tbsp) champagne or
   sparkling white wine, chilled*
julienne strips of mango, to garnish
*fresh raspberries, or strawberry
   slices, to garnish*
*tiny mint sprigs, scented geranium
   or lemon balm leaves, to garnish*

MANGO AND PAPAYA PARFAIT

*This is an elegant dessert made with fresh mango and papaya,
two of the Caribbean's most mouthwatering fruits.*

Serves 6–8

Press the mango and papaya flesh through a sieve or purée in a blender or food processor. Stir in the lemon juice.

Place the egg yolks and sugar in a bowl over a pan of hot water. Whisk for about 5 minutes, or until the mixture is pale, light and thick. Remove the bowl from the heat and continue whisking for a further 2 minutes.

Whip the cream until stiff. Fold the fruit purée into the egg yolk mixture and then add the cream. Mix until evenly blended. Pour into a rigid plastic container and freeze for 3 hours or until firm. Alternatively, freeze the parfait in a decorative mould. Dip the mould in very hot water for about 30 seconds before turning out.

INGREDIENTS
*1 small ripe mango, peeled,
   stoned and roughly chopped*
*1 ripe papaya, peeled, seeded and
   roughly chopped*
15 ml (1 tbsp) lemon juice
4 egg yolks
100 g (4 oz) icing sugar
200 ml (7 fl oz) double cream

MELON AND STRAWBERRIES WITH CHAMPAGNE

*This is a perfect dessert for a picnic. The preparation is minimal,
and the melon halves form individual serving dishes.
Use strawberries, raspberries, seedless grapes and cherries to fill the centre of the melon.*

Serves 4

Cut the melons in half and scrape out the seeds.

Hull the strawberries and place in each melon half. Sprinkle the sugar over the fruit if wished, and pour about 50 ml (2 fl oz) champagne over each serving. Eat at once, served with the remaining champagne.

INGREDIENTS
2 Charentais or Ogen melons
*500 g (1 lb) strawberries, or other
   fruit*
*20 ml (4 tsp) caster sugar
   (optional)*
*700 ml (1¼ pints) champagne or
   sparkling dry white wine*

LYCHEE AND MELON BASKET WITH GINGER CREAM

PORTWINE JELLY WITH FROSTED GRAPES

*This clear shimmering jelly, served with sparkling frosted grapes, is both light
and refreshing. To ensure a cloudless jelly, allow the liquid to drip through the muslin
in its own time—one squeeze will result in a murky mixture.*

Serves 6–8

INGREDIENTS

pared rind of 4 lemons
300 ml (½ pint) lemon juice
900 ml (1½ pints) water
275 g (10 oz) caster sugar
150 ml (¼ pint) port
*50 g (2 oz) powdered gelatine,
    dissolved in 180 ml (6 fl oz)
    hot water*
4 egg whites
4 egg shells, crushed
*375 g (12 oz) black and green
    grapes*

Place the lemon rind, juice, water, 225 g (8 oz) sugar and port in a saucepan and stir well. Place the pan over a gentle heat and stir until the sugar dissolves. Stir in the gelatine.

Beat three egg whites until frothy, then add the egg shells to the egg whites and gently whisk them into the jelly mixture. Continue whisking, until the mixture comes to the boil.

Stop whisking as the foam begins to rise and remove the pan from the heat. Return the pan to the heat and repeat this procedure twice, allowing the foam to rise and fall without any further whisking. Cool for 10 minutes.

Place a sieve lined with a double thickness of muslin over a large bowl. Slowly pour the jelly into the sieve, allowing the foam to fall in last. Set the sieve over another bowl and slowly pour the strained jelly on to the egg shells and whites. Leave the mixture to seep through. Gently remove the sieve and pour the jelly into a dampened 1.2 litre (2 pint) mould. Leave overnight in a cool place to set.

To frost the grapes, wash and dry them, and cut into clusters. Beat the remaining egg white lightly with a fork, but do not allow it to foam. Put the remaining sugar into a shallow bowl, or on to a sheet of greaseproof paper. Paint the grapes with egg white using a small brush and roll them in the sugar. Allow to dry.

To serve, dip the mould up to the rim in hot water for 5 seconds, then place a plate upside down over the mould. Invert the two, giving them a good shake. Lift off the mould and decorate with the frosted grapes.

GINGER WATER-ICE

*The flavour of this water-ice is reminiscent of the ginger beer sold in stone
bottles years ago. For those who loathe ginger, follow the recipe,
omitting the ginger, and you will have a refreshing lemon water-ice.*

Makes 600 ml (1 pint)

INGREDIENTS

225 g (8 oz) sugar
450 ml (¾ pint) water
175 ml (6 fl oz) lemon juice
*75 g (3 oz) preserved stem ginger,
    very finely chopped*

Dissolve the sugar in the water over gentle heat, stirring frequently. Increase the heat and boil for 5 minutes. Remove the syrup from the heat and allow to cool.

Stir in the lemon juice and the stem ginger. Set the freezer to its coldest setting. Pour the syrup into a shallow container and freeze until it starts to freeze around the edges. Turn into a chilled bowl and beat to remove the ice crystals. Return to the freezer and freeze until solid.

Remove from the freezer 15 minutes before serving, to soften.

GRAPE TARTLETS

*These elegant tartlets are decorated with black and green grapes and glazed
with lemon marmalade and brandy.*

Makes 12

INGREDIENTS

*pâte sucrée made with 175 g (6 oz)
plain flour (see page 248)*
1 large egg, beaten
40 g (1½ oz) caster sugar
75 ml (3 fl oz) double cream
75 g (3 oz) ground almonds
*finely grated rind and juice of
½ large lemon*
few drops of almond essence
*45 ml (3 tbsp) lemon marmalade,
sieved*
15 ml (1 tbsp) brandy
15 ml (1 tbsp) water
*225 g (8 oz) grapes, peeled, halved
and pips removed*

Roll the pâte sucrée out very thinly on a lightly floured surface with a lightly
floured rolling pin. Cut out 12 × 6 cm (2½ inch) circles with a round cutter and use
to line 12 tartlet tins. Prick the base of each tartlet lightly, then cover and chill for
at least 30 minutes.

Bake blind at 200°C (400°F) mark 6 for about 8–10 minutes or until the pastry
has set and is lightly coloured.

Meanwhile, lightly beat together the egg, sugar, cream, ground almonds,
lemon rind and juice, and almond essence. Divide equally between the tartlet
cases. Reduce the oven temperature to 180°C (350°F) mark 4 and bake for about
10 minutes or until the filling is lightly set and coloured. Cool slightly then
carefully transfer the tartlets to a wire rack to cool completely.

Gently heat the marmalade with the brandy, and the water if necessary, until
the marmalade has melted. Leave to cool. Arrange the grapes in the tartlet cases,
then carefully spoon over the marmalade glaze. Serve cold.

PEARS POACHED WITH QUINCE IN CASSIS

Serve with lightly whipped cream and almond tuiles.

Serves 4

INGREDIENTS

500 ml (18 fl oz) dry white wine
75 ml (3 fl oz) crème de cassis
½ cinnamon stick
40 g (1.5 oz) sugar, to taste
2 quinces
4 firm but ripe pears

Mix the wine, crème de cassis, cinnamon stick and sugar together in a saucepan
that will just fit the pears when standing upright. Heat to simmering point.

Peel, core and slice the quinces and put into the pan. Peel the pears and stand
them upright in the pan. Cover and poach about 20 minutes until the pears are
just tender.

Leave the pears to cool in the liquid then remove them with a slotted spoon.
Cover and chill them.

Remove the cinnamon stick from the liquid then purée in a blender or food
processor. Cover and leave in the refrigerator for ar least 2 hours to allow the
flavour to mature. Adjust the sweetness with caster sugar, if necessary, just
before serving.

Leave the pears at room temperature for about 15 minutes before serving on
cold plates with some of the purée spooned to the side.

SOUTH PACIFIC SORBET

SOUTH PACIFIC SORBET

*A delectable trio of tropical fruit sorbets which can be served on
individual plates or arranged into a pyramid shape with alternating colours.*

Serves 12–14

Place the mango purée, kiwi fruit purée and the pineapple juice in 3 separate bowls.

To make the sugar syrups, place the water in 3 separate saucepans, add the respective amounts of sugar, stir until dissolved, then boil for 5 minutes. Cool the syrups, then add to their respective purées and juice.

Add the lemon juice and rind to the kiwi sorbet and the orange flower water to the pineapple sorbet.

Pour the mixtures into separate shallow containers and freeze for $2\frac{1}{2}$ hours. Remove from the freezer, turn into chilled bowls and beat to break up the ice crystals. Return to the freezer, and leave until frozen.

To serve, remove from the freezer, and allow to soften for 30 minutes at room temperature. Place scoops of sorbet on to baking trays and place in the freezer for 30 minutes to harden. Arrange in a pyramid or on individual serving plates and decorate with mint or fruit if wished.

Note

Due to the varying acidity of each fruit a different concentration of sugar syrup is required for each one to ensure a smooth texture and a complementary balance of flavours.

INGREDIENTS

MANGO SORBET

*2 ripe mangoes, peeled, stoned
and puréed*
300 ml ($\frac{1}{2}$ pint) water
150 g (5 oz) sugar

KIWI FRUIT SORBET

4 kiwi fruits, peeled and puréed
450 ml ($\frac{3}{4}$ pint) water
225 g (8 oz) sugar
*juice and finely grated rind
of 1 lemon*

PINEAPPLE SORBET

450 ml ($\frac{3}{4}$ pint) pineapple juice
5 ml (1 tsp) orange flower water
150 ml ($\frac{1}{4}$ pint) water
100 g (4 oz) sugar

GOOSEBERRY ICE CREAM IN BRANDY SNAP CASES

*The rich smoothness of the ice cream is complemented by the crunchy texture
of the brandy snap cases.*

Serves 8

Place the gooseberries, sugar, orange rind and water in a saucepan, cover and poach over low heat until they are soft. Remove the orange rind, then rub the gooseberry mixture through a sieve. Leave to cool, cover and place in the refrigerator for about 1 hour. Add a few drops of green colouring if necessary.

Lightly whip the cream then fold into the mixture. Pour into a shallow container, cover and freeze for 45 minutes. Tip the gooseberry mixture into a chilled bowl and beat to break down the ice crystals. Return to the container, cover and repeat once more. Return to the container and leave until frozen.

Meanwhile, to make the brandy snaps, gently heat the syrup, butter and sugar together, stirring occasionally until the sugar has dissolved. Remove from the heat and stir in the remaining brandy snap ingredients. Drop about 45 ml (3 tbsp) of the mixture on to a lightly greased baking tray, leaving plenty of room for the mixture to spread. Bake at 180°C (350°F) mark 4 for 7–10 minutes until golden brown. Quickly but carefully remove the cooked mixture with a fish slice and while still hot, mould it around the base of an oiled orange, large apple or small bowl or dish. Leave to set. Remove the mould and leave the baskets to cool on a wire rack. Bake and shape the remaining mixture in the same way.

About 30 minutes before serving, transfer the ice cream to the main part of the refrigerator. Scoop the ice cream into the baskets and decorate with shreds of orange rind.

INGREDIENTS
1 kg (2 lb) gooseberries
175 g (6 oz) caster sugar
2 long strips pared orange rind,
  plus extra for decoration
45 ml (3 tbsp) water
few drops green food colouring
  (optional)
450 ml (¾ pint) double or whipping
  cream, chilled
shredded orange rind for
  decorating
BRANDY SNAP CASES
40 g (1½ oz) golden syrup
40 g (1½ oz) butter
90 g (3½ oz) caster sugar
40 g (1½ oz) plain flour
4 ml (¾ tsp) ground ginger
2.5 ml (½ tsp) finely grated orange
  rind
1.25 ml (¼ tsp) orange juice

ORANGE CURACAO ICE CREAM

*A perfect dessert for a dinner party. It is made beforehand, and served either in glass
dishes, or orange shells. Garnish with spirals of orange rind and serve with
langue-de-chat biscuits or brandy snaps.*

Makes about 600 ml (1 pint)

Beat the egg yolks with the sugar until pale. Gradually beat in the orange rind and juice, and the Curaçao, then mix in the cream. Set the freezer at the lowest setting.

Place the mixture in a shallow container and freeze until the ice-cream begins to set around the edges. Turn it into a chilled bowl and beat to break up the ice crystals until smooth. Return it to the shallow container and freeze until firm. If a smoother ice cream is preferred, repeat the beating and freezing process once or twice more. Remove from the freezer about 15 minutes before serving to soften slightly.

INGREDIENTS
5 egg yolks
175 g (6 oz) sugar
finely grated rind and juice
  of 2 oranges
30–45 ml (2–3 tbsp)
  orange Curaçao or Grand
  Marnier
300 ml (½ pint) double cream,
  lightly whipped

DESSERTS, CAKES AND BREADS

DESSERTS

— ◆ —

With their tempting arrays of tarts, cheesecakes, Apfel Strudel,
flans and mousses, Harrods never fails to provide a delicious dessert
for an impromptu dinner party. Far more enjoyable to make yourself,
puddings are always popular, and who could resist Hazelnut and
Passion Fruit Roulade, Crème Brulée avec Cerises,
or Grand Marnier Mousse with Chocolate Crust?

CHOCOLATE-SHERRY CHEESECAKE

The extra flavour of sherry makes this an out of the ordinary cheesecake.
It can be made a day in advance and served chilled.

Serves 10–12

INGREDIENTS

150 g (5 oz) butter
45 ml (3 tbsp) golden syrup
225 g (8 oz) digestive biscuits
50 g (2 oz) plain chocolate
few drops of vanilla essence
500 g (1 lb) cream cheese
3 eggs, separated
225 g (8 oz) caster sugar
30 ml (2 tbsp) sherry
30 ml (2 tbsp) powdered gelatine
300 ml (½ pint) double cream

Place 100 g (4 oz) of the butter and 30 ml (2 tbsp) syrup in a pan and heat until the butter has melted. Crush the biscuits; stir in and mix well. Press the mixture into a greased 25 cm (10 inch) springform tin. Chill.

Melt the chocolate with the remaining butter, remaining syrup and vanilla essence in a bowl placed over a pan of hot water. Stir occasionally until melted and glossy.

Beat the cream cheese until smooth, then beat in the egg yolks, sugar and sherry. Sprinkle the gelatine over 6 ml (4 tbsp) cold water and leave to soften for 2 minutes. Stand in a pan of hot water and stir until dissolved. Cool slightly.

Whisk the egg whites until stiff. Whip the cream until it just holds its shape. Stir the cooled gelatine into the cream cheese mixture in a steady stream. Fold in the cream and egg whites.

Pour the mixture into the lined tin. Quickly drizzle the chocolate sauce over the top and swirl with a skewer. Chill until set.

FRESH DATE AND BANANA PUDDING

There is no added sweetener in this dessert as the natural fruit sugar
in the dates and bananas is sufficient.

Serves 8

INGREDIENTS

750 g (1½ lb) fresh dates, weighed
  before stoning
3 large bananas, peeled and sliced
300 ml (½ pint) double cream
finely grated rind of 1 orange
45 ml (3 tbsp) orange juice
30 ml (2 tbsp) orange flower
  water
banana slices, dates and slices of
  orange, to decorate

Skin, stone and halve the dates, then arrange half of them in a serving dish. Place the sliced bananas on top of the dates, then cover with the remaining dates.

Pour the cream into a bowl and gradually stir in the orange rind, juice and flower water, stirring constantly to prevent the cream from separating. Pour the flavoured cream evenly over the layers of fruit and leave in a cool place for at least 30 minutes for the flavours to develop. Decorate with fruit before serving.

CRÈME BRULEE AVEC CERISES

CRÈME BRULEE AVEC CERISES

*This is a crème brûlée with a fruity variation; once the caramel topping has been
cracked open to reveal the velvety cream, a layer of dark cherries in
kirsch can be found underneath.*

Serves 6

Place the cherries, 150 ml (¼ pint) water and the caster sugar in a pan over
moderate heat. Stir to dissolve the sugar, bring to the boil, then reduce the heat
and simmer for 3 minutes. Mix the arrowroot with 10 ml (2 tsp) cold water and
stir it into the cherries. Simmer for 2 minutes, stirring occasionally. Pour the
cherries into a shallow, ovenproof serving dish, or individual ramekins and leave
to cool. Stir in the kirsch.

Meanwhile, scald the cream. Mix the egg yolks with the vanilla sugar, then
gradually whisk in the hot cream. Strain the mixture into a saucepan. Cook over
very gentle heat, stirring constantly, for 10 minutes, or until the mixture coats the
back of the spoon. Do not boil or it will curdle. Cover the cream with a circle of
greaseproof paper and leave until cool and thickened. When cool, remove the
paper and spoon it over the cherries, making sure that they are covered
completely. Cover with clingfilm and chill for 3 hours or overnight until firm.

Sprinkle the caster sugar over the surface. Cook under a hot grill until the sugar
melts, bubbles and darkens slightly. Cool, then chill.

INGREDIENTS
*350 g (12 oz) dark cherries, stoned
    weight*
water
50 g (2 oz) caster sugar
10 ml (2 tsp) arrowroot
30 ml (2 tbsp) kirsch
600 ml (1 pint) double cream
5 egg yolks
30 ml (2 tbsp) vanilla sugar
50 g (2 oz) caster sugar

RAINBOW SOUFFLE

*Raspberries and pistachio nuts add colour as well as an interesting taste
to this creamy soufflé. This is an ideal dessert to serve for any festive occasion.*

Serves 6–8

INGREDIENTS

6 eggs, separated
225 g (8 oz) caster sugar
25 g (1 oz) powdered gelatine
60 ml (4 tbsp) cold water
450 ml (¾ pint) double cream
10 ml (2 tsp) vanilla essence
150 ml (¼ pint) raspberry purée
50 g (2 oz) pistachio nuts,
  pounded in a mortar
few drops of green food colouring

DECORATION

100 g (4 oz) plain chocolate
rose leaves
300 ml (½ pint) double cream,
  stiffly whipped
additional chopped pistachio nuts

Whisk the egg yolks and sugar in a bowl placed over hot water for 10 minutes or until pale and thick and the mixture just holds the trail of a whisk. Remove the pan from the heat and whisk for a further 2 minutes.

Sprinkle the gelatine over the water in a bowl and leave to soften for 2 minutes. Stand in a pan of hot water and stir until dissolved. Cool slightly then gradually stir it into the egg mixture.

Whip the cream until it just holds its shape then fold it into the egg mixture. Divide the mixture evenly between three bowls.

Stir the vanilla into one bowl of mixture, the raspberry purée into another, and the pistachios and a little green food colouring into the third. Whisk the egg whites until stiff. Divide between the bowls and fold in carefully.

Pour the raspberry mixture into a 1.5 litre (3 pint) glass soufflé dish with a wide strip of greaseproof paper tied around the edge and secured with string. Place in the fridge for about 10 minutes or until lightly set. Pour the vanilla soufflé mixture over the top and chill again. Finally, pour over the pistachio mixture and chill for about 4 hours until firm.

Meanwhile, make the decoration. Melt the chocolate and paint the underside of the rose leaves with the chocolate. Leave to set, then carefully remove the leaves. Fill a piping bag fitted with a star nozzle with the cream. Carefully peel off the paper from the soufflé. Decorate around the top edge with whirls of cream and chopped pistachio nuts.

CHOCOLATE SNOWBALL

*This luscious dessert should be left for at least 24 hours before eating.
The outer layer forms a crust while the centre remains a soft fudge.*

Serves 4–6

INGREDIENTS

100 g (4 oz) plain chocolate
5 ml (1 tsp) instant coffee
45 ml (3 tbsp) boiling water
100 g (4 oz) caster sugar
100 g (4 oz) unsalted butter, diced
2 large eggs
15 ml (1 tbsp) dark rum
225 ml (8 fl oz) double cream
crystallized rose petals and violet
  petals, to decorate (optional)

Break up the chocolate and place it in a saucepan. Dissolve the coffee in the water and add it to the pan with the sugar. Heat gently until the chocolate has melted. Transfer the chocolate mixture to a bowl and beat well with an electric hand-held mixer or a balloon whisk. Slowly whisk in the butter until evenly combined, then whisk in the eggs one at a time. Stir in the rum.

Pour the mixture into a 750 ml (1¼ pint) basin lined with aluminium foil. Bake at 180°C (350°F) mark 4 for about 40 minutes or until risen and firm, but still slightly wobbly like a soufflé, with a thick, cracked crust.

Leave to cool at room temperature then press down with your fingertips to level the surface. Cover and chill for at least 24 hours. Unmould on to a serving plate.

Whip the cream until it holds its shape. Fill a piping bag fitted with a star nozzle and pipe rosettes on the pudding until it is completely covered. Decorate with a sprinkling of crystallized petals if wished.

CLEMENTINE CHARLOTTE MALAKOFF

CLEMENTINE CHARLOTTE MALAKOFF

A tempting dessert flavoured with clementines and orange liqueur.
The final result looks as spectacular as it tastes.

Serves 6—8

Mix half the Grand Marnier with the water. Quickly dip the sponge fingers in the liquid then line the base and sides of a 900 ml (1½ pint) charlotte mould, trimming to fit.

Roughly chop 3 of the clementines and reserve the fourth clementine for decoration.

Beat the butter and sugar together until pale, light and fluffy. Beat in the remaining liqueur and the ground almonds.

Whip 300 ml (½ pint) of the cream until it just holds its shape, then fold it into the creamed mixture with the chopped clementines. Pour this mixture into the mould and smooth the top. Chill for about 3 hours or until firm.

Whip the remaining cream until stiff and fill a piping bag fitted with a star nozzle. Turn the dessert out on to a serving plate. Pipe whirls of cream around the top and bottom edge of the dessert and decorate with the reserved clementine segments.

INGREDIENTS

60 ml (4 tbsp) Grand Marnier
30 ml (2 tbsp) water
20—24 sponge fingers
4 clementines, peeled and
  segmented
225 g (8 oz) unsalted butter,
  softened
225 g (8 oz) caster sugar
225 g (8 oz) ground almonds
450 ml (¾ pint) double cream

MERINGUE BASKET WITH SUMMER FRUITS

*Melt in-the-mouth meringue and luscious seasonal fruits make the
perfect light dessert for summer entertaining.*

Serves 6–8

INGREDIENTS

4 egg whites

225 g (8 oz) icing sugar

300 ml (½ pint) whipping cream

*30 ml (2 tbsp) kirsch or orange-
flavoured liqueur*

*225 g (8 oz) fruit, such as, grapes,
seeded; cherries, stoned;
strawberries and raspberries,
hulled; peaches, sliced*

Line three baking sheets with non-stick baking parchment (turn rimmed baking sheets upside down and use the bases), and draw a 19 cm (7½ inch) circle on each. Turn the paper over so that the pencilled circle is visible but does not come into contact with the meringues and mark them.

Put 3 egg whites in a clean, dry heatproof bowl, and place the bowl over a pan of simmering water. Sift in 175 g (6 oz) of the icing sugar.

Whisk the egg whites and sugar vigorously over the simmering water until the mixture stands in very stiff peaks. Do not allow the bowl to get too hot or the meringue will crust around edges.

Fit a piping bag with a large star nozzle. Spoon in one third of the meringue mixture. Secure the paper to the baking sheets with a little meringue.

Pipe a ring of meringue about 1 cm (½ inch) thick inside two of the circles on the paper. Fill the bag with the remaining meringue and, starting from centre, pipe a continuous coil of meringue on the third sheet of paper. Place all in the oven at 100°C (200°F) gas mark Low for 2½–3 hours to dry out.

Whisk the remaining egg white until stiff, then sift and fold in the remaining sugar. Put into the piping bag. Remove the cooked meringue rings from the paper and put one on top of the other on the base, piping a ring of fresh meringue between each. Return to the oven for a further 1½–2 hours. Slide on to a wire rack and peel off base paper when cool.

Just before serving, stand the meringue shell on a flat serving plate. Whisk the cream and liqueur until stiff then fold in the prepared fruit, reserving some pieces for decoration. Fill the basket with the cream and fruit mixture and decorate with the remaining pieces of fruit.

RUM SOUFFLE OMELETTE

*This fluffy soufflé omelette is delicious as a special treat for one or to round off
an intimate supper for two.*

Serves 1–2

INGREDIENTS

2 eggs, separated

5 ml (1 tsp) caster sugar

15 ml (1 tbsp) dark rum

15 g (½ oz) butter

*15 ml (1 tbsp) apricot jam,
warmed*

30 ml (2 tbsp) icing sugar

Put the egg yolks in a bowl with the caster sugar and rum. Mix well together. Whisk the egg whites in a clean dry bowl until they are stiff and standing in peaks.

Melt the butter in a heavy-based omelette pan until foaming. Fold the egg whites quickly into the egg yolk mixture, then pour into the foaming butter.

Cook over moderate heat for 2–3 minutes until the underside of the omelette is golden brown, then place the pan under a preheated hot grill and cook for a few minutes more until the top is golden brown.

Slide the omelette on to a sheet of aluminium foil placed on a warmed serving plate. Spread with the warmed jam, then tip the aluminium foil to fold over the omelette.

Sift the icing sugar thickly over the top of the omelette, then mark in a criss-cross pattern with hot metal skewers, if liked. Remove the aluminium foil and serve immediately.

GRAND MARNIER MOUSSE WITH CHOCOLATE CRUST

A rich orange mousse enclosed in a thin crust of chocolate. Great care is needed when turning out of the pan in order not to damage the chocolate band.

Serves 4—6

Melt the chocolate in a bowl placed over a pan of hot water. Pour it into an oiled 900 ml (1½ pint) charlotte mould and swirl evenly over the base and sides, spreading with a knife if necessary. Leave to set.

Place the orange rind and juice, egg yolks, caster sugar and Grand Marnier in a bowl over hot water. Whisk for about 10 minutes until pale and thick. Remove from the heat and whisk for a further 2 minutes.

Sprinkle the gelatine over the water and leave to soften for 2 minutes. Stand in a pan of hot water and stir until dissolved. Cool slightly, then fold it into the egg mixture.

Whisk the egg whites until stiff. Whip the cream until it just holds its shape. Using a metal spoon, fold the cream, then the egg whites into the egg mixture.

Pour into the lined mould and chill for about 3 hours or until set.

Just before serving, very carefully loosen the edge of the chocolate case with a sharp pointed knife and turn out on to a serving plate.

INGREDIENTS
175 g (6 oz) plain chocolate
finely grated rind and juice of
1 orange
2 eggs, separated
75 g (3 oz) caster sugar
30 ml (2 tbsp) Grand Marnier
10 ml (2 tsp) powdered gelatine
15 ml (1 tbsp) water
150 ml (¼ pint) double cream

APRICOT BAVARIAN CREAM

Bavarian creams are among the lightest and creamiest fruit desserts.
The apricot purée adds a delicate flavour.

Serves 6—8

Place the apricots in a small pan and cook in their soaking water to cover for about 25—30 minutes or until tender. Place the apricots in a blender or food processor and blend with sufficient cooking liquid to make a thick purée. Set aside to cool.

Whisk the egg yolks and 175 g (6 oz) of the sugar together in a bowl until thick. Whisk in the cornflour. Gradually whisk in the warm milk. Place the bowl over a pan of hot water and cook, stirring, until the custard coats the back of a wooden spoon. Remove from heat.

Pour the lemon juice into a bowl, sprinkle the gelatine over and leave to soften for 2 minutes. Stand the bowl in a pan of hot water and stir until dissolved. Stir into the hot custard with the apricot purée.

Whisk the egg whites until stiff then whisk in the remaining sugar. Fold them into the custard using a metal spoon. Chill until just beginning to set, stirring occasionally.

Whip the cream until it just holds its shape and fold it into the custard. Pour the mixture into a rinsed-out 1.5 litre (3 pint) metal mould and chill for at least 3 hours or until set.

To unmould, quickly dip the base of the mould into hot water. Run the tip of a sharp knife around the edge and turn out on to a serving plate.

INGREDIENTS
225 g (8 oz) dried apricots, soaked
overnight
5 eggs, separated
200 g (7 oz) caster sugar
10 ml (2 tsp) cornflour
450 ml (¾ pint) milk, scalded
15 g (½ oz) powdered gelatine
45 ml (3 tbsp) lemon juice
150 ml (¼ pint) double cream

COEURS A LA CREME

*This delicate dessert, ideally served with tiny wild strawberries,
derives its name from the heart-shaped dishes in which it is made.
The holes in the base of the dish allow the whey to drain away.*

Serves 6

INGREDIENTS

100 g (4 oz) ricotta, sieved
225 g (8 oz) cream cheese
225 ml (8 fl oz) crème fraîche
30 ml (2 tbsp) vanilla sugar
30 ml (2 tbsp) caster sugar
*150 ml (¼ pint) double cream,
   lightly whipped*
100 g (4 oz) wild strawberries
strawberry leaves, to garnish
double cream, to serve

Mash the ricotta and cream cheese together. Stir in the crème fraîche, vanilla and caster sugars and fold in the whipped cream.

Rinse 12 pieces of muslin in water and wring out well. Line 6 heart-shaped coeur à la crème moulds with a double layer of muslin, pressing it well into the corners.

Spoon the cheese mixture into the lined moulds and place on a large plate to catch the liquid. Cover with clingfilm to avoid the dessert absorbing any odours or flavours from the fridge. Leave to drain overnight.

Discard the liquid on the plate. Invert the moulds on to individual serving plates and gently remove the muslin.

Arrange the strawberries around the hearts and serve with cream.

Hazelnut and Passion Fruit Roulade

*Roulades are much easier to make than they look, the important factor being
to allow yourself enough time for the rolling. Passion fruit adds an
exotic taste to this luscious dessert.*

Serves 6

Whisk the egg yolks and sugar in a bowl over hot water for 10 minutes or until pale and thick. Remove from the heat and whisk for a further 2 minutes.

Whisk the egg whites until stiff, then gradually whisk in the golden syrup. Fold the egg whites into the egg yolk and sugar mixture, then fold in the ground hazelnuts. Pour the mixture into a greased and lined 33 × 23 cm (13 × 9 inch) Swiss roll tin. Shake the tin to level the mixture. Bake at 180°C (350°F) mark 4 for 12–15 minutes, until firm to the touch. Cover with aluminium foil and leave to cool in the tin.

Cut the passion fruit in half and scoop out the seeds. Whip the cream until stiff then fold in the passion fruit seeds.

Dust a sheet of greaseproof paper with icing sugar. Turn the cooked cake out on to the paper and carefully remove the lining paper. Spread with the cream and roll up from one short edge, using the greaseproof paper to lift the cake. Carefully transfer to a serving plate and dust with more icing sugar.

INGREDIENTS

5 eggs, separated
175 g (6 oz) caster sugar
30 ml (2 tbsp) golden syrup
75 g (3 oz) ground hazelnuts
3 passion fruit
300 ml ($\frac{1}{2}$ pint) double cream
icing sugar, sifted, to decorate

(Left) COEURS A LA CREME
HAZELNUT AND PASSION
FRUIT ROULADE *(Below)*

SPICED FIG AND GINGER PUDDING

*This spicy pudding is a possible alternative to traditional Christmas pudding.
Served with rum butter and decorated with holly, it looks and tastes seasonal.*

Serves 8

INGREDIENTS

75 g (3 oz) plain flour
5 ml (1 tsp) baking powder
100 g (4 oz) grated beef suet
150 g (5 oz) fine fresh breadcrumbs
175 g (6 oz) dried figs, chopped
175 g (6 oz) dried dates, chopped
75 g (3 oz) stoned raisins
50 g (2 oz) mixed candied peel
50 g (2 oz) preserved stem ginger,
*   finely chopped*
5 ml (1 tsp) mixed ground spice
large pinch of grated nutmeg
finely grated rind and juice of
*   1 orange*
2 eggs, lightly beaten
45 ml (3 tbsp) dark rum
RUM BUTTER
100 g (4 oz) unsalted butter
100 g (4 oz) soft light brown sugar
finely grated rind of ½ an orange
45–60 ml (3–4 tbsp) dark rum

Sift the flour and baking powder into a large bowl. Stir in the suet, breadcrumbs, dried fruits, ginger and spices. Add the orange rind and juice, the eggs and rum, and mix well. Spoon the mixture into a 1.2 litre (2 pint) pudding basin. Cover with pleated greaseproof paper and aluminium foil, then tie string around the rim of the basin to secure the cover.

Place a trivet in a heavy-based saucepan, lower the pudding into the pan and pour in enough boiling water to come two-thirds of the way up the sides of the basin. Cover and steam over gentle heat for 4 hours, topping up with more boiling water if necessary.

To make the rum butter, cream the butter and sugar until pale, light and fluffy. Beat in the orange rind. Gradually beat in the rum. Chill until required.

Turn the pudding out on to a serving dish and serve hot, with the rum butter.

RHUBARB AND ORANGE CRUMBLE

*A traditional English pudding, that is delicious served warm or cold
with cream or custard.*

Serves 6

INGREDIENTS

800 g (1¾ lb) rhubarb, trimmed
*   and chopped*
juice of ½ orange
finely grated rind of 1 orange
75 g (3 oz) Demerera sugar
25 g (1 oz) preserved stem ginger,
*   finely chopped (optional)*
TOPPING
100 g (4 oz) plain flour
100 g (4 oz) wholemeal flour
5 ml (1 tsp) baking powder
100 g (4 oz) Demerera sugar
75 g (3 oz) blanched almonds,
*   coarsely chopped*
100 g (4 oz) butter

Bring the rhubarb, orange juice and rind and sugar to the boil in a saucepan. Cover and simmer for 15 minutes. Cool slightly and stir in the ginger. Pour the mixture into a 1.5 litre (3 pint) dish.

To make the topping, sift the flours and baking powder together. Tip any bran from the sieve back into the bowl. Add the sugar and almonds and mix well.

Rub the butter into the flour until the mixture resembles breadcrumbs then spread it over the fruit. Bake at 180°C (350°F) mark 4 for 35–40 minutes, or until the crumble is golden and crisp.

SUMMER FRUITS IN A BLACKCURRANT RING

*In this dessert, whole strawberries, raspberries and cherries are set in blackcurrant jelly
in a ring mould, with fresh fruit piled into the centre.*

Serves 8–10

Bring the blackcurrants and 150 ml ($\frac{1}{4}$ pint) water to the boil, reduce the heat and
simmer, covered, for 10 minutes. Remove from the heat and rub the fruit through
a fine nylon sieve. Pour the purée into a measuring jug and add sufficient cold
water to make the purée up to 600 ml (1 pint).

Return the purée to the pan and stir in the sugar. Stir over gentle heat to
dissolve the sugar, then bring it to the boil. Remove from the heat and add the
strawberries, raspberries and cherries. Pour the hot water into a small bowl and
sprinkle over the gelatine. Leave to soften for 2 minutes, then place the bowl in a
pan of hot water and stir the gelatine until dissolved. Stir it into the jelly and set
aside to cool.

Pour the jelly into a 1.4 litre (2$\frac{1}{2}$ pint) rinsed-out ring mould. Leave to set
overnight. Unmould on to a serving dish and pile the fruit for decoration into the
centre.

If available, arrange blackcurrant leaves under the jelly and a few bunches of
blackcurrants outside the ring.

INGREDIENTS
500 g (1 lb) blackcurrants
150 g (5 oz) caster sugar
225 g (8 oz) strawberries, hulled
225 g (8 oz) raspberries
*225 g (8 oz) black cherries, stoned
weight*
100 ml (4 fl oz) hot water
40 ml (8 tsp) powdered gelatine
DECORATION
*225 g (8 oz) strawberries
with their leaves*
225 g (8 oz) black cherries, stoned
225 g (8 oz) raspberries
*small bunches fresh blackcurrants
(optional)*
blackcurrant leaves (optional)

BISCUITS AND CAKES

—◆—

Everything stops for tea, and no-one takes their tea more seriously than the British, which is probably why Harrods stocks such a varied selection of cakes and biscuits. Traditional Madeira and Dundee cakes are four o'clock favourites, while Florentines and Orange and Hazelnut Vacherin are irresistible alternatives.

SIMNEL CAKE

Simnel cake is traditionally served on Easter Sunday, the eleven balls of marzipan representing the eleven faithful disciples. The centre of the cake may be covered with glacé icing, if wished, then decorated with sugar or fabric flowers, Easter chicks and ribbon.

Makes one 20 cm (8 inch) cake

INGREDIENTS

225 g (8 oz) plain flour

50 g (2 oz) potato flour

5 ml (1 tsp) baking powder

2.5 ml (½ tsp) ground mixed spice

225 g (8 oz) currants

175 g (6 oz) sultanas

50 g (2 oz) raisins

75 g (3 oz) mixed candied peel

50 g (2 oz) glacé cherries, quartered

225 g (8 oz) butter, softened

225 g (8 oz) soft light brown sugar

4 eggs, plus 1 egg, beaten, to glaze

finely grated rind of 1 lemon

15–30 ml (1–2 tbsp) brandy

45 ml (3 tbsp) apricot jam,
 warmed and sieved

MARZIPAN

225 g (8 oz) ground almonds

100 g (4 oz) icing sugar, sifted

100 g (4 oz) caster sugar

1 egg yolk

15 ml (1 tbsp) lemon juice

15 ml (1 tbsp) orange flower water

2–3 drops vanilla essence

GLACE ICING

100 g (4 oz) icing sugar, sifted

15 ml (1 tbsp) warm water

5 ml (1 tsp) orange flower water

First make the marzipan. Mix the ground almonds, icing and caster sugar together. Add the remaining ingredients and mix to a smooth paste. Knead the marzipan lightly but do not over-work, or the almonds will become oily. Divide in half and shape into rounds. Wrap in a double layer of clingfilm and set aside.

Sift the plain and potato flour, baking powder and mixed spice together. In a separate bowl, mix together the dried fruits, peel, glacé cherries and 45 ml (3 tbsp) of the sifted flour.

Cream the butter and sugar together until pale, light and fluffy.

Roll out half the marzipan into a circle, just under 20 cm (8 inches) wide.

Add the eggs to the creamed butter, beating well after each addition. Add a little flour if the mixture starts to separate. Add the lemon rind and fold in the flour. Fold in the fruit mixture and stir in the brandy. Spoon half the mixture into a 20 cm (8 inch) round cake tin, double-lined with greaseproof paper. Place the layer of marzipan over the cake mixture, then spoon the remaining cake mixture on top, making a slight hollow in the centre.

Wrap the outside of the cake tin with a double layer of brown paper and secure with string. Bake at 170°C (325°F) mark 3 for 3 hours. Do not test the cake in the normal way with a skewer, as the marzipan layer tends to stick to it and gives the appearance of underdone cake mixture. Simply press the top of the cake with your fingers—it should feel firm. Cover the top of the cake with greaseproof paper if it becomes too brown. Leave to cool in the tin for 30 minutes, then turn out on to a wire rack to cool. Wrap in aluminium foil and leave the cake for 24 hours before decorating.

Divide the remaining marzipan in half. Roll out one half into a 20 cm (8 inch) circle to fit the top of the cake. Turn the cake over, trimming the base if necessary. Glaze the top with apricot jam and place the marzipan circle on top. Divide the remaining marzipan in half. Divide one half into 11 small balls and place on a baking tray. Divide the second half in half again and roll each half into strips, long enough to go around the top of the cake. Twist these strips together and press

180

SIMNEL CAKE

around the outer edge of the cake. Place a circle of greaseproof paper over the circle of marzipan. Brush the ring and marzipan balls with beaten egg. Place the cake under a hot grill, for 1—2 minutes, to brown the marzipan. Remove the paper carefully, then grill the marzipan balls until brown.

Make the glacé icing by sifting the icing sugar into a bowl and adding the water and orange flower water. Mix until smooth then pour immediately into the centre of the cake. Leave to set for 2—3 hours before placing the marzipan balls around the edge and adding any decorations. Tie a ribbon around the outside of the cake, if wished.

DUNDEE CAKE

Dundee cake originated in the city of Dundee in Scotland, also famous for its marmalade. Candied orange peel and orange rind are used in the making of this popular fruit cake, which is easily recognised by the circles of blanched almonds on the surface.

Makes one 20 cm (8 inch) cake

INGREDIENTS
225 g (8 oz) butter
grated rind of 1 lemon
grated rind of 1 orange
225 g (8 oz) caster sugar
150 g (5 oz) raisins
150 g (5 oz) currants
150 g (5 oz) sultanas
100 g (4 oz) mixed candied peel
300 g (11 oz) self-raising flour
pinch of salt
50 g (2 oz) ground almonds
4 eggs
30 ml (2 tbsp) brandy or dark rum
50 g (2 oz) blanched almonds, halved
25 ml (1 fl oz) milk

Cream the butter and gradually work in the citrus rind. Add the sugar and cream together until pale, light and fluffy. Place the raisins, currants, sultanas and mixed peel in a bowl. Sift the flour with the salt twice, and add 50 g (2 oz) of it to the dried fruits. Mix well to ensure that they are completely covered in flour.

Add the ground almonds to the butter and sugar, mix well, then gradually add the eggs one at a time, beating well after each addition. Gradually fold in half the remaining flour, then add the fruit little by little. Fold in the remaining flour, then add the brandy. Spoon the mixture into a greased and lined 20 cm (8 inch) round cake tin and smooth the surface. Dip the blanched almonds into the milk, then arrange them in circles on the top of the cake.

Bake on the centre shelf, at 170°C (325°F) mark 3, for 2–2½ hours. The cake is cooked when a small skewer inserted into the centre comes out clean. Cool in the tin for 10 minutes then turn out on to a wire rack and leave until cold.

CARAWAY SEED CAKE

Most Victorian English cookery books include a recipe for seed cake. This plain buttery cake, with a hint of caraway, is best eaten a day after baking. It keeps very well in an airtight tin.

Makes one 20 cm (8 inch) cake

INGREDIENTS
250 g (9 oz) butter
250 g (9 oz) caster sugar
125 g (4½ oz) potato flour
125 g (4½ oz) plain flour
5 ml (1 tsp) baking powder
4 eggs, size 2
5 ml (1 tsp) vanilla essence
15 ml (1 tbsp) brandy
15 ml (1 tbsp) caraway seeds

Cream the butter with half the sugar until pale, light and fluffy. Sift the potato flour, plain flour and the baking powder together. Gradually add 1 whole egg and 3 egg yolks to the creamed butter and sugar, beating well between each addition. Should the mixture start to separate, add a little flour. Stir in the vanilla essence and the brandy, then gradually fold in the sifted flour. Add the caraway seeds and mix lightly.

Whisk the egg whites until they hold stiff peaks. Gradually add the remaining sugar and whisk for another 30 seconds or until glossy. Gently fold the beaten egg whites into the cake mixture.

Pour the mixture into a greased and floured 20 cm (8 inch) round cake tin, and bake on the centre shelf at 180°C (350°F) mark 4 for 1 hour and 20 minutes. The cake is cooked when a small skewer inserted into the centre comes out clean. Cool in the tin for 10 minutes, then turn out on to a wire rack and leave until cold.

CROQUEMBOUCHE

This tower of tiny choux buns is the traditional wedding cake of France.
The buns are built up around a metal cone which is removed when they are set.
You could use a large conical strainer, or make your own with several thicknesses of foil.

Serves 18—20

Roll out the pastry to line an 18 cm (7 inch) fluted flan case. Prick the pastry and bake at 190°C (375°F) mark 5 for 20 minutes until golden brown. Cool on a wire rack. Fill a piping bag fitted with a small plain tube with the choux pastry mixture. Pipe small buns onto greased baking sheets, leaving space for spreading. You should have about 60—70 buns. Bake at 220°C (425°F) mark 7 for 15 minutes, then reduce the temperature to 190°C (375°F) mark 5 for a further 10—12 minutes, until the buns are puffy and golden brown. Make a small hole in the base of each bun and cool on a wire rack. Whip half the cream and fill the buns.

Place the sugar and water in a heavy based saucepan. Stir over a low heat until the sugar has dissolved. Add the cream of tartar, put in a sugar thermometer and boil steadily, without stirring, until it registers 150°C (300°F) or brittle strands will hang from a fork. Place the pan in hot water to stop further browning.

Oil the cone and place it on non-stick paper. Spear each bun on to a fine skewer and dip in the caramel. Build the buns up around the cone until it is completely covered. Pour over remaining caramel and leave to set. Carefully remove the cone from the buns and place on top of the pastry base. Whip half the remaining cream and pile in the centre of the pastry base with fresh fruit of your choice.

Spoon the remaining cream into a piping bag fitted with a star nozzle. Pipe rosettes at random between the buns and decorate with crystallised flowers or fruits.

INGREDIENTS
rich shortcrust pastry made with
   500 g (1 lb) flour (see page 248)
choux pastry made with 180 g
   (7 oz) flour (see page 249)
450 g (1 lb) cube sugar
200 ml (7 fl oz) water
2.5 ml ($\frac{1}{2}$ tsp) cream of tartar
600 ml (1 pint) double cream
450 g (1 lb) fresh fruit
DECORATIONS
small fruits or edible flowers tossed
   in egg white and caster sugar,
   or bought crystallised mimosa

VIENNESE FINGERS

These chocolate-coated biscuits are a teatime treat.

Makes about 18

INGREDIENTS
*125 g (4 oz) butter or block
    margarine*
25 g (1 oz) icing sugar
125 g (4 oz) plain flour
1.25 ml ($\frac{1}{4}$ tsp) baking powder
few drops of vanilla flavouring
50 g (2 oz) plain chocolate

Grease two baking sheets. Put the butter into a bowl and beat until pale and soft, then beat in the icing sugar. Sift in the flour and baking powder. Beat well, adding a few drops of vanilla flavouring.

Spoon into a piping bag fitted with a medium star nozzle and pipe finger shapes about 7.5 cm (3 inches) long on to the prepared baking sheets, allowing room between each for the mixture to spread. Bake at 190°C (375°F) mark 5 for 15–20 minutes until crisp and pale golden. Cool on a wire rack for 30 minutes.

When the fingers are cold, break the chocolate into a heatproof bowl. Stand the bowl over a pan of simmering water and stir until the chocolate has melted. Remove from the heat and dip both ends of the fingers into the melted chocolate. Leave on a wire rack for 30 minutes to set.

CHOCOLATE, ORANGE AND HAZELNUT VACHERIN

*This is the perfect dessert for a special occasion, as it looks and tastes wonderful,
and can be prepared in advance. The meringues may be made up to 2 weeks ahead
and stored in an airtight tin.*

Serves 8–10

INGREDIENTS
6 egg whites
350 g (12 oz) caster sugar
75 g (3 oz) plain chocolate
45 ml (3 tbsp) water
1.25 ml ($\frac{1}{4}$ tsp) instant coffee
900 ml (1$\frac{1}{2}$ pints) double cream
finely grated rind of 1 orange
15 ml (1 tbsp) Grand Marnier
15 ml (1 tbsp) fresh orange juice
HAZELNUT PRALINE
75 g (3 oz) hazelnuts
40 g (1$\frac{1}{2}$ oz) caster sugar
15 ml (1 tbsp) water
DECORATION
5 ml (1 tsp) icing sugar, sifted
8 hazelnuts
*thinly pared orange rind or
    chocolate caraque (optional)*

To make the meringues, whisk the egg whites until they are stiff but not dry. Whisk in the sugar, one tablespoon at a time, whisking well between each addition. Spoon the meringue into a large piping bag fitted with a 2.5 cm ($\frac{1}{2}$ in) plain nozzle. Pipe the meringue in a spiral pattern on to a baking sheet lined with non-stick silicone paper or oiled aluminium foil to form a 21.5 cm (8$\frac{1}{2}$ inch) circle. Pipe the remaining meringue on to 3 more sheets to make 4 circles. Bake at 140°C (275°F) mark 1 for 1$\frac{1}{2}$ hours.

Remove from the oven and allow to cool. Peel off the paper very carefully.

Meanwhile, make the praline. Place the hazelnuts on a baking sheet and roast at 190°C (375°F) mark 5 for 10 minutes or until they begin to colour slightly. Rub them in a tea towel to remove the skins.

Dissolve the sugar in the water over gentle heat, stirring frequently. Bring to the boil and boil gently for 5 minutes or until the syrup is a light golden colour. Stir in the hazelnuts. Immediately pour on to a lightly oiled baking tray lined with non-stick silicone paper and leave to cool. When the praline is cold, crush in a blender or food processor or with a rolling pin. Set aside.

Melt the chocolate with the water over gentle heat. Remove from the heat and stir in the instant coffee. Leave to cool.

Whip a quarter of the cream until it just holds its shape. Fill a piping bag fitted with a large star nozzle with the cream and chill.

Whisk the cream until stiff then stir one-third into the praline, half the remaining cream into the cooled chocolate mixture and the remaining cream into the orange rind, Grand Marnier and orange juice.

Place one layer of meringue on a serving dish and cover with the praline cream. Place the second layer on top and cover with the chocolate cream then put the third layer on top, cover with the orange cream and finally top with the fourth layer of meringue.

Sift the icing sugar over the top and pipe 8 rosettes with the cream around the edge. Lightly press a hazelnut into each of the rosettes. Sprinkle with orange rind or chocolate caraque, if desired.

CHOCOLATE GATEAU

This luscious gâteau consists of layers of light 'biscuit de Savoie' spread with chocolate ganache and 'wrapped' in a chocolate frill. Tia Maria or Grand Marnier can be used instead of the brandy, if preferred.

Makes one 24 cm (9½ inch) cake

INGREDIENTS

15 ml (1 tbsp) cocoa powder

65 g (2½ oz) potato flour

65 g (2½ oz) plain flour

225 g (8 oz) icing sugar, sifted, plus 2.5 ml (½ tsp)

6 eggs, separated

300 g (11 oz) plain chocolate

60 ml (4 tbsp) brandy

1.25 ml (¼ tsp) salt

5 ml (1 tsp) caster sugar mixed with 5 ml (1 tsp) plain flour

CHOCOLATE GANACHE

225 g (8 oz) plain chocolate

350 ml (12 fl oz) double cream

1.25 ml (¼ tsp) vanilla essence

Sift the cocoa, potato and plain flours together three times. Whisk 200 g (7 oz) of the icing sugar with the egg yolks until pale and thick enough to make a ribbon trail. Grate 75 g (3 oz) of the chocolate, then gradually fold it in with 30 ml (2 tbsp) of the brandy and sifted flours.

Whisk the egg whites and salt until stiff then whisk in the remaining icing sugar. Carefully fold the egg whites into the mixture a little at a time.

Grease and base-line a 24 cm (9½ inch) springform tin. Grease the paper, then dust the tin with the caster sugar and plain flour—this prevents a crisp 'crust' forming. Spoon the mixture into the tin and bake at 180°C (350°F) mark 4 for 50 minutes. The cake is cooked when a small skewer inserted into the centre comes out clean. Cool in the tin for 5 minutes then leave upside down on a wire rack.

When the cake is cold, peel off the paper and cut it into 3 equal layers. Brush with the remaining brandy.

To make the ganache, melt the chocolate in a bowl placed over a pan of simmering water. Remove from the heat and stir in the cream and vanilla essence. Whisk until the mixture cools and thickens. Sandwich the layers together with the ganache, then spread over the top and sides.

Cut out a strip of non-stick silicone paper long enough to wrap around the cake, and 4 cm (1½ inches) higher than the depth. Melt the remaining chocolate and spread 175 g (6 oz) over the paper strip with a palette knife, to the edge of one long side, making a straight edge for the base. Spread roughly to the corresponding edge. Spread the remaining melted chocolate on to the non-stick silicone paper to 3 mm (⅛ inch) thickness.

When the chocolate strip begins to cool, but before it has hardened, carefully wrap it around the gâteau with the uneven edge at the top. Press gently into place. Carefully pinch the chocolate above the cake into slight 'pleats' using the paper. Leave the chocolate to harden, then peel away the paper. Scrape the remaining chocolate into caraque. Arrange on top and sprinkle with icing sugar.

MADEIRA CAKE

A classic cake which is recognised by the large slice of candied citron peel on the top. This cake is best eaten a day after baking. It keeps well in an airtight container.

Makes one 18 cm (7 inch) round cake

INGREDIENTS

115 g (4½ oz) potato flour

115 g (4½ oz) plain flour

5 ml (1 tsp) baking powder

pinch of salt

175 g (6 oz) butter

175 g (6 oz) caster sugar

3 large eggs

finely grated rind and juice of ½ lemon

1 large slice citron peel

Sift the flours, baking powder and salt together 2 or 3 times. Beat the butter until soft, then cream it with the sugar until pale, light and fluffy. Beat in the eggs one at a time, beating well after each addition. Should the mixture begin to separate, add a spoonful of the sifted flour. Gradually fold in the sifted flour alternately with the lemon rind and juice.

Spoon the cake mixture into a greased and lined 18 cm (7 inch) round cake tin. Smooth the top, make a slight dip in the centre and place the citron peel in the indentation. Bake on the centre shelf at 170°C (325°F) mark 3 for 1–1¼ hours. The cake is cooked when a small skewer inserted into the centre comes out clean. Cool in the tin for 10 minutes, then turn out on to a wire rack and leave until cold.

CLEMENTINE GATEAU

This rich but light gâteau makes a sumptuous dessert.

Makes one 24 cm (9½ inch) gâteau

Sift the potato and plain flour together. Grease a 24 cm (9½ inch) round spring-form cake tin and line the base. Grease the paper. Mix the reserved 5 ml (1 tsp) of plain flour and 5 ml (1 tsp) of the caster sugar together and dust the tin.

Sift all but 30 ml (2 tbsp) of the icing sugar into a bowl and add the egg yolks. Whisk until pale and thick enough to make a ribbon trail. Add the orange rind and gradually stir in 15 ml (1 tbsp) of the Grand Marnier and the orange juice. Fold in the flours.

Whisk the egg whites with the salt until stiff, but not dry, then whisk in the reserved icing sugar. Carefully fold the egg whites into the egg yolk mixture. Turn into the prepared tin and bake at 180°C (350°F) mark 4 for 50 minutes. The cake is cooked when a small skewer inserted into the centre comes out clean. Cool in the tin for 5 minutes, then turn out on to a wire rack and leave to cool.

Meanwhile, make the sugar syrup. Place the granulated sugar and water in a pan and stir over low heat until the sugar has dissolved. Boil for 4–5 minutes or until the temperature reaches 108°C (225°F) on a sugar thermometer. Cool the syrup, then stir in the remaining Grand Marnier. Pour it over the clementines.

When the cake is cold, peel off the paper and cut it into 3 equal layers. Brush the cake layers with syrup. Arrange the clementines on two layers only, reserving 100 g (4 oz) for decoration. Whip the cream, orange flower water and remaining caster sugar together. Spread some of the cream over the fruit and assemble the gâteau, with the plain layer on the top. Spread some of the cream around the sides and press on the almonds. Place the remaining cream in a piping bag fitted with a large star nozzle. Arrange the reserved clementines in the centre of the gâteau and pipe cream rosettes around the clementines.

INGREDIENTS
65 g (2½ oz) potato flour
65 g (2½ oz) plain flour, plus 5 ml (1 tsp)
30 ml (2 tbsp) caster sugar
225 g (8 oz) icing sugar
6 eggs, separated
finely grated rind of ½ orange
45 ml (3 tbsp) Grand Marnier
15 ml (1 tbsp) orange juice
1.25 ml (¼ tsp) salt
175 g (6 oz) granulated sugar
90 ml (3½ fl oz) water
1 kg (2 lb) clementines, peeled and segmented
750 ml (1¼ pints) double cream
5 ml (1 tsp) orange flower water
175 g (6 oz) flaked almonds, toasted

CELEBRATION CAKE

For that special celebration, this cake makes a really spectacular centrepiece.
The use of fresh flowers adds a delightful touch.

Makes one 25 cm (10 inch) cake

INGREDIENTS
SPONGE
350 g (12 oz) butter
350 g (12 oz) caster sugar
6 eggs, size 2
350 g (12 oz) self-raising flour
FILLING
75 g (3 oz) granulated sugar
45 ml (3 tbsp) water
75–90 (5–6 tbsp) Grand Marnier
225 g (8 oz) unsalted butter
500 g (1 lb) icing sugar, sifted
ALMOND PASTE
350 g (12 oz) ground almonds
175 g (6 oz) caster sugar
175 g (6 oz) icing sugar, sifted
almond essence
6 egg yolks, size 2
sieved apricot jam
ICING AND DECORATION
8 egg whites, size 2
2 kg (4 lb) icing sugar, sifted
25 ml (1½ tbsp) glycerine
few drops acetic acid
yellow food colouring
fresh freesias

For the sponge, cream the butter and sugar together until pale, light and fluffy, then beat in the eggs one at a time, beating well after each addition. Carefully fold in the flour. Spoon the mixture into a greased and lined 25 cm (10 inch) cake tin and smooth the top. Bake at 180°C (350°F) mark 4 for about 1½ hours, or until well risen, firm to the touch, and slightly shrunk away from the sides of the tin. Cool in the tin for 10 minutes, then turn out on to a wire rack to cool completely.

For the filling, put the granulated sugar and water into a small saucepan and heat gently until the sugar has dissolved. Bring to the boil and boil for 2 minutes. Remove from the heat and stir in 30–45 ml (2–3 tbsp) of the Grand Marnier. Allow the syrup to cool.

Beat the butter until very soft then gradually beat in the icing sugar, beating well after each addition. Beat in the remaining Grand Marnier, or flavour to taste.

Slice the cake horizontally, into three even layers. Place the bottom layer on a 30 cm (12 inch) round cake board. Brush the sponge with some of the syrup, then spread with the filling. Place the centre layer of sponge on top, brush with more syrup and spread with filling. Brush the cut side of the remaining layer of sponge with syrup then place it on top of the cake. Press the layers firmly but gently together, making sure that the cake is level.

For the almond paste, mix the almonds and sugars together in a large mixing bowl. Add a few drops of almond essence, and mix together with the egg yolks to make a stiff paste. Knead lightly until smooth. Cut off one-third of the almond paste and set it aside.

Roll out the remaining almond paste to a long strip, long enough and wide enough to fit around the cake. Brush the sides of the cake with apricot jam then fit the strip of almond paste neatly around the sides, pressing it firmly to the cake. Roll out the remaining piece of almond paste to a round large enough to fit the top of the cake. Brush the top of the cake with apricot jam and cover with the round of almond paste, rolling it gently into place with a rolling pin. Leave for 24 hours before icing.

For the icing, lightly whisk 6 of the egg whites. Gradually beat in 1.5 kg (3 lb) of the icing sugar to make a smooth royal icing. Beat in the glycerine.

Spread a good layer of the icing over the top of the cake with a palette knife, working it backwards and forwards to remove as many air bubbles as possible. Pull a ruler, preferably a metal one, across the top of the cake to smooth the icing. Remove the excess icing from the top edge of the cake. Place the cake on a turntable, or an up-turned cake tin, and spread the sides with icing, spreading it as evenly as possible. Pull a cake scraper around the side to smooth the icing. Leave overnight, in a cool place, to dry. Put the remaining icing into a clean mixing bowl and cover the surface closely with clingfilm. Cover the bowl with clingfilm, and refrigerate until the next day. Beat the icing well before using again. Store the icing in this way after each application.

Next day, scrape away the rough icing from the top edge of the cake, and from the board with a small sharp knife. Brush off loose icing from the cake with a clean, dry, pastry brush. Give the cake three more coats of icing, allowing each coat to dry overnight before applying the next.

For the narcissi, beat the remaining egg whites and icing sugar together to make a smooth royal icing, then beat in a few drops of acetic acid. Put about 15 ml (1 tbsp) of the icing into a small basin and colour with a few drops of

yellow colouring. Place in a paper piping bag. Put a little of the white icing into another paper piping bag, flatten the point between your finger and thumb, then cut into a 'V' shape with scissors. Cut a small hole in the bag containing the yellow icing.

Secure a small square of non-stick baking paper on to an icing nail with a little icing. Pipe five, slightly overlapping, white petals on to the paper to form a flower, then make a centre with the yellow icing. Remove the paper from the flower nail and place it on a flat tray. Make about 80 flowers in the same way. Leave the flowers in cool dry place for at least 24 hours to harden. Make the flowers when you apply the first coat of icing to the cake.

To decorate, mark a double row of evenly spaced scallops around the side of the cake, marking the second row about 4 cm (1½ inches) below the first. Pipe a small 'blob' of icing on each narcissus, and press them gently on to the side of the cake, following the first row of scallops.

Place a little icing in a paper piping bag fitted with a small 8 point star nozzle, then pipe a row of stars around the side of the cake, following the second row of scallops. Pipe two more rows of stars under the first row, continuing them on to the board. Pipe three rows of stars around the top edge of the cake. Place eight narcissi on top of the cake.

Finally, just before presenting the cake, place a small arrangement of fresh freesias on top of the cake.

SHORTBREAD

*Shortbread moulds transform this simple recipe into a decorative teatime treat.
Press the dough into the mould and chill for 1 hour.*

Makes 8 pieces

INGREDIENTS
150 g (5 oz) plain flour
pinch of salt
25 g (1 oz) ground rice
100 g (4 oz) butter
*50 g (2 oz) caster sugar, plus
    extra for sprinkling*

Sift the flour with the salt and the ground rice. Cream the butter with the sugar until pale, light and fluffy. Gradually add the flour mixture and mix lightly until the ingredients form into a smooth dough.

Roll out the dough on a lightly floured board to an 18 cm (7 inch) circle. Place on a baking sheet. Alternatively, press the shortbread into an 18 cm (7 inch) sandwich tin and roll the surface level with a smooth glass tumbler. Pinch the edge into a pattern and prick the surface with a fork to prevent the dough from rising during cooking. Chill for 1 hour. Bake on the centre shelf at 170°C (325°F) mark 3 for about 45 minutes. While the shortbread is still hot, cut it into 8 even-sized wedges. Sprinkle with caster sugar and cool in the tin.

CHOCOLATE AND WALNUT COOKIES

*These cookies usually disappear the moment they are placed on the cooling rack,
probably because they taste wonderful when slightly warm.*

Makes about 24

INGREDIENTS
175 g (6 oz) plain flour
1.25 ml ($\frac{1}{4}$ tsp) baking powder
pinch of salt
100 g (4 oz) butter
175 g (6 oz) Demerera sugar
1 egg
few drops of vanilla essence
*100 g (4 oz) plain chocolate,
    coarsely chopped*
75 g (3 oz) walnuts, chopped

Sift the flour, baking powder and salt together. Cream the butter and sugar together, until pale. Beat the egg and vanilla essence together, then gradually beat it into the butter and sugar. Fold in the flour a little at a time, then add the chocolate and the walnuts.

Place heaped tablespoons of the mixture on to greased baking sheets, spaced well apart to allow room for the cookies to spread during cooking. Press very gently to flatten slightly.

Bake at 180°C (350°F) mark 4 for 15–20 minutes or until the cookies are golden brown around the outside and firm to the touch. Leave to cool for 2 minutes, then transfer to a wire rack. Store in an airtight container.

TREACLE TART

*This is a favourite nursery pudding that few people grow out of. In spite of the name,
this English recipe is made with golden syrup and not treacle.*

Serves 6–8

INGREDIENTS
*rich shortcrust pastry made with
    225 g (8 oz) flour (see page 248)*
75 ml (5 tbsp) golden syrup
*90 ml (6 tbsp) white or wholemeal
    breadcrumbs*
*finely grated rind and juice of $\frac{1}{2}$
    lemon*

Roll out the pastry and use it to line a 20 cm (8 inch) pie tin. Re-roll the trimmings and cut into four 1 cm ($\frac{1}{2}$ inch) wide strips, a little longer than the width of the tin. Heat the syrup over gentle heat and stir in the breadcrumbs then stir in the lemon rind and juice. Remove the pan from the heat and leave to cool.

Spread the filling over the pastry base. Twist the pastry strips, one by one, and place across the tart, making 8 sections. Press the ends of the pastry strips into the edges of the pie. Bake on the centre shelf at 190°C (375°F) mark 5 for 30 minutes. Serve warm or cold.

IRISH APPLE CAKE

*This apple cake is more like a pudding than a cake. It can be served warm
with a good dollop of whipped cream, or served cold.*

Makes one 23 cm (9 inch) round cake

Cream the butter with the caster and vanilla sugar until pale, light and fluffy.
Add the eggs one at a time, beating well after each addition. Stir in the lemon
rind.

Sift the plain flour, potato flour and baking powder together twice. Gradually
fold it into the cake mixture, then stir in the milk.

Spoon the mixture into a greased and floured 23 cm (9 inch) round spring form
cake tin with a removable base. Arrange the apple quarters, rounded sides up, on
top.

Bake the cake on the middle shelf of the oven at 190°C (375°F) mark 5 for 1
hour. The cake is cooked when a small skewer inserted into the centre comes out
clean. Cool in the tin for 10 minutes, then remove the ring.

Heat the apricot jam with the water then rub it through a sieve. Brush the top
of the cake with the glaze while it is still hot.

If it is to be served cold, leave the cake until it has cooled completely, then
sprinkle the top with icing sugar.

INGREDIENTS
115 g (4½ oz) butter
115 g (4½ oz) caster sugar
15 ml (1 tbsp) vanilla sugar
3 eggs, lightly beaten
finely grated rind of 1 lemon
115 g (4½ oz) plain flour
115 g (4½ oz) potato flour
10 ml (2 tsp) baking powder
30 ml (2 tbsp) milk
*400 g (14 oz) eating apples, peeled
    weight, cored and quartered*
30 ml (2 tbsp) apricot jam
5 ml (1 tsp) water
5 ml (1 tsp) icing sugar, sifted

LIQUEUR-FLAVOURED CREAM HORNS

*Cointreau, Grand Marnier, Kahlua and Tia Maria are among the endless variety of
liqueurs suitable for this filling. Serve these delicate pastries with coffee
or as part of an English tea party.*

Makes 8

Roll out the pastry on a lightly floured working surface to a strip measuring
66 × 10 cm (26 × 4 inches). Cut the pastry lengthways with a sharp knife into
eight 1 cm (½ inch) ribbons.

Grease eight cream horn tins. Moisten one edge of each pastry strip and wind
each strip around a horn tin starting at the tip, overlapping 3 mm (⅛ inch) and
finishing neatly on the underside. The pastry should not overlap the metal rim.
Brush with beaten egg.

Dampen a baking sheet and arrange the cream horns on it, join-side down.
Bake at 220°C (425°F) mark 7 for 10 minutes until golden brown.

Cool for a few minutes, then carefully twist each tin, holding the pastry lightly
in the other hand, to ease it out of the pastry horn. Leave the horns for about 30
minutes to cool completely.

When cold, fill the tip of each horn with a little jam. Whip the cream with the
liqueur until stiff peaks form and fill the horns down to the jam. Sift the icing
sugar on each horn to decorate.

INGREDIENTS
*puff pastry made with 50 g (2 oz)
    flour (see page 248) or 212 g
    (7½ oz) packet frozen puff
    pastry*
beaten egg, to glaze
strawberry jam
300 ml (½ pint) double cream
*15 ml (1 tbsp) fruit flavoured
    liqueur*
icing sugar, to decorate

FLORENTINES

*Florentines are a luscious mixture of nuts and dried fruits, coated on one side
with plain chocolate.*

Makes 16

INGREDIENTS

50 g (2 oz) butter

75 g (3 oz) caster sugar

*50 g (2 oz) almonds, blanched and
coarsely chopped*

*25 g (1 oz) hazelnuts, blanched
and coarsely chopped*

25 ml (1½ tbsp) plain flour

50 g (2 oz) mixed candied peel

6 glacé cherries, coarsely chopped

45 ml (3 tbsp) single cream

175 g (6 oz) plain chocolate

Melt the butter over a gentle heat and add the remaining ingredients, except the
chocolate. Stir over gentle heat for 2 minutes, or until the sugar has dissolved and
the mixture is well blended.

Place 15 ml (1 tbsp) of the mixture on greased baking sheets, leaving room
between each one, as the mixture spreads during cooking. With damp fingers
flatten the mixture slightly. Bake at 180°C (350°F) mark 4 for 10 minutes, or until
golden brown. The mixture will have spread during baking, so push the edges
into a tidy circle with a palette knife. Cool on the baking sheets for 2 minutes,
then cool on a wire rack.

Melt the chocolate in a bowl set over simmering water. When the florentines
are cool, turn them over, and coat the undersides with melted chocolate. As the
chocolate begins to set, make a wavy pattern across the base of each one with a
fork. Store in a cool, dry place.

CHOCOLATE ECLAIRS

*Chocolate eclairs are always a welcome treat. Serve these as a dessert after
a dinner party or for a special afternoon tea.*

Makes 12

Spoon the choux pastry into a large piping bag fitted with a large star nozzle.
Pipe into about twelve 12.5 cm (5 inch) lengths on an aluminium foil-lined baking
sheet. Leave space for the mixture to puff up.

Bake at 220°C (425°F) mark 7 for 35—40 minutes. Reduce the temperature to
190°C (375°F) mark 5 and bake for a further 20—25 minutes. Remove from the
oven and pierce each eclair to allow the steam to escape. Return to the oven for 5
minutes to dry, then cool on a wire rack.

Whip the cream with the sugar and vanilla until stiff. Spoon into a piping bag
fitted with a small star nozzle and fill the eclairs.

Melt the chocolate with the water in a bowl set over a pan of simmering water.
Stir in the butter. Dip the tops of the eclairs in chocolate and leave on a wire rack
until set.

INGREDIENTS

*1 quantity choux pastry made
with 90 g (3½ oz) plain flour
(see page 249)*
300 ml (½ pint) double cream
25 g (1 oz) icing sugar, sifted
few drops of vanilla essence
100 g (4 oz) plain chocolate
40 ml (3½ fl oz) water
25 g (1 oz) butter

BLACK FOREST GATEAU

This chocolate and cherry gâteau is a popular dessert. It is too tempting to resist, with its generously piped cream, cherries and chocolate caraque.

Serves 8–10

INGREDIENTS
3 large eggs
175 g (6 oz) caster sugar
175 g (6 oz) plain flour
25 g (1 oz) cocoa powder
10 ml (2 tsp) baking powder
75 ml (5 tbsp) hot water
600 ml (1 pint) double cream
60 ml (4 tbsp) kirsch
100 g (4 oz) plain chocolate
 caraque
450 g (1 lb) canned black cherries,
 pitted and well drained

Place the eggs and sugar in a bowl over a pan of simmering water. Whisk until the mixture is pale and thick and just holds the trail of the whisk. Remove the bowl from the heat and whisk for a further 2 minutes. Sift the flour, cocoa powder and baking powder on to a plate. Carefully fold it into the egg mixture, cutting through with a metal spoon until evenly mixed. Gently stir in the hot water.

Spoon the mixture into a greased and base-lined 23 cm (9 inch) round cake tin. Bake at 190°C (375°F) mark 5 for 35–40 minutes or until firm to the touch. Turn out, remove the paper and cool on a wire rack.

When the cake is cold, split it into three layers. Whip the cream until stiff and spoon one-third into a piping bag fitted with a star nozzle. Sprinkle the bottom layer of the cake with a little kirsch and pipe a band of cream around the edge. Reserve 8–10 cherries for decoration and spread the remainder inside the cream.

Place the middle layer of sponge on top of the cherries and sprinkle it with kirsch. Spread the sponge with cream. Sprinkle the underside of the top layer of sponge with the remaining kirsch and invert on to the cream layer.

Cover the top and sides of the cake with cream. Sprinkle with the chocolate caraque. Pipe cream around the top edge of the cake and decorate. Chill.

MERINGUES

Light as air, meringues are everyone's favourite at tea time. They can be filled with a variety of creams, or used as a base for topping. Stored in an airtight container, they will keep for several weeks.

Makes 10

INGREDIENTS
4 egg whites
215 g (7½ oz) caster sugar
15 g (½ oz) vanilla sugar
CHOCOLATE CREAM FILLING
75 g (3 oz) plain chocolate
40 ml (1½ fl oz) water
1.25 ml (¼ tsp) instant coffee
300 ml (½ pint) double cream,
 lightly whipped
LIQUEUR FILLING
300 ml (½ pint) double cream,
 lightly whipped
15 g (½ oz) caster sugar
15–25 ml (1–1½ tbsp) liqueur
 (such as Grand Marnier,
 Curaçao or kirsch)
FRUIT FILLING
300 ml (½ pint) double cream,
 lightly whipped
15 g (½ oz) caster sugar
50 g (2 oz) strawberries or
 raspberries, puréed

Whisk the egg whites until stiff but not dry. Whisk in half the sugar, then fold in the remainder with the vanilla sugar. Put spoonfuls of the meringue on to baking sheets lined with non-stick silicone paper. This amount of mixture will make 20 7 cm (2¾ inch) wide meringues. Bake at 140°C (275°F) mark 1 for 1½ hours.

Leave the meringues to cool in the oven.

For the chocolate cream filling, melt the chocolate, water and coffee together. Leave until cool, then stir into the cream. Beat the ingredients for the liqueur filling together. Repeat for the fruit filling.

When the meringues are cold, arrange in pairs and fill with one of the cream mixtures.

COTTAGE LOAF

A cottage loaf is easily recognisable by its shape—a squat round base with a smaller round on top. The potato flour glaze gives the loaf a lovely golden crust.

Makes two 600 g (1¼ lb) loaves

Crumble the yeast into a warm bowl and mash with the sugar. Mix the water with the milk and whisk into the yeast mixture. Cover with clingfilm and leave in a warm place for 20 minutes or until the yeast is puffed up and frothy.

Sift the flour with the salt and rub in the butter. Make a well in the centre and pour in the yeast mixture. Mix to a smooth dough. Turn out on to a lightly floured surface and knead for 10 minutes. Return the dough to the bowl, cover it with clingfilm and leave in a warm place for 45–60 minutes, or until doubled in size.

Knead the dough for 5 minutes then divide it into 2 equal pieces. Take one third from each piece and roll the larger pieces into round balls. Roll the two smaller pieces into balls and place one small ball on top of each large ball. Flour the handle of a wooden spoon and push it through the two balls to secure them together. Place the loaves on greased and floured baking trays, cover with cling film then leave to rise in a warm place for 15 minutes.

To make the glaze, mix the potato flour with the cold water, then add the boiling water. Stir until slightly cooled. Brush the loaves with the glaze and bake at 230°C (450°F) mark 8 for 10 minutes. Reduce the temperature to 200°C (400°F) mark 6 and bake for a further 20–25 minutes. Cool on a wire rack.

INGREDIENTS

25 g (1 oz) fresh yeast
5 ml (1 tsp) sugar
225 ml (8 fl oz) water, lukewarm
200 ml (7 fl oz) milk, lukewarm
750 g (1½ lb) strong plain flour
7.5 ml (1½ tsp) salt
25 g (1 oz) butter
GLAZE
4 ml (¾ tsp) potato flour
4 ml (¾ tsp) cold water
75 ml (3 fl oz) boiling water

HEDGEHOG ROLLS

Hedgehog rolls are very popular with children. A pair of small scissors is all that is necessary to make the hedgehog 'spines', with currants forming the eyes and nose.

Makes 16

INGREDIENTS

25 g (1 oz) fresh yeast
5 ml (1 tsp) sugar
25 ml (8 fl oz) water, lukewarm
200 ml (7 fl oz) milk, lukewarm
700 g (1½ lb) strong white flour
7.5 ml (1½ tsp) salt
25 g (1 oz) butter
48 currants
1 egg, lightly beaten, to glaze

Crumble the yeast into a warm bowl and mash with the sugar. Mix the water and milk together and whisk it into the yeast mixture. Cover with clingfilm and leave in a warm place for 20 minutes or until puffed up and frothy. Sift the flour with the salt and rub in the butter. Make a well in the centre, pour in the yeast mixture and mix to a smooth dough. Turn the dough out on to a lightly floured surface and knead for 10 minutes. Return the dough to the bowl, cover with clingfilm and leave to rise in a warm place for 45–60 minutes, or until doubled in size. Knead the dough for 5 minutes.

Divide the dough into 16 even-sized pieces. Shape each one into an oval. Press one end slightly flat, then press the sides in to make the hedgehog's face. Place the piece of dough on a greased and floured baking sheet, with the face away from you. Cut into the dough with a small pair of scissors, starting behind the head, and snip small points to make hedgehog 'spines' all over the body. Place two currants on the face for eyes, and one for the nose. Glaze with the beaten egg. Cover with clingfilm and leave in a warm place for 15 minutes. Bake at 230°C (450°F) mark 8 for 15–18 minutes or until shiny golden brown and the base sounds hollow when tapped. Cool on a wire rack.

HEDGEHOG ROLLS

CHEESE AND HERB BREAD

*Use any of your favourite herbs when they are in season to make this recipe.
Serve with unsalted butter.*

Makes two 500 g (1 lb) loaves

Grease two 500 g (1 lb) loaf tins. Sift the flour, salt, mustard and pepper into a large bowl. Stir in the chives, parsley and three quarters of the cheese. Blend the fresh yeast and water together. If using dried yeast, sprinkle it into the water with the sugar and leave in a warm place for 20 minutes until frothy. Add to the dry ingredients and mix to a soft dough. Turn on to a floured surface and knead for 10 minutes. Place in a bowl, cover with a clean tea towel and leave to rise in a warm place for about 1 hour, or until doubled in size.

Turn the dough on to a floured surface and knead for 5 minutes. Divide the dough into two and shape to fit the tins. Cover with a clean tea towel and leave to prove in a warm place for about 30 minutes, until the dough reaches the top of the tins.

Sprinkle the tops of the loaves with the remaining cheese. Bake at 190°C (375°F) mark 5 for 40–45 minutes until well risen and golden brown. Turn out and cool on a wire rack.

INGREDIENTS
500 g (1 lb) strong white flour
10 ml (2 tsp) salt
5 ml (1 tsp) mustard powder
pepper
10 ml (2 tsp) snipped fresh chives
30 ml (2 tbsp) chopped fresh
   parsley
175 g (6 oz) Cheddar cheese,
   grated
15 g (½ oz) fresh yeast or
   7.5 ml (1½ tsp) dried yeast with
   a pinch of sugar
300 ml (½ pint) tepid water

BLACK RYE BREAD

*This bread is traditionally made using the sour dough method, which is
time consuming. The quicker version below includes natural yogurt
to give the loaf a pleasantly acidic tang.*

Makes 1 large loaf

Blend the fresh yeast with the water. If using dried yeast, sprinkle it into the milk with the sugar and leave in a warm place for 20 minutes, until frothy. Sift the flours, salt and caraway seeds together in a large bowl. Tip the bran remaining in the sieve back into the bowl. Stir in the oil, yeast liquid and yogurt. Mix to a soft dough.

Knead the dough for 10 minutes then return it to the rinsed-out bowl. Cover with clingfilm and leave in a warm place for 1–1½ hours or until doubled in size.

Knead the dough for 5 minutes then shape it to fit a 1 kg (2 lb) greased loaf tin. Prick the surface of the loaf with a fork. Cover with clingfilm and leave in a warm place for about 30 minutes or until the dough reaches the top of the tin. Bake at 200°C (400°F) mark 6 for 45 minutes. Remove the loaf from the tin and return it to the oven for 5 minutes more. Place on a wire rack and cover with a tea towel until cool.

INGREDIENTS
25 g (1 oz) fresh yeast or 15 g (½ oz)
   dried yeast with a pinch of
   sugar
175 ml (6 fl oz) lukewarm water
225 g (8 oz) wholemeal flour
225 g (8 oz) rye flour
5 ml (1 tsp) salt
5 ml (1 tsp) caraway seeds
10 ml (2 tsp) oil
150 ml (¼ pint) natural yogurt

WHOLEMEAL BUNS

These soft buns may be made with all wholemeal flour, or half wholemeal and half strong plain flour. The latter combination gives a lighter texture.

Makes 12

INGREDIENTS

25 g (1 oz) fresh yeast
5 ml (1 tsp) caster sugar
150 ml (¼ pint) milk, lukewarm
150 ml (¼ pint) water, lukewarm
225 g (8 oz) wholemeal flour, plus 10 ml (2 tsp)
225 g (8 oz) strong plain flour
7.5 ml (1½ tsp) salt
25 g (1 oz) butter

Crumble the yeast into a warm bowl and mash with the sugar. Mix the milk and water together and whisk into the yeast mixture. Cover with clingfilm and leave the bowl in a warm place for 20 minutes or until puffed up and frothy.

Meanwhile, sift the flours together with the salt. Tip the bran from the sieve back into the bowl. Rub in the butter and make a well in the centre. Pour in the yeast mixture and mix to a smooth dough. Turn out on to a lightly floured surface and knead for 10 minutes. Return the dough to the bowl, cover with clingfilm and leave to rise in a warm place for 1 hour or until doubled in size.

Knead the dough for 5 minutes. Divide into 12 even-sized pieces, and roll each one into a ball. Flatten the balls of dough with your hand into 7.5 cm (3 inch) rounds. Place the rolls on greased and floured baking sheets, leaving enough space between to allow for expansion during cooking. Cover with clingfilm and leave to rise in a warm place for 20 minutes.

Dust the rolls with the remaining wholemeal flour and bake at 220°C (425°F) mark 7 for 15 minutes. Cool on a wire rack.

IRISH SODA BREAD

Brown soda bread and jam is an essential part of the Irish high tea. If you prefer a white loaf, use plain white flour only.

Makes 1 large or 2 small loaves

INGREDIENTS

500 g (1 lb) wholemeal flour
225 g (8 oz) plain flour
5 ml (1 tsp) bicarbonate of soda
5 ml (1 tsp) salt
600 ml (1 pint) buttermilk or natural yogurt

Sift the flours, bicarbonate of soda and salt together into a large mixing bowl. Tip the bran in the sieve back into the bowl and stir to mix. Pour the buttermilk into the bowl, all at once, and mix quickly and lightly to form a soft dough.

Knead briefly on a lightly floured surface, then shape the dough into 1 large or 2 small rounds, flattening each slightly. Cut a deep cross in the dough with a sharp knife. Dust with flour and place on a floured baking sheet. Bake at 200°C (400°F) mark 6 for 35–40 minutes for small loaves, or 45–50 minutes for a large one. When cooked, the loaf will be well browned and sound hollow when tapped on the base. Cool on a wire rack and eat the same day, if possible, as it quickly becomes stale.

MUFFINS

*Muffins are traditionally cooked on a griddle; however a heavy-based
frying pan can be used instead. Alternatively, cook on a greased baking sheet in the oven.*

Makes 12

Crumble the yeast into a warm bowl and mash with the sugar. Mix the milk and water together and whisk into the yeast mixture. Cover with clingfilm and leave in a warm place for 20 minutes until puffed up and frothy.

Sift the flour with the salt and make a well in the centre. Pour in the yeast mixture and mix to a smooth dough. Turn out on to a lightly floured surface and knead for 10 minutes. Return to the bowl, cover with clingfilm and leave to rise in a warm place for 1 hour or until doubled in size.

Turn the dough out on to a lightly floured surface. Roll out to 1 cm ($\frac{1}{2}$ inch). thick. Using a 7.5 cm (3 inch) round cutter, cut out 12 circles. Re-roll the trimmings as necessary. Place the muffins on a floured baking tray, dust the tops with the remaining flour mixed with the semolina. Cover the trays with clingfilm and leave to rise in a warm place for 40 minutes.

Grease a griddle or heavy-based frying pan lightly and heat over moderate heat. Place the muffins on the griddle and cook over low heat for about 7 minutes on each side. Alternatively, bake at 220°C (425°F) mark 7 for 10 minutes. Turn the muffins over and bake for a further 4–5 minutes. Cool on a wire rack.

Serve the muffins split in two and buttered. If serving cold, split in half, toast lightly and spread with butter.

INGREDIENTS
15 g ($\frac{1}{2}$ oz) fresh yeast
5 ml (1 tsp) caster sugar
150 ml ($\frac{1}{4}$ pint) milk, lukewarm
150 ml ($\frac{1}{4}$ pint) water, lukewarm
*500 g (1 lb) strong plain flour, plus
5 ml (1 tsp)*
5 ml (1 tsp) salt
*5 ml (1 tsp) fine unbleached
semolina*
oil, for greasing

SESAME BREAD STICKS

Serve with soups, starters and snacks.

Makes about 20

Blend the fresh yeast with a little of the milk and water liquid, then whisk in the remainder. If using dried yeast, sprinkle into the liquid with the sugar and leave in a warm place for 20 minutes until frothy. Sift the flour and salt together and rub in the butter. Stir in the sugar and make a well in the centre. Stir in the yeast liquid and mix to a soft dough.

Turn the dough out on to a lightly floured surface and knead for 10 minutes. Return to the rinsed-out bowl, cover with clingfilm and leave to rise for 1$\frac{1}{2}$ hours, or until doubled in size.

Knead for 5 minutes. Break off pieces of the dough, about 50 g (2 oz) each, and roll out to 30 cm (12 inch) lengths. Place on greased baking sheets, brush with the egg white and sprinkle liberally with sesame seeds. Cover with clingfilm and leave in a warm place for 15 minutes. Bake at 220°C (425°F) mark 7 for 12–15 minutes, or until very crisp and golden brown. Cool on a wire rack.

INGREDIENTS
*15 g ($\frac{1}{2}$ oz) fresh yeast or
7.5 ml (1$\frac{1}{2}$ tsp) dried with a
pinch of sugar*
*450 ml ($\frac{3}{4}$ pint) lukewarm milk and
water mixed*
750 g (1$\frac{1}{2}$ lb) strong white flour
10 ml (2 tsp) salt
75 g (3 oz) butter
10 ml (2 tsp) sugar
beaten egg white, for glazing
sesame seeds, for sprinkling

HOT CROSS BUNS

These Easter buns should be served hot, dripping with butter. Halve and toast any that do not get eaten immediately.

Makes 12

INGREDIENTS

500 g (1 lb) plain flour
50 g (2 oz) caster sugar plus
  5 ml (1 tsp)
25 g (1 oz) fresh yeast or
  15 g (½ oz) dried yeast
100 ml (4 fl oz) milk, lukewarm
125 ml (4 fl oz) water, lukewarm
5 ml (1 tsp) salt
15 ml (1 tbsp) ground mixed spice
50 g (2 oz) butter, melted and
  cooled
1 egg, lightly beaten
50 g (2 oz) currants
50 g (2 oz) mixed candied peel
10 ml (2 tsp) clear honey, to glaze
DECORATION
25 g (1 oz) plain flour, sifted
cold water

Mix 25 g (1 oz) of the flour with 5 ml (1 tsp) of the sugar and the fresh or dried yeast. Stir in the milk and water. Cover and leave in a warm place, for 20 minutes or until puffed up and frothy.

Sift the remaining flour with the salt and mixed spice, make a well in the centre and add the 50 g (2 oz) sugar, butter, egg and yeast mixture. Mix to a dough and knead for 10 minutes. Place the dough in a clean bowl and cover with clingfilm, leave in a warm place until doubled in size. Knock back the risen dough, then knead in the currants and candied peel.

Divide the dough into 12 equal pieces and knead each one into a smooth ball. Place on a greased baking sheet, cover with clingfilm and leave to rise in a warm place for 45 minutes to 1 hour or until doubled in size.

For the decoration, blend the flour with enough cold water to make a paste. Fill a small piping bag with the paste and pipe a cross over each bun. Bake at 220°C (425°F) mark 7 for 20 minutes. Remove the buns from the oven and glaze with the honey. Return to the turned-off oven for 3 minutes. Leave the buns on the baking tray for 2 minutes, then cool on a wire rack.

FRUIT MALT LOAF

Popular throughout the British Isles, this sticky, fruited bread, spread with butter, makes a nutritious snack.

Makes one 500 g (1 lb) loaf

INGREDIENTS

15 g (½ oz) fresh yeast or
  7.5 ml (1½ tsp) dried yeast with
  2.5 ml (½ tsp) sugar
40 ml (1½ fl oz) milk, lukewarm
40 ml (1½ fl oz) water, lukewarm
2.5 ml (½ tsp) sugar
225 g (8 oz) plain flour
2.5 ml (½ tsp) salt
50 g (2 oz) malt extract
15 ml (1 tbsp) black treacle
15 g (½ oz) butter
75 g (3 oz) sultanas
25 g (1 oz) mixed candied peel
5 ml (1 tsp) honey

Blend the fresh yeast in the milk and water. If using dried yeast, mix with the milk and water, adding the sugar. Leave in a warm place for 20 minutes or until puffed up and frothy.

Meanwhile, sift the flour with the salt into a large bowl. Melt the malt extract, treacle and butter together over gentle heat, stirring frequently. Leave until lukewarm. Stir the yeast mixture and the treacle mixture into the flour and mix to a dough. Knead for 10 minutes. Knead in the sultanas and candied peel. Place in the rinsed-out bowl, cover with clingfilm and leave in a warm place for 45 minutes. The dough will not rise very much at this stage.

Knead the dough for a further 5 minutes, then place in a greased 500 g (1 lb) loaf tin. Cover with clingfilm and leave in a warm place for 45 minutes or until the dough has risen to the top of the tin.

Bake at 200°C (400°F) mark 6, for 45 minutes.

While the bread is hot, glaze the top of the loaf with the honey, and return to the oven for 3 minutes. Cool the loaf in the tin for 10 minutes, then turn it out on to a wire rack. Serve warm or cold, spread with butter.

CHELSEA BUNS

CHELSEA BUNS

*Chelsea buns make a delicious accompaniment to morning coffee,
or serve as part of a traditional tea.*

Makes 12

INGREDIENTS

225 g (8 oz) strong plain flour

15 g (½ oz) fresh yeast or 7.5 ml
(1½ tsp) dried yeast

2.5 ml (½ tsp) caster sugar

50 ml (2 fl oz) milk, lukewarm

50 ml (2 fl oz) water, lukewarm

2.5 ml (½ tsp) salt

15 g (½ oz) lard

1 egg, lightly beaten

75 g (3 oz) currants

50 g (2 oz) mixed candied peel

50 g (2 oz) soft light brown sugar

25 g (1 oz) butter, melted

15 ml (1 tbsp) clear honey

Sift 50 g (2 oz) of the flour into a warmed bowl. Crumble in the yeast, add the caster sugar and pour in the milk and water. Leave in a warm place for 20 minutes or until puffed up and frothy.

Sift the remaining flour with the salt and rub in the lard. Make a well in the centre and pour in the yeast mixture and the egg. Mix to a dough and knead for 10 minutes. Place the dough in a bowl, cover with clingfilm and leave in a warm place for 1½ hours or until doubled in size.

Turn the dough out on to a lightly floured surface and knead lightly. Roll the dough out into a 30 cm × 23 cm (12 × 9 inch) rectangle.

Mix the currants, mixed peel and brown sugar together. Brush the dough with melted butter and sprinkle with the fruit mixture to within 2.5 cm (1 inch) of the edge. Roll the dough tightly, starting from one long edge. Press the edges to seal. Slice the roll into 12 pieces and pack into a greased baking tray with sides.

Cover with clingfilm and leave in a warm place for 30 minutes or until risen slightly, then bake at 190°C (350°F) mark 5 for 30 minutes.

Remove from the oven and brush with honey. Leave to cool in the tin.

RUM AND WALNUT GUGELHOPF

RUM AND WALNUT GUGELHOPF

The name Gugelhopf, or Kugelhopf, is derived from the shape of the
fluted ring mould used, 'kugel' meaning ball.
This Austrian recipe is a cross between a cake and a sweet bread,
and is said to have been a favourite of Emperor Franz Joseph I. Serve sliced,
spread with butter if wished.

Serves 8–10

Blend the yeast in 45 ml (3 tbsp) of the milk and blend in 5 ml (1 tsp) of the sugar and 10 ml (2 tsp) of the flour. Cover and leave in a warm place for 20–30 minutes, or until puffed up and frothy.

Pour boiling water over the raisins and currants, stir for 1 minute, drain thoroughly and dry on a tea towel. Place in a bowl and sprinkle with the 15 ml (1 tbsp) of flour. Add the mixed candied peel and walnuts. Mix the vanilla sugar with the remaining caster sugar.

Sift the remaining flour with the salt into a bowl and make a well in the centre. Pour in the yeast mixture, with the remaining milk, rum, eggs, butter and lemon rind. Mix to a dough and knead for 10 minutes. Knead in the dried fruits and nuts.

Place the dough into a large warmed bowl, cover with clingfilm and leave to rise in a warm place for 1½–2 hours or until doubled in size. Knead for 5 minutes, then place in a greased gugelhopf mould. Cover and leave to rise in a warm place for 20–30 minutes or until risen.

Bake at 180°C (350°F) mark 5 for 1 hour.

Cool in the mould for 10 minutes, then turn out on to a wire rack to cool completely.

To make the icing, sift the icing sugar into a bowl and stir in the water and the rum. Place the bowl over simmering water and stir until the icing is just lukewarm. Dribble over the top of the cake and leave to set.

INGREDIENTS
45 g (1¾ oz) fresh yeast or 20 g
 (¾ oz) dried yeast
150 ml (¼ pint) milk, lukewarm
115 g (4½ oz) caster sugar
550 g (1 lb 2 oz) plain flour,
 plus 15 ml (1 tbsp)
100 g (4 oz) raisins
50 g (2 oz) currants
75 g (3 oz) mixed candied peel
75 g (3 oz) walnuts, chopped
10 ml (2 tsp) vanilla sugar
pinch of salt
30 ml (2 tbsp) rum
3 eggs, lightly beaten
150 g (5 oz) unsalted butter,
 softened
finely grated rind of 1 lemon
ICING
100 g (4 oz) icing sugar
15 ml (1 tbsp) hot water
25 ml (1½ tbsp) rum

THE CONFECTIONERY HALL

CONFECTIONERY

RUM AND RAISIN FUDGE

*Enriched with cream, milk and butter, this fudge has a fine smooth
texture obtained by cooling, then beating the mixture until it thickens.*

Makes about 1 kg (2 lb)

INGREDIENTS

150 ml (¼ pint) single cream
150 ml (¼ pint) milk
800 g (1¾ lb) sugar
100 g (4 oz) butter
15 ml (1 tbsp) dark rum
100 g (4 oz) seedless raisins

Pour the cream and milk into a saucepan and heat gently. Add the sugar, butter
and rum, then stir until the sugar has completely dissolved. Using a pastry brush
dipped in cold water, wash down the sugar crystals that form around the sides of
the pan. Do not allow the syrup to boil until the sugar has dissolved. Boil the
mixture, without stirring, to the soft ball stage or until a temperature of 116°C
(240°F) is reached on a sugar thermometer.

Remove the pan from the heat and immediately plunge the base into cold
water. Leave the fudge to cool for 5 minutes, then beat it until thick and creamy.
Stir in the raisins. Pour the mixture into a greased 23 cm (9 inch) square tin and
leave to cool completely. Mark the fudge into 2.5 cm (1 inch) squares, cut into
pieces and serve.

BUTTERSCOTCH

*Butterscotch is made with butter, Demerara sugar and water, but is more
delicious made with added double cream. This recipe includes instructions
for brittle butterscotch and delicious butterscotch caramels.*

Makes about 600 g (1¼ lb)

INGREDIENTS

500 g (1 lb) Demerara sugar
150 ml (¼ pint) water
150 ml (¼ pint) double cream
100 g (4 oz) butter
2.5 ml (½ tsp) vanilla essence

Place the sugar, water, cream and butter in a pan and heat gently for 10 minutes,
stirring, until the sugar has dissolved.

Place a warmed sugar thermometer into the pan and heat the syrup, stirring
occasionally, to 137°C (280°F) for butterscotch caramels, or to 154°C (310°F) for
a harder, brittle butterscotch. Stir in the vanilla essence, remove from the heat and
plunge the base of the pan into cold water.

Pour the mixture into a greased 20 cm (8 inch) square tin. When cooled, mark
into squares with an oiled knife.

When completely cold, snap the butterscotch into squares, wrap in waxed
paper and store in an airtight container.

GAELIC TRUFFLES

GAELIC TRUFFLES

These truffles may be made with Irish or Scotch whisky. Roll them in chopped walnuts, icing sugar, cocoa powder, grated chocolate or chocolate vermicelli. Home-made truffles make an ideal gift when presented in a pretty box.

Makes about 30

Rinse out a saucepan with cold water. Pour in the cream and bring to boiling point over moderate heat. Remove from the heat and add the chocolate. Stir the mixture constantly, until the chocolate melts and no lumps remain. Allow the mixture to cool to room temperature then stir in the whisky. Sift in the icing sugar and add the dissolved coffee. Beat until well blended, then chill until the paste is firm enough to roll into balls.

Place the chocolate vermicelli on a plate. Using two forks, roll a little of the chocolate paste into a walnut-sized ball. Do not roll the mixture in your hands. Roll the truffles in the chocolate vermicelli or walnuts to cover completely. Place in paper cases and arrange on a serving dish. These truffles will keep up to 2 days in the refrigerator.

INGREDIENTS
150 ml (¼ pint) double cream
225 g (8 oz) plain chocolate,
 broken into small pieces
45 ml (3 tbsp) whisky
75 g (3 oz) icing sugar
5 ml (1 tsp) instant coffee,
 dissolved in 15 ml (1 tbsp) hot
 water and left to cool
chocolate vermicelli or 100 g (4 oz)
 walnuts, finely chopped

FRUITS DIPPED IN FONDANT

These exquisite confections are perfect to serve after dinner with coffee.
Other fruits ideal for dipping are Chinese gooseberries, tangerines, cherries and grapes.
Apricot or cherry brandy may be used instead of Grand Marnier.

Makes about 500 g (1 lb)

INGREDIENTS

225 g (8 oz) granulated sugar
7.5 ml (1½ tsp) liquid glucose
75 ml (3 fl oz) water
5 ml (1 tsp) Grand Marnier
350 g (12 oz) strawberries, with
stalks and leaves, washed
and completely dry
50 g (2 oz) caster sugar

Heat the sugar, glucose and water together over gentle heat in a heavy-based saucepan. Stir until the sugar dissolves. Using a brush dipped in water, brush any sugar crystals down from the sides of the pan. Stir until the sugar has dissolved.

Bring to the boil and boil without stirring until the temperature reaches 116°C (240°F) on a sugar thermometer, or to the soft ball stage. Plunge the base of the pan immediately into cold water and pour the syrup on to a dampened baking sheet.

Leave the syrup to cool for 5 minutes. Using a dampened metal scraper, keep scraping the syrup in from the edges, until it cools slightly and becomes tinged with yellow. Work the fondant in a figure 8 pattern with a wooden spatula until it thickens. When very stiff, white and cold, knead it with damp hands. This process takes about 15 minutes.

Place the fondant in a rinsed-out bowl, cover with a damp cloth and leave in the fridge overnight.

Place the bowl of fondant over a pan of simmering water. Stir as it begins to melt, add the Grand Marnier, and place a sugar thermometer in the fondant. The fondant only takes about 4 minutes to reach the correct temperature for dipping and should not be allowed to reach 66°C (150°F), or it will crack. Holding the strawberries by the stalk, dip two-thirds of it into the fondant. Allow the excess fondant to drip off, then roll it in the caster sugar. Place on a baking sheet lined with non-stick silicone paper. Leave to dry. Arrange the sweets on a serving dish.

NOUGAT

To make this nougat, the syrup is first boiled to 138°C (280°F) on a sugar
thermometer, before adding the honey, as lengthy boiling at a high temperature
impairs the delicate flavour of the honey.

Makes 800 g (1¾ lb)

INGREDIENTS

225 g (8 oz) blanched almonds,
toasted
100 g (4 oz) pistachio nuts,
coarsely chopped
50 g (2 oz) glacé cherries, rinsed,
dried and coarsely chopped
225 g (8 oz) granulated sugar
25 ml (1½ tbsp) liquid glucose
100 ml (4 fl oz) water
100 g (4 oz) clear honey, warmed
2 egg whites, stiffly beaten
5 ml (1 tsp) vanilla essence
2 sheets rice paper

Mix the almonds, pistachios and glacé cherries together and reserve. Place the sugar, glucose and water in a heavy-based saucepan and heat gently, stirring until the sugar has dissolved. Dip a brush in water and brush any sugar crystals down from the sides of the pan. Stir until the sugar has dissolved. Bring to the boil and boil without stirring until the temperature reaches 138°C (280°F) on a sugar thermometer, or to the soft crack stage. Stir in the warmed honey and continue to boil, until a temperature of 143°C (290°F) is reached.

Immediately pour the syrup in a thin stream on to the egg whites, beating constantly. Stir in the vanilla essence, nuts and cherries. Beat the mixture for 5 minutes, or until the nougat begins to thicken. Pour into an 18 × 28 cm (7 × 11 inch) shallow tin lined with rice paper. Spread the nougat into the tin and place a second sheet of rice paper on the top. Place a weight on top to knock out the air bubbles and leave to set overnight.

Remove the weight and cut the nougat into bars or squares. Wrap in waxed paper and store in an airtight container for up to 10 days.

GRAND MARNIER TRUFFLES

*These deliciously rich truffles are made by whisking melted chocolate and
cream together. Many variations are possible, using different flavourings, nuts and
liqueurs. They will keep in the refrigerator for up to 2 days.*

Makes 35

INGREDIENTS
150 ml (¼ pint) double cream
*275 g (10 oz) plain chocolate,
    broken into small pieces*
75 ml (3 fl oz) Grand Marnier
*100 g (4 oz) blanched almonds,
    finely chopped*
finely grated rind of 1 orange
25 g (1 oz) cocoa powder, sifted

Rinse out a saucepan with cold water. Pour in the cream and bring to boiling
point over moderate heat. Remove from the heat and add the chocolate.
Stir the mixture constantly, until the chocolate melts and no lumps remain. Allow
the mixture to cool to room temperature then stir in the Grand Marnier, almonds
and orange rind. Beat the mixture until well blended, then chill until the paste is
firm enough to roll into balls.

Using two forks, roll the chocolate paste into walnut-sized balls. Do not roll
the mixture in your hands. Lightly roll the truffles in the cocoa powder—do
not press them into the powder as this gives too thick a coating, and will make
the truffles bitter.

Place the truffles in paper cases, and arrange on a serving dish.

MARZIPAN SWEETMEATS

*Marzipan is quite delicious when made with walnuts instead of almonds. Many
flavourings can be used—Grand Marnier, vanilla essence, orange flower water,
rum or brandy are just a few.*

Makes about 750 g (1½ lb)

INGREDIENTS
*500 g (1 lb) dates, weighed before
    stoning*
225 g (8 oz) ground walnuts
225 g (8 oz) caster sugar
1 small egg, beaten
5 ml (1 tsp) brandy
25 g (1 oz) slivered almonds

Cut the dates lengthways on one side only and remove the stones. Mix the
walnuts with the caster sugar. Gradually mix in the egg and brandy, and
stir until the mixture is well blended. Stuff the dates with some of the marzipan
mixture. Place in paper cases and arrange on a serving dish.

Shape the remaining marzipan into small pear-shaped sweets. Press a small
piece of almond into the wide end of the sweet, to form a stalk. Roll in caster
sugar and place on a serving dish. These pear-shaped sweets may also be made
with almond marzipan, coloured a pale green with a few drops of green food
colouring, and a slither of pistachio to form the stalk.

EVERTON TOFFEE

Everton toffee is made with black treacle and has a rich, buttery flavour.

Makes 800 g (1¾ lb)

INGREDIENTS
100 g (4 oz) butter
350 g (12 oz) Demerara sugar
350 g (12 oz) black treacle

Melt the butter over gentle heat then stir in the sugar and the treacle. Place a
warmed sugar thermometer into the toffee, and cook over moderately low heat,
stirring frequently, until the temperature reaches 130°C (266°F) or the light crack
stage.

Immediately plunge the base of the pan into a bowl of cold water. Pour the
toffee into a greased 20.5 cm (8 inch) square tin. As the toffee begins to set, cut it
into 2.5 cm (1 inch) squares.

Store in an airtight tin, individually wrapped, if desired.

MARSHMALLOWS

Marshmallows should be delicately flavoured and coloured. Rose or orange flower water are ideal as they lend a subtle fragrance as well as flavour.

Makes about 600 g (1¼ lb)

Sift the 5 ml (1 tsp) icing sugar and 5 ml (1 tsp) cornflour together and use to coat the sides of an oiled 18 × 25 cm (7 × 11 inch) shallow tin. Shake out any excess.

Place the sugar, glucose and 200 ml (7 fl oz) of the water in a heavy-based pan. Stir over gentle heat until the sugar dissolves. Using a brush dipped in water, brush any sugar crystals down from the sides of the pan. Stir until the sugar has dissolved. Bring to the boil and boil, without stirring, until the temperature reaches 127°C (260°F) on a sugar thermometer.

Meanwhile, place the remaining water and the rose water in a bowl. Sprinkle the gelatine over the liquid. Leave to soften for 5 minutes, then place the bowl over a pan of hot water and stir the gelatine until dissolved. Add the colouring then stir the gelatine into the syrup. Remove the pan from the heat immediately. Be very careful at this stage as the syrup bubbles. Pour the syrup in a thin stream on to the egg whites, beating constantly. Beat for 3 minutes, or until thickened. Pour the mixture into the prepared tin and leave to set for 4 hours.

Ease the mixture away from the sides of the tin with a greased knife, then gradually ease it away from the base. Sift the remaining icing sugar and cornflour on to a baking tray and turn the slab of marshmallow on to it. Turn over, and coat on the other side. Cut into 2.5 cm (1 inch) squares and store in an airtight, paper-lined container for up to 10 days.

INGREDIENTS
30 ml (2 tbsp) icing sugar,
  plus 5 ml (1 tsp)
30 ml (2 tbsp) cornflour, plus
  5 ml (1 tsp)
500 g (1 lb) granulated sugar
25 ml (1½ tbsp) liquid glucose
300 ml (½ pint) water
45 ml (3 tbsp) rose water
25 g (1 oz) powdered gelatine
1 drop of red food colouring
2 egg whites, stiffly beaten

MARSHMALLOWS

THE PANTRY

PRESERVES

PRESERVES

◆•◆

Preserves are ideal to give as gifts, to serve at breakfast and teatime, and on special occasions such as Christmas. The Pantry stocks a wide variety of preserves, but making your own—such as Apricot and Date Chutney and peaches in Brandy—when the produce is in season, is a delightful way to pass an afternoon.

SEVILLE ORANGE AND WHISKY MARMALADE

Seville oranges are imported from Spain and are available from December to February. This sour fruit makes the best marmalade. Incidentally, the juice of the Seville orange is a delicious accompaniment to grilled or fried fish.

Makes 2.3 kg (5 lb)

INGREDIENTS

750 g (1½ lb) Seville oranges
juice of 1 lemon
2 litres (3 pints) water
1.5 kg (3 lb) sugar
45 ml (3 tbsp) whisky

Wash and dry the oranges thoroughly, as they are frequently sprayed to improve their colour and keeping qualities.

With a sharp knife, remove the rind, leaving all of the white pith behind. Cut the rind into 5 mm (¼ inch) strips.

Squeeze the juice from the oranges and reserve the pips. Roughly chop the squeezed flesh and pith, and place it, with the pips, in a large piece of muslin. Tie into a bundle.

Put the cut rind, orange and lemon juice, the muslin bag of pith and pips, and the water into a large preserving pan. Bring to the boil and simmer for 2 hours or until the contents of the pan have reduced by half.

Remove the muslin bag, add the sugar, and stir over gentle heat, until the sugar has dissolved. Bring to the boil and boil rapidly for 15–20 minutes until setting point is reached (see note below). Remove the pan from the heat and add the whisky. Return it to the heat, and boil for 1 minute. Skim the marmalade and leave it to cool for 30 minutes. Stir the marmalade then pour it into warm, dry, sterilized jars. When the marmalade is cold, cover with wax discs and seal. Store in a cool, dry place.

Note

To test for setting point, spoon a little of the conserve on to a saucer. Leave for a few minutes, then push with your finger. If the surface wrinkles, setting point has been reached.

QUINCE AND GERANIUM JELLY

*The golden, down-covered quince changes colour when it is cooked to give a
pinkish-amber jelly. This autumnal fruit is high in pectin and is therefore
ideal for jams, jellies and preserves.
Serve with meat or poultry, or spread on bread and butter. This recipe
may also be made with japonica quince.*

Makes 2.3 kg (5 lb)

Wash and chop the quinces. Put them into a preserving pan with sufficient water
to just cover them. Bring to the boil, reduce the heat, and simmer for 25 minutes
until soft and pulpy. As the fruit softens, mash it slightly from time to time.

Pour the fruit and juice into a jelly bag, or strain through a muslin cloth, and
leave to drip into a container overnight. On no account must you squeeze the
jelly bag, as this results in a cloudy, murky jelly.

Measure the juice and pour it into the pan with the correct amount of sugar.
Heat gently, stirring until the sugar has dissolved, then bring to the boil. Add the
rose leaves, tied together, and boil for 10 minutes or until setting point is reached
(see note opposite). Remove the leaves and pour the jelly into warm, dry,
sterilized jars. When cold, cover with wax discs and seal. Store in a cool, dry
place.

INGREDIENTS
2.3 kg (5 lb) quinces
water
*500 g (1 lb) sugar to every
600 ml (1 pint) juice*
*3–4 rose or lemon geranium
leaves*

LIME MARMALADE

Limes have a refreshing tangy flavour and make a particularly fragrant marmalade.

Makes 1.8 kg (4 lb)

INGREDIENTS
750 g (1½ lb) fresh limes
2 litres (3 pints) water
1.5 kg (3 lb) sugar

Wash and dry the limes. With a sharp knife or potato peeler, remove the rind, leaving all white pith on the fruit. Cut the rind into 5 mm (¼ inch) strips.

Place the rind and half the water in a pan. Bring to the boil, cover, reduce the heat and simmer very gently for 2 hours, or until the rind is tender. Meanwhile, roughly chop the peeled limes on a plate, so that none of the juice is lost. Place them in a pan with the remaining water. Bring to the boil, cover, reduce the heat, and simmer gently for 1½ hours.

Strain the limes and liquid through a piece of muslin, into the pan with the lime rind. Add the sugar and heat gently, stirring until the sugar has dissolved. Boil rapidly for 15–20 minutes or until setting point is reached (see note on page 216). Allow the marmalade to cool for 30 minutes. Stir gently and pour into warm, dry, sterilized jars. When cold, cover with waxed discs and seal. Store in a cool, dry place.

TANGERINE AND ALMOND JAM

The addition of orange flower water makes this a fragrant and delicate jam.

Makes about 1.5 kg (3 lb)

INGREDIENTS
1 kg (2 lb) tangerines
1 kg (2 lb) sugar
50 ml (2 fl oz) orange flower water
75 g (3 oz) slivered almonds

Halve the tangerines and squeeze out the juice. Reserve in a covered jar. Scrape the flesh and white pith from the rind and discard. Simmer the rind in water for 10 minutes then drain. Cover the rind with cold water and leave to soak for 12 hours or overnight.

Drain the rind and roughly chop. Pour the reserved tangerine juice, sugar and chopped rind into a preserving pan. Heat gently until the sugar dissolves, then bring to the boil. Boil for 15–20 minutes or until setting point is reached (see note page 216). Remove from the heat and stir in the orange flower water and almonds. Stir and boil again for 2 minutes.

Pour into warm, dry, sterilized jars. When cold, cover with wax discs and seal. Store in a cool, dry place.

KIWIS IN COGNAC

This recipe demonstrates the simplest method of preserving fruits in Cognac or brandy. Other fruits suitable for preserving in this way are greengages, peaches, cherries and apricots.

Fills one 1.4 kg (2 lb) jar

INGREDIENTS
6 kiwi fruits
45 ml (3 tbsp) sugar
about 600 ml (1 pint) Cognac or brandy

Do not peel the kiwi fruits. Prick each fruit with a needle in several places. Pack the fruit into clean, dry jars and sprinkle with sugar. Pour the Cognac or brandy over the fruit to cover completely.

Seal the jars and store for 4–6 months in a cool, dry place.

STRAWBERRY, PINEAPPLE
AND KIRSCH CONSERVE

STRAWBERRY, PINEAPPLE AND KIRSCH CONSERVE

Rich in flavour and colour, this conserve is easy and quick to prepare.
It can be made in summer when fruit is plentiful and stored until winter if wished.

Makes 1 kg (2 lb)

Place the pineapple, strawberries and sugar into a preserving pan. Heat gently, stirring until the sugar has dissolved, then bring to the boil. Boil the conserve for 15–20 minutes, or until setting point is reached (see note page 216). Remove from the heat, and stir in the kirsch. Return the pan to the heat and boil for 1 minute.

Pour the conserve into warm, dry, sterilized jars. When cold, cover with wax discs and seal. Store in a cool, dry place.

INGREDIENTS
225 g (8 oz) fresh pineapple,
  chopped into small pieces
750 g (1½ lb) strawberries, hulled
750 g (1½ lb) sugar
100 ml (4 fl oz) kirsch

219

LOGANBERRY JAM

Plump loganberries are in season during summer and are available in all the markets.
They can be used for pie fillings or to make this rich purple jam.

Makes 3.2 kg (7 lb)

INGREDIENTS
1.8 kg (4 lb) loganberries
1.8 kg (4 lb) sugar

Place the fruit in a preserving pan. Simmer over a gentle heat until the juices run. Add the sugar and heat gently, stirring until the sugar has dissolved. Bring to the boil, and boil rapidly for 20 minutes or until setting point is reached (see note on page 216).

Pour the jam into warm, dry, sterilized jars. When the jam is cold, cover with wax discs and seal. Store in a cool, dry place.

BRAMBLE JELLY

This delightful jelly is like a sweet breath of country air. Elderberries should be
gathered on a dry day and removed from the stems with the prongs of a fork.
If elderberries are unobtainable, use only blackberries.

Makes 2.3 kg (5 lb)

INGREDIENTS
1.5 kg (3 lb) blackberries
500 g (1 lb) elderberries
600 ml (1 pint) water
juice of 2 lemons
500 g (1 lb) sugar to each
*   600 ml (1 pint) of juice*

Place the blackberries, elderberries, water and lemon juice in a preserving pan. Bring to the boil, reduce the heat and simmer for 1 hour or until tender. Strain the cooked fruit through a jelly bag or a piece of muslin.

Measure the juice and pour it into the pan with the correct amount of sugar. Heat gently, stirring until the sugar has dissolved, then bring to the boil. Boil for 10 minutes, or until setting point is reached (see note on page 216). Pour into warm, dry sterilized jars. When cold, cover with wax discs and seal. Store in a cool, dry place.

CHERRY AND APPLE JAM

This jam preserves two of summer's freshest fruits.

Makes 2.3 kg (5 lb)

INGREDIENTS
1 kg (2 lb) sour cooking apples
900 ml (1½ pints) water
2 kg (4 lb) Morello or May Duke
*   cherries*
juice of 1 lemon
1.75 kg (3½ lb) sugar
a knob of butter

Slice the apples without peeling or coring. Put them into a large saucepan with the water and simmer for 30–40 minutes, until they are well pulped. Spoon them into a jelly bag and leave to strain for several hours.

Put the apple extract, which should weigh about 300 g (10 oz), into a preserving pan with the cherries and lemon juice. Simmer gently for about 30 minutes, until most of the moisture from the cherries has evaporated. Remove from the heat and stir in the sugar. Add the knob of butter, then bring to the boil and boil for 10 minutes.

Test for a set (see note on page 216) and, when setting point is reached, take the pan off the heat and remove any scum from the surface with a slotted spoon. Pour into warm, dry, sterilized jars. When the jar is cold, cover with wax discs and seal. Store in a cool, dry place.

Apricot and Amaretto Conserve

This luscious, glowing conserve makes an ideal gift. It is delicious eaten with warm buttered bread.

Makes about 1 kg (2 lb)

Halve the apricots and remove the stones. Place the stones in boiling water for a few minutes, then drain. Wrap the stones in a cloth, and crack them with a hammer or a rolling pin. Remove the kernels from their shells and blanch in boiling water. Split the kernels and reserve.

Place the apricots, sugar and water in a preserving pan, and heat gently, stirring until the sugar has dissolved. Add the kernels and bring to the boil.

Boil the conserve for 15–20 minutes, or until setting point is reached (see note on page 216). Remove from the heat, stir in the Amaretto, and return to the boil for 1 minute. Pour the conserve into warm, dry, sterilized jars. When cold, cover with waxed discs and seal. Store in a cool, dry place.

INGREDIENTS
750 g (1½ lb) fresh apricots
750 g (1½ lb) sugar
150 ml (¼ pint) water
45 ml (3 tbsp) Amaretto liqueur

Pickled Walnuts

Pickled walnuts are often associated with Boxing Day, along with cold turkey and bread sauce but they are quite delicious with any cold meats, poultry or cheese. The walnuts must be picked during July, from the beginning to the middle of the month, while they are still green, and before the shells have hardened; insert a needle into the nut, and push it through—there should be no hard shell. They will be ready to eat after 6 weeks and will keep for about 2 years.

Makes 900 g (2 lb)

Make the brine by boiling the water and pouring it over the salt. Cool.

Wear rubber gloves to prepare the walnuts, as they will stain your hands. Prick the walnuts with a fork or knitting needle and place in a bowl. Cover with brine. Put a plate on top to immerse them, and leave them to soak for 12 days, changing the brine every 4 days.

Drain the walnuts and spread them on a large plate. Leave them to dry in the sun for 2–3 days, or until they have turned completely black. Pack the walnuts into jars.

Boil the vinegar with the spices for 10 minutes, then pour over the walnuts until completely covered. Cover the jars and keep in a dry place. If you need extra spiced vinegar, make up another batch in the same proportion of spices to vinegar.

INGREDIENTS
900 g (2 lb) green walnuts
BRINE
200 g (7 oz) salt to every
  1.2 litres (2 pints) water
SPICED VINEGAR
1.2 litres (2 pints) white malt
  vinegar
40 g (1½ oz) peppercorns
25 g (1 oz) allspice berries
25 g (1 oz) bruised fresh root
  ginger

PICCALILLI

This bright golden pickle is quite delicious served with cold gammon or tongue, or a variety of cold meat and cheese. Use only the freshest, undamaged vegetables, and a good quality vinegar, such as distilled white malt, or a white wine vinegar.

Makes 2.3 kg (5 lb)

Place the prepared vegetables into a large bowl, sprinkle with salt, cover and leave for 12 hours or overnight.

Rinse the vegetables under cold water and drain. Pour 900 ml (1½ pints) of the vinegar into a large heavy-based saucepan with the pickling spice. Bring to the boil and boil for 5 minutes. Strain and return the vinegar to the pan.

Mix the remaining pickling sauce ingredients with the remaining vinegar, and add to the vinegar in the pan. Bring to the boil and add the vegetables. Simmer the pickle for 10 minutes.

Cool and pour into dry, sterilized jars. Cover with a non-metallic lid and store in a cool, dark, dry place.

This recipe makes an ideal gift. It keeps for up to 6 months and makes a special meal with crusty bread and cold sliced ham and pork.

INGREDIENTS
225 g (8 oz) French beans, cut into 2.5 cm (1 inch) lengths
500 g (1 lb) small onions or shallots, roughly chopped
500 g (1 lb) courgettes, sliced crossways
1 cucumber, peeled and diced
1 small marrow, peeled, seeded and diced
2 cauliflowers, divided into florets
75 g (3 oz) salt
PICKLING SAUCE
1.2 litres (2 pints) distilled white malt, or white wine vinegar
25 g (1 oz) pickling spice
15 ml (1 tbsp) turmeric
15 ml (1 tbsp) mustard powder
15 ml (1 tbsp) ground ginger
15 ml (1 tbsp) cornflour
225 g (8 oz) Demerara sugar

LIME CURD

Curds are usually made in small quantities as they contain butter and eggs, and are more perishable than jam. When cooled, the curd should be stored in the refrigerator, where it will keep for about 2 months.
Fruit curds may be spread on buttered bread, or used as a filling for a sponge cake or pastry tart.

Makes 450 ml (¾ pint)

Place the lime rind and juice, sugar and butter in a double boiler. Grate the limes directly into the bowl of the double boiler so that none of the rind is wasted. Stir over simmering water until the butter melts and the sugar dissolves. Beat the eggs in a small bowl and strain them through a sieve into the lime mixture. Stir the mixture constantly, for 15 minutes, or until the curd thickens and coats the back of a spoon. Pour into warm, dry, sterilized jars. When cold, cover with waxed discs, and seal. Store in the refrigerator.
Tangerine curd
Use the finely grated rind and juice of 3 tangerines instead of the limes.

INGREDIENTS
finely grated rind and juice of 4 limes
175 g (6 oz) sugar
100 g (4 oz) butter
3 large eggs

PICCALILLI

PEACHES IN BRANDY

This is an economical way of preserving fruit in brandy, by mixing a thick sugar syrup with the alcohol.
Buy the peaches in August and bottle them for Christmas. They are delicious served in their syrup, with a rich velvety vanilla ice-cream.

Serves 12

INGREDIENTS
12 large ripe peaches
water
1.3 kg (2½ lb) sugar
about 600 ml (1 pint) brandy

Half-fill a large saucepan with water, and bring to the boil. Immerse the peaches in the water and poach them for 4 minutes. Drain and skin, leaving the fruit whole.

Make a thin syrup by placing 225 g (8 oz) of the sugar in a saucepan with 600 ml (1 pint) water. Stir over gentle heat until the sugar dissolves, then bring to the boil. Boil for 2 minutes. Add the skinned peaches and simmer for 1 minute. Remove the peaches, drain and cool.

Measure 600 ml (1 pint) of the syrup and place it in a saucepan. Add the remaining sugar, and heat gently, stirring until the sugar dissolves. Using a pastry brush dipped in warm water, wash down any sugar crystals which have formed on the side of the pan; this prevents the syrup from crystallizing. Bring to the boil and boil steadily for 2 minutes until the syrup reaches 102°C (216°F) on a sugar thermometer. Immediately plunge the base of the pan in cold water to prevent the syrup from cooking any further. Cool. Pack the peaches into a large 2 litre (3½ pint) kilner jar. Pour an equal quantity of syrup and brandy over them to cover. Seal and store in a cool, dry place for 4–6 months.

APRICOT AND DATE CHUTNEY

This delicious fruity chutney makes an excellent accompaniment to cheese, cold meats, poultry and curry.

Makes 2.8 kg (6 lb)

INGREDIENTS
500 g (1 lb) dried apricots or
1 kg (2 lb) fresh apricots
1 kg (2 lb) dates, weighed before stoning
250 g (9 oz) preserved ginger, chopped
4 garlic cloves, crushed
500 g (1 lb) Demerara sugar
500 g (1 lb) stoned raisins
65 g (2½ oz) sea salt
about 1.2 litres (2 pints) white wine vinegar

If using dried apricots, cover them with cold water, and soak overnight. If using fresh apricots, stone them.

Stone the dates. Drain the apricots and place all of the ingredients in a pan. Add sufficient vinegar to cover and bring to the boil. Reduce the heat, and simmer for about 2 hours, or until the fruit is soft and the chutney is thick. Pour into warm, dry, sterilized jars and seal with non-metallic lids. Store in a dark, cool, dry place.

SPECIAL
OCCASIONS

CHRISTMAS

Make merry with a traditional family Christmas feast with all the trimmings.

Serves 6—8

Chestnut and Apple Soup
***

Roast Goose with Fruit and Nut Stuffing
Spiced Cranberries with Port and Orange
***

Roast Potatoes and Parsnips
Brussels Sprouts with Almonds
Glazed Carrots
***

Polly Basset's Christmas Pudding with Brandy Butter
***

Christmas Cake
Mince Pies

CHESTNUT AND APPLE SOUP

*All the flavours in this recipe combine beautifully to create a delicate
but tasty soup which is ideal to serve before a large meal.*

Serves 6—8

INGREDIENTS

50 g (2 oz) butter

3 shallots, finely chopped

*2 slices unsmoked streaky bacon,
rinded and finely chopped*

2 celery stalks, finely chopped

*75 g (3 oz) cooking apple, peeled
and roughly chopped*

*750 g (1½ lb) canned unsweetened
chestnuts, drained*

*1.5 litres (3 pints) chicken stock
(see page 247)*

2.5 ml (½ tsp) mace

2.5 ml (½ tsp) sugar

salt and pepper

45 ml (3 tbsp) medium dry sherry

40 g (1½ oz) butter

*150 g (5 oz) cooking apple, peeled
and sliced*

7.5 ml (1½ tsp) sugar

*45 ml (3 tbsp) single cream,
to garnish*

Melt the butter and fry the shallots and bacon for 5 minutes. Add the celery and apple, and cover with a piece of buttered greaseproof paper. Cover the pan with a lid, and sweat the vegetables over gentle heat for 10 minutes. Remove the paper and stir in the chestnuts. Pour in the stock, add the mace and sugar, and bring to a gentle boil. Cover the pan and cook for 30 minutes.

Season to taste with salt and pepper. Purée the soup and stir in the sherry. For the garnish, melt the butter, add the apple slices, sprinkle over the sugar and fry until golden.

To serve, either pour the soup into a tureen or individual bowls, swirl in the cream, and garnish with the apples.

ROAST GOOSE WITH FRUIT AND NUT STUFFING

Goose is in season from September to February and is at its best around Christmas time. A 4.5 kg (10 lb) bird will only feed about 8 people due to the high percentage of bone and fat. Goose is virtually self-basting and an excellent bird for roasting.

Serves 6—8

To make the giblet stock, place the giblets, onion, carrot, bay leaf, parsley sprigs, peppercorns and water in a saucepan, and bring to the boil. Skim the scum from the surface, reduce the heat, partially cover the pan and simmer gently for about 4 hours. Strain the stock, and skim any fat from the surface. Measure 600 ml (1 pint) and reserve.

Meanwhile, soak the prunes and apricots in the red wine for 3—4 hours. Wipe the goose inside and out, remove any fat from the cavity and season. Melt the butter in a frying pan and fry the onion until soft. Add the liver and fry for 2 minutes, or until it changes colour. Cool slightly and place in a large bowl. Add the remaining stuffing ingredients together with the prunes, apricots and the wine in which they were soaking.

Mix and season well then stuff the neck end of the goose loosely with the mixture.

Truss the goose neatly and place it on a rack in a roasting pan. Prick the lower legs, breast and sides of the bird, and roast it breast side up for 20 minutes at 200°C (400°F) mark 6.

Remove the bird from the oven and turn it over on to its breast. Reduce the oven temperature to 170°C (325°F) mark 3 and roast for 2 hours. Turn the goose on to its back and roast, breast side up, for a further 1—1¼ hours. The bird is cooked sufficiently if the juices run clear when a skewer is inserted into the leg. During cooking, pour off excess fat from the roasting pan several times.

When the goose is cooked, leave it in a warm oven, with the door open, for about 15 minutes before carving. Meanwhile, make the gravy. Skim off most of the fat from the juices in the roasting tin then stir in the flour, over gentle heat. Add the measured stock gradually, then add the wine. Simmer, stirring, for about 10 minutes. Season and strain into a gravy boat. Serve with the goose and stuffing.

INGREDIENTS

175 g (6 oz) stoned prunes, roughly chopped
100 g (4 oz) dried apricots, roughly chopped
225 ml (8 fl oz) red wine
3.5—4.5 kg (8—10 lb) goose, trussed weight
salt and pepper
40 g (1½ oz) butter
1 onion, finely chopped
the goose liver, finely chopped
175 g (6 oz) fresh breadcrumbs
500 g (1 lb) cooking apples, peeled and roughly chopped
100 g (4 oz) walnuts, roughly chopped
45 ml (3 tbsp) chopped fresh parsley
5 ml (1 tsp) oregano
GIBLET GRAVY
goose giblets, minus the liver
1 onion, quartered
1 small carrot, roughly chopped
1 bay leaf
few parsley sprigs
4 black peppercorns
1.5 litres (2½ pints) water
30 ml (2 tbsp) flour
300 ml (½ pint) red wine
salt and pepper

SPICED CRANBERRIES WITH PORT AND ORANGE

An excellent accompaniment to poultry, game and cold meats.

Serves 6—8

INGREDIENTS

350 g (12 oz) fresh cranberries
225 g (8 oz) sugar
150 ml (¼ pint) orange juice
finely grated rind of 1 orange
75 ml (3 fl oz) water
45 ml (3 tbsp) port
1 cinnamon stick

Place all the ingredients in a pan over moderate heat. Stir until the sugar dissolves, then bring to the boil. Reduce the heat and simmer for 20 minutes. Remove the cinnamon stick and serve.

This dish can be served hot or made in advance and served chilled.

ROAST POTATOES AND PARSNIPS

Roast potatoes are traditionally served with the Christmas bird and trimmings.
The sweet parsnip is also particularly good cooked in this way.

Serves 6—8

INGREDIENTS

1 kg (2 lb) medium potatoes,
   halved
1 kg (2 lb) medium parsnips,
   halved
salt
100 g (4 oz) butter

Cook the potatoes and parsnips in a large saucepan of lightly salted boiling water for 10 minutes. Drain. Place the butter in a baking dish, and put into the oven heated to 200°C (400°F) mark 6 to melt. Scratch the surface of the potatoes only with a fork, to give them a crunchy skin when cooked.

When the butter is hot and sizzling, add the potatoes and parsnips, and toss in the butter. Roast for about 1 hour, or until crunchy and golden.

BRUSSELS SPROUTS WITH ALMONDS

Few things could taste worse than soggy 'sprouts', but when served slightly crunchy
with a lemon almond butter, they are delicious.

Serves 6—8

INGREDIENTS

750 g (1½ lb) Brussels sprouts
75 g (3 oz) butter
40 g (1½ oz) slivered almonds
finely grated rind and juice of
   ½ a lemon
salt and pepper

Steam or boil the sprouts until just tender. Drain well.

Melt the butter, add the almonds and cook until slightly golden. Add the lemon rind and juice and remove from the heat.

Place the sprouts in a serving dish and pour over the hot butter. Season to taste.

From Left to Right: CHESTNUT AND APPLE SOUP, POLLY BASSET'S CHRISTMAS PUDDING,
CHRISTMAS CAKE, MINCE PIES, BRANDY BUTTER, ROAST PARSNIPS, GLAZED CARROTS,
ROAST GOOSE WITH FRUIT AND NUT STUFFING, ROAST POTATOES, BRUSSELS SPROUTS
WITH ALMONDS, SPICED CRANBERRIES WITH PORT AND ORANGE.

GLAZED CARROTS

*For this recipe the carrots may be peeled and cut into even 'barrel' shapes,
sliced into quarters lengthways, or left whole, depending on their size.*

Serves 6—8

INGREDIENTS

500 g (1 lb) carrots

300 ml ($\frac{1}{2}$ pint) water

10 ml (2 tsp) sugar

1.25 ml ($\frac{1}{4}$ tsp) salt

50 g (2 oz) butter

*chopped fresh herbs—thyme,
   parsley, sage etc (optional)*

Place the carrots, water, 2.5 ml ($\frac{1}{2}$ tsp) sugar, salt and 15 g ($\frac{1}{2}$ oz) butter in a pan and bring to the boil. Boil slowly, uncovered for about 30 minutes, until the water evaporates. Turn down the heat and add the remaining sugar and butter. Cook the carrots until glazed, shaking the pan from time to time. A few chopped herbs may be added at this point if desired.

POLLY BASSET'S CHRISTMAS PUDDING

*This dates back to the late 19th century. Although Christmas puddings
should be made well in advance, it is possible to make this pudding on
Christmas Eve with very successful results.*

Serves 8—10

INGREDIENTS

225 g (8 oz) currants

225 g (8 oz) sultanas

225 g (8 oz) stoned raisins

225 g (8 oz) Barbados sugar

100 g (4 oz) grated beef suet

100 g (4 oz) fresh breadcrumbs

100 g (4 oz) ground almonds

*100 g (4 oz) blanched almonds,
   chopped*

100 g (4 oz) mixed candied peel

*175 g (6 oz) cooking apple, peeled
   and finely chopped*

225 g (8 oz) plain flour

finely grated rind of 1 lemon

finely grated rind of 1 orange

30 ml (2 tbsp) lemon juice

75 ml (3 fl oz) stout

4 eggs, beaten

15 g ($\frac{1}{2}$ oz) ground mixed spice

1.25 ml ($\frac{1}{4}$ tsp) grated nutmeg

1.25 ml ($\frac{1}{4}$ tsp) ground cinnamon

pinch of salt

75 ml (5 tbsp) brandy

Mix all the ingredients together in a large bowl with 30 ml (2 tbsp) of the brandy. Pour the mixture into a greased 2 litre (3$\frac{1}{2}$ pint) pudding basin and cover with a double layer of greased, greaseproof paper or aluminium foil, pleated in the middle to allow for expansion. Tie string under the rim and across the top to make a handle. Place a trivet in the base of a large saucepan. Lower the pudding into the saucepan and fill with enough boiling water to come two thirds of the way up the sides of the basin. Cover and cook in simmering water for 8 hours. Pour in more boiling water as necessary.

When the pudding is cooked, pour the remaining brandy over the surface and re-cover. To reheat, boil gently for 3—4 hours.

To serve, decorate with a sprig of holly and flambé at the table with warmed brandy, if wished.

BRANDY BUTTER

Brandy butter may be made up to 3 weeks before Christmas, sealed in a jar and stored in the refrigerator.

Makes 225 g (8 oz)

Cream the butter until pale, light and fluffy. Beat in the sugar and lemon rind until well mixed. Gradually add the brandy, beating constantly until well blended. Serve slightly chilled.

Rum butter

Use soft brown sugar instead of white, orange rind instead of lemon and replace the brandy with rum.

INGREDIENTS
100 g (4 oz) unsalted butter
100 g (4 oz) caster or icing sugar
finely grated rind of 1 lemon
45–60 ml (3–4 tbsp) brandy

MINCE PIES

Hot mince pies served on Christmas Eve herald the beginning of the holiday.
Serve them warm rather than hot, with brandy or rum butter.
For the mincemeat flavours to blend, make the mixture at least 2 weeks in advance.

Makes 24

Mix all the ingredients for the mincemeat together in a large bowl. Spoon into clean, dry screw-top jars, seal and store in a cool dry place for at least 2 weeks until required.

Roll out half the pastry on a lightly floured board.

With a 7.5 cm (3 inch) fluted cutter, cut out 24 rounds and line the bases of 24 patty tins. Fill them two-thirds full with mincemeat.

Roll out the remaining dough and using a 6.5 cm (2½ inch) fluted cutter, cut out 24 lids. Dip the lids in milk on both sides and press gently on to the filled bases. Make a small hole in the top of each pie and bake at 180°C (350°F) mark 4, for 25–30 minutes.

Place the pies on a wire rack and sprinkle them with caster sugar.

Note
The recipe for mincemeat will make 1.5 kg (3 lb). You will need approximately 500 g (1 lb) for the mince pies. Any leftover mincemeat can be put in an airtight container and kept for a maximum of 1 year.

INGREDIENTS
rich shortcrust pastry made with
    225 g (8 oz) plain flour (see
    page 248)
milk
caster sugar
MINCEMEAT
225 g (8 oz) currants
225 g (8 oz) sultanas
225 g (8 oz) stoned raisins
225 g (8 oz) dark soft brown
    sugar
175 g (6 oz) cooking apples, peeled
    and finely chopped
100 g (4 oz) mixed candied peel
100 g (4 oz) grated beef suet
75 g (3 oz) walnuts, coarsely
    chopped
100 ml (4 fl oz) dark rum
finely grated rind of 1 orange
finely grated rind of 1 lemon
30 ml (2 tbsp) lemon juice
15 g (½ oz) mixed spice
pinch of grated nutmeg

CHRISTMAS CAKE

*A traditional, spicy and rich fruit cake, which should be made during October,
or early November.*
*To decorate the Christmas cake, cover it first with marzipan, then with
icing. The icing may be piped, or rough iced. A most effective alternative
decoration, is to cover the top of the cake only with marzipan and to
arrange an assortment of nuts and glacé fruits on the top. Cover the marzipan
with a little apricot glaze, and make a pattern with brazils, almonds and
walnuts, glacé cherries, glacé pineapple, and angelica. Brush the top with
more apricot glaze and tie a wide satin ribbon around the cake.*

Makes one 20 cm (8 inch) round cake

INGREDIENTS

*100 g (4 oz) glacé cherries, washed,
dried and quartered*
100 g (4 oz) mixed candied peel
225 g (8 oz) sultanas
225 g (8 oz) currants
*225 g (8 oz) stoned raisins,
chopped*
225 g (8 oz) plain flour
2.5 ml ($\frac{1}{2}$ tsp) salt
2.5 ml ($\frac{1}{2}$ tsp) ground cinnamon
1.25 ml ($\frac{1}{4}$ tsp) grated nutmeg
1.25 ml ($\frac{1}{4}$ tsp) ground cloves
5 ml (1 tsp) ground mixed spice
225 g (8 oz) butter
225 g (8 oz) dark brown sugar
finely grated rind of 1 lemon
finely grated rind of 1 orange
4 eggs
2.5 ml ($\frac{1}{2}$ tsp) vanilla essence
15 ml (1 tbsp) black treacle
50 g (2 oz) ground almonds
*50 g (2 oz) blanched almonds,
chopped*
45 ml (3 tbsp) brandy

Place the cherries, candied peel, sultanas, currants and raisins in a bowl. Sift the flour, salt and spices together. Stir 50 g (2 oz) of the spiced flour into the fruits, making sure they are completely coated in the flour; this prevents the fruit from sinking to the bottom of the cake during baking.

Cream the butter until pale and fluffy. Gradually add the sugar, and beat well. Add the lemon and orange rind.

In a small bowl, lightly beat the eggs, then add the vanilla essence and treacle. Gradually add the egg mixture to the butter and sugar, beating well between each addition to prevent curdling (a little flour added with the last of the egg mixture will also prevent this).

Gradually add the remaining flour to the egg mixture, then the fruit, together with any flour left in that bowl.

Add the ground and chopped almonds and the brandy. Mix thoroughly, and pour the mixture into a 20 cm (8 inch) round cake tin, double-lined with greased greaseproof paper. Make a slight indentation in the centre of the cake so that it will have an even surface when cooked.

Wrap brown paper around the outside of the cake tin to prevent the cake from browning too much. Place the cake in the centre of the oven and bake at 150°C (300°F) mark 2 for 1½ hours. Reduce the temperature to 140°C (275°F) mark 1 and continue baking for another 2¼ hours. Should the cake be browning too much, place a circle of aluminium foil over the top. To test whether the cake is cooked, insert a skewer into the centre of the cake. If it comes out clean, the cake is ready, but if any mixture clings to the skewer, bake for a further 30 minutes.

Leave the cake in the tin for 30 minutes, then turn it out on to a wire rack and leave until cold. Wrap in aluminium foil and store in an airtight container.

To 'feed' the cake during storage, make a few holes with a small skewer, and pour a little brandy over the cake from time to time.

MARZIPAN
*If decorating the cake with royal icing, it must first be covered with marzipan.
You will need 750 g (1½ lb) for a 20 cm (8 inch) cake.*

Makes 1 kg (2 lb)

INGREDIENTS

500 g (1 lb) ground almonds
175 g (6 oz) caster sugar
175 g (6 oz) icing sugar, sifted
30 ml (2 tbsp) lemon juice
5 ml (1 tsp) orange flower water
2.5 ml ($\frac{1}{2}$ tsp) vanilla essence
1 whole egg
1–2 egg yolks

Place the almonds, caster and icing sugar into a bowl. Mix well and add the remaining ingredients. Knead the mixture lightly, with your hand until it forms a smooth paste. Do not knead the paste for too long, as the almonds will become very oily. Wrap the paste in clingfilm until needed.
To decorate
Measure the circumference of the cake with a piece of string. Take two thirds of the marzipan and roll it into a long strip, trim to the height and circumference of the cake. Brush a little apricot glaze on to the sides of the cake and cover with the marzipan strip.

To cover the top of the cake with marzipan, use the baking tin as a guide. Roll the remaining marzipan into a circle and cut it slightly larger than the diameter of the cake.

Brush the top of the cake with more apricot glaze and press the marzipan circle into place. Trim the edges and press into place. Wrap the cake loosely in foil, and leave for 1 week before icing.

ICING

ALBUMEN BASED ICING

Albumen based powder makes the best quality royal icing.

Makes 500 g (1 lb)

Sprinkle the powder into the water. The mixture will become quite lumpy. Leave to soak for at least 15 minutes, then stir and strain the mixture into a bowl. Sprinkle the sifted icing sugar on to the solution and beat for 20 minutes. If mixing the icing by machine, beat on the very slowest speed, for the same amount of time.

INGREDIENTS
15 g (½ oz) albumen powder
75 ml (3 fl oz) cold water
500 g (1 lb) icing sugar

FRESH EGG WHITE ICING

Makes 500 g (1 lb)

Sift the icing sugar into a bowl.

Whisk the egg whites until frothy, then gradually add the icing sugar, a little at a time, beating well between each addition. Stir in the lemon juice and beat for 20 minutes.

Glycerine is added to the icing to make it softer. Use it for covering a cake, but not for piping. Add the glycerine at the same time as the lemon juice, if using. Lastly, a few drops of blue colouring can be added to whiten the icing. Place the icing in a tightly sealed plastic container and leave overnight before using.

INGREDIENTS
500 g (1 lb) icing sugar
2 egg whites
5 ml (1 tsp) lemon juice
5 ml (1 tsp) glycerine (optional)
few drops of blue food colouring (optional)

SMOOTH ICING

With a pastry brush, remove any crumbs or sugar from the top of the marzipan. Pour sufficient icing to give a good coat on the top of the cake, and work it across the top and sides with a palette knife. You will need about 1 kg (2 lb) in total. Take a metal ruler and place it on the top of the cake at a slight angle. Push it away from yourself across the top of the cake. Now press the farthest edge of the ruler on to the cake, and draw it back across the top towards you. Once again, press the ruler edge nearest to you down on to the surface of the cake. Lift the ruler up—the top surface should be completely smooth.

To smooth the sides of the cake, place the cake on an icing turntable. Hold a scraper or metal ruler against the side of the cake, with your right hand. With your left hand, grasp the turntable and rotate anti-clockwise, to complete a full circle.

Leave the cake to dry, in a cool airy place, for 24 hours. Scrape away any rough edges. Repeat this process twice more, before decorating with piped icing.

Note
When icing a cake, *never* place icing on the centre of the cake board to secure the cake to it, as it turns the cake mouldy.

PICNIC
HAMPER

*Savour the long, lazy days of summer with this portable
banquet for a special occasion.*

Serves 8–10

Yogurt Cheese Balls (see page 100)
Smoked Eel Pâté (see page 47)

***

Granny Smith's Salad (see page 154)
Fennel and Salami with Black Olives (see page 125)
Raised Pork and Apple Pie (see page 31)
Sesame Bread Sticks (see page 196)

***

Grape Tartlets (see page 164)
Melon and Strawberries with Champagne (see page 161)
Rum and Raisin Fudge (see page 208)

AFTERNOON TEA
—VICTORIAN STYLE

*Recapture the elegance of an English afternoon
with this classic Victorian tea.*

Serves 8–10

Cucumber Sandwiches
Egg and Cress Sandwiches
Meringues (see page 194)
Chocolate Eclairs (see page 193)
Irish Apple Cake (see page 191)
Scones with Jam and Clotted Cream (see page 196)
Dundee Cake (see page 182)

IRISH APPLE CAKE AND SCONES

GARDEN
PARTY MENU

Celebrate a special birthday, an engagement or anniversary with
this splendid buffet served in the garden. The combined dishes
in this menu have been made to serve 50 people,
although the portions per recipe vary.

Serves 50

Parma Ham and Figs with Caper Dressing
Black and Red Caviar served with Blinis
Satay Sticks with Peanut Sauce

***

Poached Salmon
New Potatoes with Mint Dressing
Avocado, Mozzarella and Tomato Salad
Chicken and Mandarin Rice
Chicory, Watercress and Orange Salad
Green Bean and Lobster Tail Salad

***

Celebration Trifle
Strawberry Flans with Praline Cream
Vanilla Soufflé with Pistachio Nuts

PARMA HAM AND FIGS WITH CAPER DRESSING

These figs look attractive as part of a buffet. They are cut into a waterlily shape,
then filled with fine strips of Parma ham.

INGREDIENTS
50 fresh figs
500 g (1 lb) Parma ham, cut into
    fine julienne strips
lettuce leave, to garnish
DRESSING
450 ml (¾ pint) sour cream
juice of 1½ lemons
25 ml (5 tsp) Dijon mustard
salt and pepper
45 ml (3 tbsp) capers, drained and
    chopped

Very carefully peel the figs, then cut through each one, from the top almost to the
bottom, to divide the fig into four. Open out the figs and fill them with the Parma
ham.

Mix all the dressing ingredients together and pour them into a serving bowl.

Place the bowl of dressing in the centre of a large serving platter, then arrange
the lettuce leaves around the bowl. Place the figs on the lettuce. Cover with
clingfilm and chill for at least 1 hour before serving.

From Left to Right: AVOCADO, MOZZARELLA AND TOMATO SALAD, POACHED SALMON AND
CHICORY, WATERCRESS AND ORANGE SALAD

BLACK AND RED CAVIAR SERVED WITH BLINIS

The blinis may be made ahead of time and re-heated in a warm oven,
wrapped in aluminium foil. Alternatively, re-heat for a few seconds in a microwave oven.

For the blinis, mix the buckwheat flour and yeast together in a large mixing bowl, then gradually stir in the tepid milk and water to make a thick batter. Cover with clingfilm, and leave in a warm place for about 30 minutes or until risen.

Meanwhile, sift the plain flour and salt into a mixing bowl, make a well in the centre and add the egg yolks and butter. Gradually beat into the flour, adding the milk as the mixture thickens.

Add the batter to the buckwheat mixture and beat together well. Cover with clingfilm and leave in a warm place for 1 hour, or until risen.

Whisk the egg whites until stiff, then gently fold them into the risen batter.

Heat a griddle, or a very large heavy-based frying pan, and grease lightly with butter. To make blinis about 6 cm (2½ inches) in diameter, drop the batter in dessertspoonfuls on to the hot griddle. Cook for about 1 minute or until golden brown underneath and bubbles appear on the surface. Turn over and cook the other side for 1 minute. Remove from the griddle and keep warm. Continue to make more blinis until all of the batter has been used or you have about 100.

For the dill butter, beat the butter until soft, then beat in the dill, seasoning and lemon juice to taste. Spoon into a serving dish.

To serve, spoon the caviars into separate serving bowls and set them on a bed of crushed iced. Serve the blinis hot in a napkin-lined basket with the dill butter.

INGREDIENTS

350 g (12 oz) black caviar, well
  chilled
350 g (12 oz) red caviar, well
  chilled
crushed ice, to serve

BLINIS

250 g (8 oz) buckwheat flour
7 g (¼ oz) sachet easy-blend dried
  yeast
300 ml (½ pint) tepid milk and
  water, mixed
225 g (8 oz) plain flour
5 ml (1 tsp) salt
2 eggs, separated
50 g (2 oz) butter, melted
450 ml (¾ pint) milk

DILL BUTTER

225 g (8 oz) butter
30 ml (2 tbsp) chopped fresh dill
salt and pepper
lemon juice

SATAY STICKS WITH PEANUT SAUCE

*The rich, nutty flavour of the peanut sauce and the tender meat form a perfect
partnership for this unusual party dish.*

INGREDIENTS

1.4 kg (3 lb) rump steak

MARINADE

50 g (2 oz) tamarind pulp

150 ml (¼ pint) boiling water

50 g (2 oz) fresh root ginger,
  chopped

2 large onions, finely chopped

2 garlic cloves, crushed

10 ml (2 tsp) ground cumin

10 ml (2 tsp) ground turmeric

10 ml (2 tsp) finely ground dried
  lemon grass

5 ml (1 tsp) ground coriander

salt and pepper

60 ml (4 tbsp) soy sauce

PEANUT SAUCE

30 ml (2 tbsp) peanut oil

2 large onions, finely chopped

2 garlic cloves, crushed

10 ml (2 tsp) finely ground dried
  lemon grass

1.25 ml (¼ tsp) ground cinnamon

5 ml (1 tsp) chilli powder

juice of 1 lemon

75 g (3 oz) creamed coconut

25 ml (1½ tbsp) dark brown sugar

350 g (12 oz) unsalted peanuts,
  skinned and ground

TO SERVE

1 cucumber, cut into 5 cm (2 inch)
  lengths

3 large onions, thinly sliced

Trim the steak and cut it into 1 cm (½ inch) cubes. Put into a large mixing bowl.

For the marinade, put the tamarind pulp into a small bowl with the boiling water and leave to stand for 30 minutes. Strain the tamarind liquid through a sieve into a mixing bowl, pressing down on the tamarind to extract the juices. Add all the remaining marinade ingredients and mix together well. Pour it over the steak, mix well, cover and leave to marinate for at least 2 hours.

Meanwhile, make the peanut sauce. Dissolve the creamed coconut in 450 ml (¾ pint) boiling water. Heat the oil in a saucepan and fry the onions until soft. Add the garlic and spices, and cook for a further 2–3 minutes, then stir in all of the remaining ingredients with the dissolved coconut. Slowly bring the sauce to the boil, stirring constantly, then reduce the heat and simmer for 20 minutes, stirring frequently. Keep the sauce hot until ready to serve.

Thread the marinated steak on to bamboo skewers, about five pieces to each skewer. Brush with peanut oil and cook under a very hot grill for 5–6 minutes, turning frequently.

Spoon the sauce into a hot serving bowl and place it on a very large hot serving platter. Arrange the cucumber and onions in another bowl and place them on the same platter. Arrange the hot satay sticks around the bowls and serve immediately.

NEW POTATOES WITH MINT DRESSING

*New potatoes and fresh mint is a traditional combination for summer.
If the mint is unavailable, substitute parsley, tarragon or chives.*

INGREDIENTS

4.6 kg (10 lb) new potatoes

150 ml (¼ pint) hot chicken stock
  (see page 247)

sprigs of fresh mint, to garnish

DRESSING

750 ml (1¼ pints) mayonnaise

600 ml (1 pint) sour cream

45 ml (3 tbsp) chopped fresh mint

salt and pepper

Cook the potatoes in boiling salted water until they are tender. Drain well.

Put the potatoes into two large bowls and spoon the stock over them while they are still hot. Allow to cool.

Mix all the dressing ingredients together. Pour the dressing over the potatoes and toss gently but thoroughly together. Spoon into serving dishes and garnish with fresh mint.

POACHED SALMON

This recipe gives instructions for cooking and decorating one salmon,
which will serve 25 people. To serve 50 people, you will need to cook two salmon.
Make sure that the fish kettle is large enough to accommodate the salmon;
it will need to be about 75 cm (30 inches) long. If you do not wish to
prepare the fish yourself, ask the fishmonger to do it for you.

For the poaching stock, put all the ingredients, except the wine, into a large saucepan. Bring to the boil, then reduce the heat and simmer gently for 30 minutes. Add the wine and simmer for a further 20 minutes. Allow to cool.

To prepare the salmon, cut off the fins with sharp scissors. Scrape the fish, with the back of a small knife, to remove as many of the loose scales as possible. Prick or remove the eyes and remove the gills, then remove the entrails of the fish through the gills: this means that the fish does not have to be slit along the belly, and will keep a better shape. Wash the salmon thoroughly under cold running water.

Place the salmon on the trivet inside the fish kettle. Strain the poaching stock into the fish kettle until it covers the salmon completely. If necessary add a little cold water.

Bring almost to the boil, until the water just begins to move. Reduce the heat and simmer for 10 minutes. Very carefully remove the fish kettle from the heat and put it in a cool place. Allow the salmon to cool in the poaching stock, preferably overnight, until it is completely cold.

Lift the salmon from the fish kettle, on the trivet, and drain well. Carefully remove the skin from one side, then turn the salmon over on to a large serving platter, or a board, and then remove the skin from the other side. Tidy the fish up by removing any small bones from the fin areas.

Chop the set aspic jelly on a sheet of wet greaseproof paper with a wet knife (this will make it sparkle). Arrange the jelly around the salmon. Decorate with the cucumber skin, dill, lemon or lime wedges and whole prawns. Glaze or brush the salmon with the remaining aspic jelly.

Keep the salmon in a cool place until ready to serve, and serve with mayonnaise.

INGREDIENTS
4.2 kg (9 lb) fresh salmon
mayonnaise, to serve
POACHING STOCK
1 large onion, sliced
4 carrots, sliced
3 celery stalks, sliced
4 bay leaves
large parsley sprig
small bunch fresh dill
15 ml (1 tbsp) salt
12 peppercorns
4 litres (7 pints) cold water
1 litre (1¾ pints) dry white wine
GARNISH
450 ml (¾ pint) set aspic jelly
30 ml (3 tbsp) mayonnaise
cucumber skin strips
fresh dill
lime or lemon wedges
whole prawns
150 ml (¼ pint) liquid aspic jelly

AVOCADO, MOZZARELLA AND TOMATO SALAD

Colourful and tasty, this salad is ideal as a side salad as well
as a light luncheon dish. Substitute any of your favourite fresh herbs for the dried herbs.

Mix all the dressing ingredients together. Cut the avocados in half lengthways, remove the stones and peel off the skin. Cut each avocado in half again, lengthways, then cut across into thin slices. Put into a large bowl and pour over the dressing.

Arrange the tomatoes in neat rows on two large flat oval serving platters. Season well and sprinkle with the herbs. Sprinkle two-thirds of the cheese over the tomatoes, then arrange the avocados, in neat lines, on top of the cheese. Sprinkle the remaining cheese over the avocados.

INGREDIENTS
4 large ripe avocados
1.4 kg (3 lb) tomatoes, seeded and
  sliced
25 ml (1½ tbsp) mixed dried herbs
400 g (14 oz) mozzarella cheese,
  grated
DRESSING
60 ml (4 tbsp) white wine vinegar
150 ml (¼ pint) olive oil
5 ml (1 tsp) Dijon mustard
salt and pepper
2 garlic cloves, crushed

CHICKEN AND MANDARIN RICE

*Mandarin orange segments add a zesty citrus taste to the rice and chicken.
Because it is prepared in advance, this dish is perfect to serve for a lunch party
as well as when catering for a large number.*

INGREDIENTS

2 vegetable stock cubes

salt and pepper

750 g (1½ lb) long-grain rice

750 g (1½ lb) cooked chicken, cut
   into thin strips

1 head of celery, thinly sliced

60 ml (4 tbsp) chopped parsley

1 bunch spring onions, sliced

200 ml (7 fl oz) mayonnaise

600 g (1¼ lb) canned mandarin
   orange segments, drained

celery leaves, to garnish

Bring a large saucepan of water to the boil, add the stock cubes and salt. Add the rice and cook gently for 20–25 minutes or until the rice is just cooked. Drain, rinse under cold running water, then drain again.

Put the rice, chicken, celery, parsley and onions into a large bowl. Add the mayonnaise, season well, and mix gently together. Carefully stir in the orange segments. Cover and leave for at least 1 hour before serving, to allow the flavours to develop.

Spoon the rice into one large, or two small, serving bowls and garnish with celery leaves.

CHICORY, WATERCRESS AND ORANGE SALAD

*This salad combines the sharp taste of the chicory and watercress
with the refreshing flavour of the orange.*

INGREDIENTS

4 large oranges

6 large heads of chicory, trimmed

4–6 bunches watercress, trimmed
   and washed

DRESSING

60 ml (4 tbsp) red wine vinegar

salt and pepper

2 garlic cloves, crushed

10 ml (2 tsp) Dijon mustard

finely grated rind of 4 oranges

150 ml (¼ pint) olive oil

Mix all the dressing ingredients together.

Remove the rind and all of the white pith from the orange. Using a sharp knife, carefully remove the segments from the oranges, cutting between the connecting tissue. Squeeze the juice from the remaining tissue into the dressing.

Cut the orange segments into small pieces and put them into a large salad bowl. Cut the chicory into fine slices, cutting across the heads, and add them to the salad bowl. Add the watercress. Cover the salad bowl and chill for at least 1 hour.

Just before serving, pour the dressing over the salad and toss lightly together.

GREEN BEAN AND LOBSTER TAIL SALAD

*The addition of lobster tail transforms this salad into a dish suitable
for any special occasion. Prepare with smaller quantities and serve as an elegant starter.*

INGREDIENTS

1.4 kg (3 lb) fine green beans,
   trimmed

500 g (1 lb) fresh lobster tail meat,
   chopped

DRESSING

90 ml (6 tbsp) lemon juice

90 ml (6 tbsp) olive oil

45 ml (3 tbsp) chopped fresh dill

salt and pepper

Cook the beans in a large saucepan of boiling salted water for 3–4 minutes or until they are just tender. Drain, rinse under cold running water and drain again. Spread them out on clean tea towels to drain thoroughly.

Cut the beans into 2.5 cm (1 inch) lengths and put them into a large salad bowl. Add the lobster meat, then cover the bowl and chill for at least 1 hour.

Mix all the dressing ingredients together. Just before serving, pour the dressing over the beans and lobster, and toss well together.

CELEBRATION TRIFLE

From Left to Right: VANILLA SOUFFLE WITH PISTACHIO NUTS, CELEBRATION TRIFLE AND STRAWBERRY FLANS WITH PRALINE CREAM

This delicious trifle will serve 8–10 guests, so you will need to make two, or more, trifles depending on the other desserts being served. Make the day before to allow the flavours to develop.

Put the raspberries into a large bowl and sprinkle with 100 g (4 oz) of the caster sugar. Cover and leave for about 1 hour or until the raspberries start to form juice.

Slice the sponge cakes in half horizontally, then sandwich together with the raspberry jam. Place in a large glass serving bowl and spread with more jam. Spoon 45 ml (3 tbsp) of the sherry over the sponge cakes.

Spoon the raspberries and their juice over the sponge cakes, then place the ratafia biscuits in a single layer on top and spoon on the remaining sherry. Arrange the sliced peach halves on top of the ratafia biscuits. Cover and leave to stand while making the custard.

Very lightly whisk the egg yolks with the remaining caster sugar until thick. Heat the milk until it is almost boiling and then whisk it into the egg yolks. Return the mixture to a heavy-based saucepan and stir over a low heat until the custard thickens, but do not allow it to boil, or to curdle. As soon as the custard thickens, remove it from the heat immediately and strain it through a nylon sieve on to the peaches. Allow to cool, then cover and chill overnight.

Whip the cream with the icing sugar and kirsch until it just holds soft peaks. Carefully spread the cream over the custard, mark into swirls and decorate with chocolate caraque. Chill until ready to serve.

INGREDIENTS
500 g (1 lb) fresh raspberries, hulled
150 g (5 oz) caster sugar
8 trifle sponge cakes
175 g (6 oz) seedless raspberry jam
90 ml (6 tbsp) medium dry sherry
100 g (4 oz) ratafia biscuits
4 large poached, or canned, peach halves, sliced
12 egg yolks
900 ml (1½ pints) milk
300 ml (½ pint) double cream
15 ml (1 tbsp) icing sugar
30 ml (2 tbsp) kirsch
chocolate caraque, to decorate

STRAWBERRY FLANS WITH PRALINE CREAM

The quantities given are for two flans, each one serving 8–10 guests.
The pastry cases may be made and frozen in their uncooked state ahead of time.
Bake from frozen.
The flans are decorated with spun sugar, but if preferred they may be decorated with
piped whipped cream instead.

INGREDIENTS

1 kg (2 lb) fresh strawberries,
  hulled

choux pastry, made with 90 g
  (3½ oz) plain flour (see page 249)

SWEET PASTRY

275 g (10 oz) plain flour

pinch of salt

50 g (2 oz) caster sugar

175 g (6 oz) butter

4 egg yolks

PRALINE CREAM

100 g (4 oz) blanched almonds

100 g (4 oz) caster sugar

600 ml (1 pint) double cream

SPUN SUGAR

225 g (8 oz) granulated sugar

90 ml (6 tbsp) water

15 ml (1 tbsp) liquid glucose

For the sweet pastry, sift the flour and salt into a mixing bowl. Stir in the sugar then rub in the butter until the mixture looks like fine breadcrumbs. Mix to a dough with the egg yolks. Wrap the pastry in clingfilm and chill for 30 minutes.

Divide the pastry into two equal pieces, and roll out each one on an upturned baking sheet to a 28 cm (11 inch) round. Prick the pastry round well with a fork. Chill.

Put the choux pastry into a piping bag fitted with a 1 cm (½ inch) plain nozzle. Pipe a single ring of choux pastry round the edge of each pastry base, piping it 5 mm (¼ inch) in from the edge. Bake at 200°C (400°F) mark 6 for 25–30 minutes or until the choux pastry is well risen and golden brown. Remove from the oven and pierce the choux pastry at intervals, to allow the steam to escape. Return to the oven for 2–3 minutes to dry. Carefully transfer the pastry cases from the baking sheets to wire racks to cool.

For the praline cream, put the almonds and sugar into a small, heavy-based saucepan and heat gently until the sugar dissolves and turns a rich caramel colour. Immediately pour on to an oiled baking sheet and allow to cool and set hard. Grind the nut mixture in an electric grinder, or crush finely with a rolling pin. Whisk the cream until it just holds soft peaks, then gently fold in the praline.

Place the pastry cases on two large flat serving plates and fill them with the praline cream. Cut the strawberries into halves, or slices, and arrange them neatly on top of the cream.

For the spun sugar, lightly oil a rolling pin. Cover the work surface with newspaper, and also cover the floor immediately below. Cover the newspaper on the work surface with greaseproof paper.

Put the sugar, water and liquid glucose into a saucepan and heat gently until every granule of sugar dissolves, brushing down the sides of the pan with a little hot water. Boil the sugar syrup to a temperature of 160°C (320°F). Immediately plunge the base of the pan into cold water to prevent further cooking. Dip two forks, held together, into the syrup then hold them up high until a fine thread starts to fall. Gently throw, or spin, the sugar threads around the rolling pin until a good quantity of threads accumulate. Remove from the rolling pin and set aside. Repeat until all the syrup has been used.

Pile the sugar nests on top of the strawberry flans and keep until required.

VANILLA SOUFFLE WITH PISTACHIO NUTS

This very light creamy soufflé, decorated with pistachio nuts, will serve about 8 guests. Make two, or more, soufflés as required. They can be made the day before.

Make a paper collar for a 16.5 cm (6½ inch) soufflé dish by cutting a double strip of greaseproof paper long enough to fit around the dish, and wide enough to stand 5 cm (2 inches) above the rim. Secure the collar firmly and place the dish on a flat plate.

Sprinkle the gelatine over the water and leave for 2 minutes to soften. Stand the bowl in a saucepan of hot water and heat gently until the gelatine dissolves.

Whisk the egg yolks with the caster sugar and vanilla until they are very thick and will hold a ribbon trail.

Whip 300 ml (½ pint) of the cream until it just holds soft peaks. Whisk the egg whites until they are very stiff.

Whisk the hot gelatine into the egg yolks then fold in the cream. Very carefully, and quickly, fold in the egg whites. Pour the soufflé mixture into the prepared dish and chill for at least 2 hours, or until set.

When set, carefully remove the paper collar. Coat the sides of the soufflé with the chopped nuts.

Whip the remaining cream until thick. Spoon into a small piping bag fitted with a small star nozzle and pipe rosettes around the top edge of the soufflé. Decorate with pistachio nuts. Chill until ready to serve.

INGREDIENTS

20 ml (4 tsp) powdered gelatine
60 ml (4 tbsp) cold water
6 eggs, separated
175 g (6 oz) caster sugar
10 ml (2 tsp) vanilla essence
450 ml (¾ pint) double cream
25 g (1 oz) pistachio nuts, skinned and chopped
whole pistachio nuts, to decorate

BASIC RECIPES

BEEF STOCK

Makes 3 litres (5½ pints)

INGREDIENTS

*1 kg (2 lb) shin of veal, on the
    bone*
25 g (1 oz) lard
*500 g (1 lb) marrow bones,
    in pieces*
3 large carrots, roughly chopped
2 celery stalks, roughly chopped
2 medium onions, quartered
2 large garlic cloves, crushed
4.5 litres (8 pints) water
1 bay leaf
8 black peppercorns
1.25 ml (¼ tsp) thyme
*1 kg (2 lb) shin of beef, sliced
    4 cm (1½ inches) thick*

Bone the veal and reserve the meat.

Place the veal bone, lard, marrow bones, carrots, celery, onions and garlic in a roasting tin. Roast at 220°C (425°F) mark 7, basting and turning them occasionally, for 45 minutes.

Transfer the bones and vegetables to a large saucepan, scraping any brown residue from the roasting tin. Add the water, bay leaf, peppercorns and thyme, and bring to the boil. Do **not** add any salt.

Skim the stock and wipe the edge of the saucepan. Partially cover the pan, and simmer for 4 hours.

Strain the stock and cool slightly. *This is bone stock.*

For beef stock, skim 60 ml (4 tbsp) of the fat from the surface of the bone stock and reserve. Return the stock to the pan. Brown the veal meat and the shin of beef in the reserved fat, turning occasionally, for about 10 minutes. Pour the strained stock over the meat and bring to the boil. Carefully skim the surface and wipe the sides of the pan. Lower the heat and partially cover the pan so that the stock simmers gently. Simmer for 3½–4 hours.

Strain the stock, cool and skim the fat from the surface when cold.

FISH STOCK

Makes about 300 ml (½ pint)

INGREDIENTS

1 fish head and bones
1 carrot, roughly sliced
1 onion, quartered
bouquet garni
a few peppercorns
water

Place all the ingredients in a large pan. Pour in about 450 ml (¾ pint) cold water to cover and bring to the boil. Skim the surface, reduce the heat, and simmer for 20–30 minutes. Strain the stock, cool, cover and refrigerate until required.

To freeze, allow the stock to cool, then strain and freeze in an ice cube tray. Place the cubes in a freezer-proof bag and freeze for up to six months. Defrost 1–2 hours at room temperature, or in a heavy-based saucepan over high heat.

COURT BOUILLON

Makes about 1.5 litres (2½ pints)

Place all the ingredients in a heavy-based saucepan and bring it to the boil. Cover the pan, reduce the heat and simmer for 30 minutes. Allow the stock to cool before using.

To freeze, rapidly boil the court bouillon until reduced to one-quarter of its original quantity. Allow to cool, then strain and freeze in an ice cube tray. Place the cubes in a freezer-proof bag and store for up to six months. Defrost overnight at room temperature or defrost over moderate heat and cool before using.

INGREDIENTS
1.2 litres (2 pints) water
1 carrot, sliced
1 onion, sliced
1 celery stalk, sliced
bouquet garni
1 slice fennel (optional)
450 ml (¾ pint) white wine
6 peppercorns
salt

CHICKEN STOCK

Makes 2.5 litres (4½ pints)

Place all the ingredients in a large saucepan. Bring to the boil slowly, skimming off any scum that rises. Reduce the heat and partially cover the pan. Simmer for 3½ hours. Skim the fat from the surface, strain the stock through a fine sieve and adjust seasoning. Cool and refrigerate until required.

If not using immediately, the stock should be boiled every day if stored in the larder and every 2–3 days if stored in the refrigerator. Freeze as for fish stock (see opposite).

INGREDIENTS
1 boiling fowl
2 chicken feet
1 veal knuckle
3.4 litres (6 pints) water
2 medium onions, quartered
2 celery stalks, roughly chopped
2 garlic cloves, crushed
1 leek, roughly sliced
4 carrots, roughly sliced
bouquet garni
6 peppercorns
salt

SHORTCRUST PASTRY

Makes 750 g (1½ lb)

Sift the flour with the salt into a bowl. Rub in the fat until the mixture resembles fine breadcrumbs. Gradually add the water and mix lightly until the mixture begins to collect together. Form the dough into a ball, wrap in clingfilm and leave to rest in the refrigerator for at least 30 minutes before rolling.
Note
When a recipe specifies, for example, 100 g (4 oz) pastry, this means pastry made using 100 g (4 oz) flour, with the other ingredients in proportion, not the combined weight of the ingredients.

INGREDIENTS
500 g (1 lb) plain flour
pinch of salt
100 g (4 oz) butter, cubed
100 g (4 oz) lard or margarine, cubed
90 ml (6 tbsp) ice-cold water

RICH SHORTCRUST PASTRY

Makes 500 g (1 lb)

INGREDIENTS
225 g (8 oz) plain flour
pinch of salt
150 g (5 oz) butter
15 ml (1 tbsp) caster sugar
1 egg yolk, size 2
about 25 ml (1½ tbsp) ice-cold
  water

Sift the flour with the salt into a bowl. Rub in the butter until the mixture resembles breadcrumbs. Stir in the sugar, add the egg yolk and sufficient water to bind the dough. Mix lightly then turn it out on to a lightly floured surface. Form into a ball, wrap in clingfilm and rest in the refrigerator for 30 minutes before rolling.

PATE SUCREE

Makes 225 g (8 oz)

INGREDIENTS
100 g (4 oz) plain flour
pinch of salt
50 g (2 oz) caster sugar
50 g (2 oz) butter
2 egg yolks, size 2
2 drops vanilla essence

Sift the flour with the salt on to a board and make a well in the centre. Place the remaining ingredients in the well. Using one hand, mix the sugar, butter, egg yolks and vanilla essence into a paste with your fingertips. Quickly draw in the surrounding flour and knead the dough lightly. Wrap in clingfilm and leave to rest in the refrigerator for 45 minutes–1 hour, before rolling.

PUFF PASTRY

Makes about 500 g (1 lb)

INGREDIENTS
225 g (8 oz) plain flour
pinch of salt
225 g (8 oz) butter
about 150 ml (¼ pint) water

Sift the flour and salt into a bowl. Lightly rub in 25 g (1 oz) of the butter. Add sufficient water to make a firm dough. Turn it out on to a floured surface and knead until smooth. Wrap the dough in clingfilm and leave to rest in the refrigerator for 30 minutes.

Lightly beat the butter into a block about 12.5 × 10 cm (5 × 4 inches). Roll out the dough on a lightly floured surface into a rectangle about 15 × 30 cm (6 × 12 inches).

Place the butter in the middle of the pastry and fold each end of the pastry over the butter to form a parcel. Press the sides together and turn it over. Roll out the pastry into an oblong shape, fold it over into three, and give the parcel a 90° anti-clockwise turn. Repeat once more, wrap and rest in the refrigerator for 30 minutes. Repeat the rolling, folding and resting process six more times, resting the dough for 15 minutes between rollings.

If the pastry appears streaky after the final turn, roll it out just once more, and only once, as it will not rise properly if handled too much. Puff pastry is usually baked in a hot oven, at 220°C (425°F) mark 7, on a wet baking sheet; the resulting steam helps the pastry to rise.

Note
It is not practical to make puff pastry in quantities smaller than 500 g (1 lb) flour weight. This quantity of puff pastry is equivalent to two 368 g (13 oz) packets of frozen.

CHOUX PASTRY

Makes about 500 g (1 lb)

Sift the flour with the salt on to a sheet of greaseproof paper. Place the water and butter in a saucepan, and heat, allowing the butter to melt before boiling point is reached. Bring to a rolling boil, and **immediately** pour in the flour. Remove the pan from the heat. Beat the mixture until it is smooth and leaves the sides of the pan. Cool, then gradually beat in the eggs. You may not need to add all of the eggs. Add just enough eggs to make the mixture glossy and smooth, and of a dropping consistency.

INGREDIENTS
90 g (3½ oz) plain flour
a pinch of salt
185 ml (7 fl oz) water
65 g (2½ oz) butter
3 eggs, beaten, size 2

WHOLEMEAL PASTRY

Makes 500 g (1 lb)

Sift the flour with the baking powder and salt into a bowl. Tip in the bran left in the sieve and mix well. Rub in the butter until the mixture resembles breadcrumbs. Gradually add the cold water and mix lightly until the dough forms a ball. Knead lightly, form into a round and cover with clingfilm. Rest in the refrigerator for 1 hour before rolling.

For a less crumbly pastry, use half wholemeal flour and half plain flour.

INGREDIENTS
275 g (10 oz) wholemeal flour
15 ml (1 tbsp) baking powder
pinch of salt
150 g (5 oz) butter
45–60 ml (3–4 tbsp) water

SUETCRUST PASTRY

Makes about 500 g (1 lb)

Sift the flour with the baking powder and salt into a large mixing bowl and mix in the pepper. Stir in the suet and add sufficient water to mix to a soft dough. Knead lightly until smooth. Form into a ball, cover and leave to rest 5 minutes. To use, roll out to 0.5 cm (¼ in) thick.

Suetcrust pastry can be used on both sweet and savoury dishes and is best boiled or steamed.

INGREDIENTS
350 g (12 oz) self-raising flour
good pinch of salt
freshly ground black pepper
175 g (6 oz) grated beef suet
water

HOT WATER CRUST PASTRY

Makes enough to line 1.5 litre (2½ pint) mould

Warm a mixing bowl and sift the flour and salt into it. Make a well in the centre and add the egg yolk. Cover the egg yolk with flour.

Heat the butter, lard and water in a saucepan and bring it to the boil. Make sure that the fat melts before boiling point is reached. When the mixture is boiling, pour it on to the flour and egg, and mix vigorously with a knife.

When the mixture has cooled slightly, turn it out on to a lightly floured surface, and knead until the pastry is smooth. Cover the dough with clingfilm and leave it to rest in a warm place for 20–30 minutes. Use at once.

INGREDIENTS
500 g (1 lb) plain flour
5 ml (1 tsp) salt
1 egg yolk, size 2
100 g (4 oz) butter
100 g (4 oz) lard
175 ml (6 fl oz) water

MAYONNAISE

Makes about 350 ml (12 fl oz)

INGREDIENTS
2 egg yolks, size 3, at room temperature
5 ml (1 tsp) Dijon mustard
salt and pepper
25 ml (1½ tbsp) white wine vinegar
300 ml (½ pint) best olive oil, at room temperature

Place the egg yolks in a bowl, with the mustard, salt and pepper, and 15 ml (1 tbsp) of the vinegar. Whisk the mixture until smooth.

Gradually add the oil, literally drop by drop, whisking vigorously.

If the oil is added too quickly, the mayonnaise will curdle. If this should happen, place another egg yolk in a clean bowl and gradually add the curdled mixture to the fresh egg yolk. If the mayonnaise is thickening too quickly, and there is still some oil to add, pour in a little more of the vinegar, and then continue to add oil. Adjust seasoning, adding a little more vinegar if necessary.

HOLLANDAISE SAUCE

Makes about 300 ml (½ pint)

INGREDIENTS
45 ml (3 tbsp) white wine vinegar
5 peppercorns
1 bay leaf
blade of mace
100 g (4 oz) butter, cut into small pieces
2 egg yolks, size 3
a pinch of salt

Place the vinegar, peppercorns, bay leaf and mace in a saucepan. Bring to the boil and reduce to 15 ml (1 tbsp). Reserve.

Place a small piece of butter, the size of a hazelnut, in a bowl, add the egg yolks and salt, and cream them together.

Strain the vinegar into the yolk mixture and set the bowl over a pan of simmering water, making sure that the water surrounding the bowl does not boil. Do not overheat the sauce or it will curdle.

Whisk the mixture constantly, until it thickens, adding the butter piece by piece. The heat may be increased as the sauce thickens, but do not boil.

Remove from the heat when sauce has thickened. Adjust seasoning.

RAGU (MEAT SAUCE)

Makes enough sauce for 750 g (1½ lb) of pasta

INGREDIENTS
50 g (2 oz) butter
15 ml (1 tbsp) olive oil
1 garlic clove, crushed
1 large onion, finely chopped
75 g (3 oz) unsmoked bacon, rinded and finely chopped
1 carrot, finely chopped
1 celery stalk, finely chopped
225 g (8 oz) minced beef
225 g (8 oz) minced pork
50 g (2 oz) chicken livers, chopped
45 ml (3 tbsp) tomato purée
175 ml (6 fl oz) dry white wine
225 ml (8 fl oz) water
1 bay leaf
2.5 ml (½ tsp) oregano
salt and pepper

Melt the butter with the oil in a large pan and fry the garlic, onion and bacon for 5 minutes. Add the carrot and celery and cook until softened.

Add the meat and livers and cook gently, stirring occasionally, until they begin to brown. Stir in the tomato purée, and cook for 2 minutes before adding any liquid—this reduces the 'raw' flavour of the tomato purée.

Add the wine, water, herbs and seasoning and bring to the boil. Cover and simmer for 1¼ hours, stirring occasionally and checking the amount of liquid from time to time. Add a little water if necessary.

Simmer for a few minutes. Serve with freshly cooked pasta.

Variation

Melt 40 g (1½ oz) butter and fry 1 crushed garlic clove for 1 minute. Add 100 g (4 oz) sliced mushrooms and cook gently for 5 minutes. Sprinkle with 15 ml (1 tbsp) chopped parsley and add to the sauce at the end of the cooking time.

TOMATO SAUCE

Makes about 1.2 litres (2 pints)

Heat the oil and fry the garlic, stirring for 1 minute. Add the tomatoes and sugar and bring to the boil. Reduce the heat, cover the pan, and simmer for 15 minutes. Sieve the tomatoes, using a soup ladle to push every scrap of pulp through, so that only the skin and seeds remain.

Return the pulp to the pan, season with salt and simmer for 10 minutes, or until the sauce has reduced to the required consistency.

INGREDIENTS
75 ml (5 tbsp) olive oil
3 garlic cloves, crushed
1.5 kg (3 lb) ripe tomatoes, quartered
10 ml (2 tsp) sugar
2.5 ml ($\frac{1}{2}$ tsp) salt

WALNUT SAUCE

Makes about 350 ml (12 fl oz)

Place the pine nuts, garlic, parsley and salt in a mortar. Pound the ingredients with a pestle for 2 minutes, then add the walnuts. Pound until well blended, then add the ricotta and water, incorporating these into the mixture. Gradually pour in the oil, and continue to pound the sauce until it is smooth and creamy.

Alternatively, place the pine nuts, garlic, parsley and salt in a blender or food processor. Mix until well blended, then add the ricotta and water and continue as above.

INGREDIENTS
40 g (1$\frac{1}{2}$ oz) pine nuts
1 garlic clove, crushed
30 ml (2 tbsp) chopped fresh parsley
pinch of salt
175 g (6 oz) ground walnuts
75 g (3 oz) ricotta
5 ml (1 tsp) water
60 ml (4 tbsp) olive oil

PASTA DOUGH

Makes about 750 g (1$\frac{1}{2}$ lb)

Sift the flour and salt on to a work surface and make a well in the centre. Pour the eggs, either whole or beaten, into the well with the oil. Gradually incorporate the flour with the eggs and oil, until a dough has formed. Knead for 10 minutes. Wrap the dough in clingfilm and rest for 1 hour.

If making pasta by hand, take one piece of dough, the size of an orange and cover the remainder until needed. On a lightly floured surface, roll out the dough until paper thin, then cut it into the desired shape (see below). Allow the pasta to dry for 30 minutes, by hanging it over a floured rack or chair back.

If rolling the pasta in a machine, it is unnecessary to knead the dough for more than a minute or two, or to rest it. Flour the pasta dough before passing it through the rollers. Take a piece the size of an orange, set the adjustable rollers to the widest setting, and gradually feed the dough through, until the desired thickness is reached. Cut into shapes (see below).

To cook the pasta, drop it into plenty of boiling, salted water with a little vegetable oil, and cook until al dente—2–3 minutes, depending on the shape.
Tagliatelle: Cut into 0.5 cm ($\frac{1}{2}$ in) strips.
Lasagne: Cut into 10–15 cm (4–6 in) strips.

INGREDIENTS
500 g (1 lb) strong white flour
5 ml (1 tsp) salt
4 eggs, size 2
30 ml (2 tbsp) olive oil

INDEX

ACKNOWLEDGMENTS

The publishers would like to thank R. J. Brimacombe, R. B. Jakeman, M. H. Macrae,
J. R. A. Walker, A. P. Guyatt, Jenny O'Donoghue, Spencer Jacobs, Tim Dale,
Margaret Baber and the staff at Harrods for their invaluable assistance and
co-operation in the making of this book.
The publishers would also like to thank Beth Cox, Vera and Alfred Chaney
and Phaedra and Roxana Aslani.
Thanks also to Osborne and Little for wallpaper and fabrics for photography;
Range Rover courtesy of H. R. Owen.

The following cookery measures have been included for American readers who are not familiar with the metric/imperial measures used throughout this book.

COOKING MEASURES

Metric (Imperial)	American
Dry Measures	
15 g (½ oz)	1 tablespoon
100 g (4 oz)	½ cup
225 g (8 oz)	1 cup

Liquid Measures	
15 ml (½ fl oz)	1 tablespoon
50 ml (2 fl oz)	¼ cup
100 ml (4 fl oz)	½ cup
225 ml (8 fl oz)	1 cup
300 ml (½ pint)	1 cup
600 ml (1 pint)	2½ cups

INGREDIENTS

Many British ingredients have different names than the American equivalents. This is a list of the most obvious differences.

British	American
Meat and Poultry	
Bacon rashers	Bacon slices
Belly pork	Parboiled salt pork
Gammon	Ham
Minced beef	Ground beef
Oven-ready chicken	Broiler/fryer
Parma ham	Prosciutto
Pigeon	Squab
Poussin	Rock Cornish Hen

Seafood	
Langoustine	Lobster tails
Prawns	Shrimp
Scampi	Jumbo shrimp

Dairy Products	
Double cream	Heavy cream
Single cream	Light cream
Lard	Shortening
Natural yogurt	Plain yogurt

Vegetables	
Aubergine	Eggplant
Beetroot	Beet
Chicory	Belgium endive
Courgettes	Zucchini
Curly endive	Chicory
Mangetout	Snow peas
Pickling onions	Pearl onions
Saltanas	Golden raisins
Spring onion	Scallions

Baking	
Plain flour	All-purpose flour
Self-raising flour	Self-rising flour
Wholemeal flour	Whole wheat flour
Shortcrust pastry	Pie dough
Caster sugar	Superfine sugar
Icing sugar	Confectioners' sugar
Golden syrup	Corn syrup
Treacle	Molassas
Plain chocolate	Semi-sweet chocolate

Miscellaneous	
Essence	Extract
Frying pan	Skillet
Ground yellow bean sauce	Miso paste
Liquid glucose	Corn syrup
Shaohsing wine	Rice wine
To grill	To broil

NOTE
1. Follow either metric or imperial measures for the recipes in this book as they are not interchangable.
2. Size 3 and 4 eggs are used unless otherwise specified.
3. All tablespoon and teaspoon measures are level unless otherwise specified.
4. Sugar is granulated unless otherwise specified.